MUSIC / CITY

MUSIC CITY

American Festivals
and Placemaking
in Austin, Nashville,
and Newport

JONATHAN R. WYNN

The University of Chicago Press / Chicago and London

JONATHAN R. WYNN is assistant professor of sociology at the
University of Massachusetts at Amherst.

The University of Chicago Press, Chicago 60637
The University of Chicago Press, Ltd., London
© 2015 by The University of Chicago
All rights reserved. Published 2015.
Printed in the United States of America

24 23 22 21 20 19 18 17 16 15   1 2 3 4 5

ISBN-13: 978-0-226-30549-3   (cloth)
ISBN-13: 978-0-226-30552-3   (paper)
ISBN-13: 978-0-226-30566-0   (e-book)
DOI: 10.7208/chicago/9780226305660.001.0001

Library of Congress Cataloging-in-Publication Data
Wynn, Jonathan R., author.
    Music / city : American festivals and placemaking in Austin, Nashville, and
Newport / Jonathan R. Wynn.
        pages cm
    Includes bibliographical references and index.
    ISBN 978-0-226-30549-3 (cloth : alkaline paper)—ISBN 978-0-226-30552-3
(paperback : alkaline paper)—ISBN 978-0-226-30566-0 (ebook)   1. Music
festivals—United States. 2. Music festivals attendees—United States.   I. Title.
    ML37.U5W96 2015
    780.78'73—dc23

                                                              2015019949

♾ This paper meets the requirements of ANSI/NISO Z39.48-1992
(Permanence of Paper).

CONTENTS

Acknowledgments / vii

Introduction: City and Stage / 1

(**1**) The Unlikely Rise in Importance of
American Music Festivals / 21

(**2**) Music in Ruins: The Newport Folk Festival / 45

(**3**) "When Country Comes to Town":
Nashville's Country Music Festival / 82

(**4**) Part-Time Indie Music Club:
Austin's South by Southwest / 125

(**5**) The Long-Term Effects of Fleeting
Moments: Part One / 167

(**6**) The Long-Term Effects of Fleeting
Moments: Part Two / 197

Conclusions: Festivalization as Good Policy / 226

Encore: Toward a Sociology of Occasions / 243

Appendix A: The Lineup (Methodological
Note and List of Interviewees) / 259

Appendix B: Music City Set List / 267

Notes / 269

References / 291

Index / 309

ACKNOWLEDGMENTS

For contributions both big and small, and work both effortless and yeo-manly . . . from providing research assistance along the way to helping with clarity of writing and ideas throughout, this book could not have been done without the help of the following: Zeenat Ahmed, Leslie Bailey, Kristina Barnett, Edward Batchelder, Howard Becker, Claudio Benzecry, Japonica Brown-Saracino, Laura Carpenter, Hanna Chandoo, Allen Chen, Ronda Chollock, Brian Connor, Andrew Deener, Karen De-Witt, Rodrigo Dominguez Villegas, Rick Fantasia, Alexandre Frenette, Jeannie Hakala, Black Hawk Hancock, Patrick Inglis, Bill Ivey, Richard Lloyd, Brittany Manley, Ally Marks, Timothy McGovern, Ashley Mears, Molly Meehan, Doug Mitchell, Chelsei Morrison-Rohlfs, Jim Neill, Jimi Nilsson, Amber Novak, Tom Pappalardo, Linda Park, Julie Slavin, Jenni-fer Reich, Betsey Robinson, Mark Shulman, Correne Spero, Andrea and Daniel Sumber, Kristin Thomson, Taro Tsujimoto, Ayse Yetis-Bayraktar, Jenna Zelenetz, and Robert Zussman. Each of these folks knows the role they played, and my immense gratitude.

The University of Massachusetts–Amherst Department of Sociology, Institute for Social Science Research, and Office of Research Develop-ment provided generous support. Additional guidance was provided by Dan Lurie at the National Endowment of the Arts, Don Cusic at the Mike Curb College of Entertainment & Music Business at Belmont University, and Matthew Seaton at the Country Music Association.

A special thanks goes to all the people within this book, who lent me their time and thoughts.

This book is dedicated to Robyn, whose presence is embedded in these pages from beginning to end. But dedications also go to the memo-ries of two who passed on in 2014: Pete Seeger, who served as the moral compass of American music for generations, and David Lamb, whose soul-shaking voice was extinguished far too soon.

Introduction
City and Stage

Within the Walls of Peace and Love

Borlänge, Sweden, is a former iron and steel town located about two and a half hours northwest of Stockholm. It's home to about 37,000 residents, as well as to the largest music festival in Sweden, the annual Peace and Love Festival. Officially, the festival focuses on fighting xenophobia and racism, and stresses diversity, solidarity, and understanding across cultural and ethnic groups; experientially, however, it's mostly a white, heavy metal crowd. Because the festival books all the city's hotel rooms, most festivalgoers commute from Stockholm or camp nearby and then walk into town.

Europe has its walled cities, but this town's fortress is different. The festival itself is held in the city center, surrounded by a temporary six-foot-tall chain-link fence covered with a blue tarp-like material—a modern and fleeting re-creation of ancient city walls dividing In from Out. Security guards stand sentry, with walkie-talkies attached to their vests, opening the gates for ticket holders.

Inside, five stages are scattered in the town's squares and parking lots, and many corners have smaller programming. A metal band called HammerFall rages on a big stage in a public plaza, the pulsing red and yellow lights bursting through smoke effects behind them transforming the musicians into four black silhouettes. Heads bounce in rhythm. A

1

A band playing the Tropico stage in a closed-off Borlänge town square.

block down, a woman is DJing from a temporary six-by-six-foot tent while a juggler handles flaming torches before a small audience, performing in sync with the throbbing techno beats. The DJ's two hands glide over the turntables, making the speakers emanate a Thum thum thum thum-ka/ Thum thum thum-ka. The crowd claps in unison. The juggler's hands move as if enslaved in a trance. All around, black T-shirted rivers of young Swedes bubble over the old cobblestone roads, with caps of blond hair cresting. One wears a shirt that says "Fuck You, I'm from Hell," and another carries a black bag with "666" and the familiar "God Save the Queen" image from the 1977 album *Never Mind the Bollocks, Here's the Sex Pistols*.

Farther down the road, the lyrics from the Waterboys' 1984 hit "The Big Music" rush over the low buildings like a swell:

> I have heard the big music, and I'll never be the same.
> Something so pure (Hey!) just called my name.
> I have drowned in the big sea, now I find I'm still alive
> and I'm coming up forever.

Their sound—a mix of folk and echoey '80s pop rock with bright backing horns, keys, and singers—was often described by the title of that first major single. From a stage the next block over, the tune rushes over the buildings on either side of the narrow street.

Most locals take the festival's presence as an opportunity to leave town, so the walled-off city center, the business district, is ceded entirely to the event. The streets terminate at the blue plastic wall encircling the area. The barbershop, the bank, the post office, the travel agency, and the optometrist are closed, and only a few places remain open to offer desirables like Thai food, sushi, ice cream, and beer. An empty storefront serves as an information kiosk.

Borlänge was the demographic and geographic equivalent of gating off Amherst, Massachusetts, the small college town where I now teach. With so many local businesses shuttered for the three-day weekend, and so many inhabitants being just plain gone, the thousands of young kids traveling in for the festival transformed the small old steel town, and Borlänge became a festival city. A Music City.

Behind the Scenes in the Music City

Fairs and festivals predate recorded time, likely having their roots in religious gatherings such as India's Maha Kumbh Mela, where millions of Hindus make a pilgrimage for a festival that occurs four times every twelve years. They serve as outlets of emotive expression, as bounded places for people to depart from their everyday routines, but, at least since the gladiatorial performances of the early Roman Empire, town and city officials have also planned them in order to provide mass entertainment and distraction. One can think of early European festivals, both secular and religious, that drew the entire community into the streets. Travelers and locals would spill into every town square, the food and music making the city a "theatre without walls." Carnival turns *il mondo alla rovescia* (the world upside down), while Midsummer or St. John's Eve, coincident with the Solstice, represents renewal. Present-day annual bacchanalia like Rio's Carnival, New Orleans's Mardi Gras, Mexico's Day of the Dead celebrations, and even the Burning Man festival in Nevada's Black Rock Desert pick up those secular and religious elements to craft celebratory rituals.[1] But even the more common county fairs and street festivals are part of this tradition.

Occurring yearly, the festivals arise and fade almost naturally with the seasons, yet they are the carefully scripted products of maneuverings and agreements between powerful stakeholders and cultural institutions. I started thinking about how these short-term events work for people and their places by delivering longer-lasting effects.

After all, today's festivals might be fun for attendees, but they are also used to attract tourists and residents, bolster existing public and private amenities, augment government services, entice business relocations, enhance territorial trademarking, and so on. At the same time, the contemporary music industry needs live events to stave off the rapid decline of profits in a new digital age, and musicians hope to capitalize upon one of their most unique assets—interactions with audiences via live performances—with larger crowds, better compensation, and more impact than the average club gig provides. And then there are the surrounding communities that also challenge, augment, and extract meanings and goods of their own. Festivals, then, illuminate some of the key struggles in our modern urban and cultural lives, as they bring some groups together and marginalize others, impose a crafted image of place for locals and visitors, and create unintended opportunities and challenges. They are the mechanisms for all these various groups to engage in cultural work through a process—which I will explain in a few pages— called *festivalization*.

One moment from early in my research did more than solidify the importance of festivals in my mind. An impromptu speech by the mayor of Austin, Texas, during the city's 2007 South by Southwest (SXSW) music festival shaped my understanding of how various actors and organizations use city resources through these short-term events.

The Mayor of Rock 'n' Roll

The event is called "Gonna Gonna Get Down 2," and it is run by the cultural-events website Austinist at a music venue known as the Mohawk. Situated in Austin's downtown entertainment district, the Mohawk fits in among the mixture of other live-music venues, but it also contrasts with the corrugated steel siding of a few light-industry buildings and fenced-in dirt lots, including one right across Red River Street.

The event features fourteen bands, split between inside and outside stages, and a stream of people flowing through a hallway between them, thick in boozy and sweaty smells; layers of unknown band stickers coat the club's murky walls and bathrooms. The capacity crowd of about 600 comprises mostly college-aged kids and, at one o'clock in the afternoon, everyone seems to be holding a two-dollar Lone Star beer can.

The band on the outdoor stage, Earl Greyhound, stops between songs in their runaway rock-and-blues set to introduce the honored guest who has just arrived. With a background in real estate development and an eye for transforming downtown, Mayor Will Wynn takes the mic with a crisp white shirt and a multicolor striped tie. After a cordial greeting—"I just want to say 'hi' and 'welcome' to, particularly, all of our out-of-town guests. How about all of those musicians coming from all around the country and the planet?"—the mayor launches into his speech:

> There are 1,725 bands in town this week; 515 local bands in town this week. It's a fabulous time to be in Austin...Remember, in order for us to be the Live Music Capital of the World, we need three things. We need venues like [the] Mohawk and some of the other venues to be successful. They gotta be in town. We gotta have a bunch of venues that are downtown, so that folks can walk to five or six or eight or ten or twelve venues in one night, and see fifteen, twenty, thirty bands during South by Southwest.
>
> You gotta have your musicians. Austin is now home to 8,000 working musicians. The vast majority of them, understandably, they're low income and uninsured. We gotta find out how to support them, you know, financially, spiritually, economically, and otherwise. And then third, we've gotta have a bunch of citizens, like me, who will turn their televisions off, get their asses off the couch, and go out and listen to live music.

The audience cheers and hoots, engaged and somewhat amused by the mayor saying "asses." Wynn continues:

> Austin is far and away the biggest city in the country that doesn't have either an NFL team, an NBA franchise, or [a] major league baseball team.

The Mohawk outdoor stage at South by Southwest with new condos.

And people ask me frequently, "So, Mayor, when is Austin going to get an NFL team?" I say, "You know what? Live music should be our sports franchise!" Instead of a family or folks going out and dropping about 400 bucks to go to an NFL game to subsidize a billionaire sports owner that the taxpayers already built a 400-million-dollar sports stadium for, why not instead, about three or four or five times a month, go out and drop twenty-five, thirty-five, fifty bucks supporting live music in a great venue, helping our 8,000 working musicians, making SXSW more productive, more experiential, for these fabulous bands to come from New York and across the planet to enjoy [the] Live Music Capital of the World: Austin, Texas!

The members of the band return to the front of the stage, getting ready to continue their set as the mayor waves good-bye. Kamara Thomas, the black, female bass player and vocalist, steps up to the mic to say, "Thank you, Mr. Mayor . . . the Mayor of Rock 'n' Roll!" The audience of hip twentysomethings sporting asymmetrical haircuts and ironic T-shirts cheers for the businessman-politician as he exits stage right.

A year later, "Gonna Gonna Get Down 3" returns to the same venue, but I now see that new condominium construction has replaced the empty lot across the street. Back in the 1980s and '90s, the neighborhood had a seedy reputation, known for its drug deals and homelessness. It certainly hasn't been transformed completely, but now men and women from the nearby Austin Resource Center for the Homeless mix with the new residents who live in downtown condos, along with the yearly influx of music industry professionals from New York and Los Angeles in town for South by Southwest. Dust kicked up from the building site settles on Styrofoam plates piled high with complimentary barbeque and smoky beans, as attendees in the VIP lounge look down from the rooftop at a band playing an operatic folk-rock set.

Studying Festivals

Mayor Wynn's speech provides some evidence of how festivals can benefit their communities today, and how something as seemingly chaotic as SXSW can reflect the goals of his mayoral administration. At another level I know that, in order to achieve their intended or unintended goals, these collective spectacles lash together a variety of different folk with different agendas through their coordinated activities: from the musician looking to further her music career to the participant who wants to see his favorite band, from the mayor who wants to bolster a local cultural scene to the music executive hoping to sell records, from the locals' frustration over corporate branding of their city to the tourist's search for a good time. They are a chance for large groups to congregate and commune, on the one hand, and yet they can also be (literally, in the case of Borlänge) walled off and exclusive.

Given that such occasions are so commonplace and well attended, it is surprising that scholars have not been particularly interested in them. Perhaps because they are so popular, and come in so many forms, sociologists mention them mostly as related to something else (e.g., an ethnic community's demonstration of pride and promotion of group solidarity, or part of a larger cultural tradition).[2] The National Endowment for the Arts found that the majority of outdoor events have music as a central or primary component.[3] By my count, there are at least 250 ongoing music festivals in the United States, ranging from the Oregon Bach Festival in Eugene to the Spirit of Bluegrass Music Fest in Live Oak, Florida. In 2014, over 90,000 people attended each day of the Coachella festival in Indio, California; Middle Tennessee's Bonnaroo, Chicago's Lollapalooza, and Las Vegas's Electric Daisy Carnival all exceeded 100,000 attendees; 160,000 went to Miami's Ultra electronic music festival; and there were 852,000 attendees over the eleven days of Milwaukee's forty-seventh annual Summerfest. The numbers increase every year.

As someone who studies cities and culture, the idea of how music adhered to certain *places* intrigued me, and helped me narrow my focus to festivals and festivalization. When one thinks of the home of the blues, for example, cities like Chicago and Memphis come to mind. Seattle is the capital when many talk of 1990s grunge rock. Detroit has its Motown, and New Orleans, its jazz.[4] But when it comes to actual festivals, only a few really stand out as having a strong connection with indigenous music, or a willingness to enhance local culture.[5] For example, despite the forty-five-year history of the Oregon Bach Festival, few think of Eugene, Oregon, with regard to mid-eighteenth-century chamber music. A place like Nashville, Tennessee, however, with the third-largest population of musicians in the country and its own legendary "Nashville Sound," is indelibly linked to country music. Austin, with its long reputation as the eccentric counterpoint to mainstream music businesses in Los Angeles, New York, and Nashville, is a natural hotbed for indie rock.[6] Although Newport, Rhode Island, lacks a homegrown music scene, it has established itself on the global music map with its long-held sister jazz and folk festivals. These three cities struck me as interesting and unstudied cases.[7]

Although Nashville and Austin have comparable sizes (pop. 601,222 and 790,390, respectively, in 2010) and growth rates, and Newport exists only as a smaller vacation outpost for New England elites (pop. 24,672 in 2010, though it quadruples in the summer), all three places exist within similar-sized geographic regions, known as Metropolitan Statistical Areas (MSAs). MSAs are territories of economic and political influence that extend beyond state and municipal lines—the New York City MSA, for example, includes areas of Pennsylvania and New Jersey. Though small within its own city limits, Newport actually sits within a larger Providence–New Bedford–Fall River, Massachusetts, MSA, which allows for a nearly identical foundation for comparison: as of 2010, Austin's was the thirty-fifth most populous MSA in the United States, while Providence's was thirty-seventh and Nashville's was thirty-eighth. With over 1.6 million residents each, the Nashville, Austin, and Providence MSAs serve as the cultural and political centers for their regions, function as central nodes for major universities, and rank as second-tier cities. Whereas Chicago, New York, and Los Angeles—like other first-tier, "global," or "alpha" cities and top MSAs—have the benefits of diverse and well-established culture industries, recognized tourist attractions, and much scholarship devoted to the dynamics at work within them, there are a greater number of smaller MSAs in need of study.[8] Scholarship on the cultural strategies of an Austin, a Nashville, or a Newport may be of greater utility and generalizability. Put another way: there are far more Charlestons striving for the success of Nashville than there are Baltimores aspiring to be New York.

((( )))

Once I narrowed my focus to these three festivals and their locales, I then thought about how to study something so big. Festivals are tricky. No rooftop VIP lounge is high enough to provide a vista for all the interactions and experiences of a festival; there is no one street corner to sit on, and no single group to query. And, like a medicine show or a traveling circus, they're gone in a few days. Festivals are what Jürgen Habermas called an *occasional public* or an *arranged public*: a moment wherein these players and organizations come together with multiple perspectives, motives, investments, and experiences.[9]

Thus, understanding these events would require an equally dynamic approach that included the producers, supporters, and consumers of music. Early in my research, I found Howard Becker's *Art Worlds* to be a good model for taking on such a complex cooperative web. The art world, for him, is a network of coconspirators whose activities and tasks—wittingly or unintentionally—produce "the kinds of art works that an art world is noted for," a perspective that assists an effort to apprehend how art is "made *and* appreciated" by that wide array of people.[10] As related to the scene at the Mohawk, for example, the mayor is there to promote his vision for a Music City, while an Austinite would tell me he's there for free entertainment; a SXSW attendee would say she flew to Austin to scout bands for her music label, while local musicians would express disappointment that they weren't invited to the city's big cultural event. Festivals are occasional publics with only a measure of consensus, and a multifaceted approach to the multiple perspectives of people seemed the best way to understand them.[11]

That there are a variety of views—and even conflicting ones—among participants of such large social gatherings is not a particularly surprising realization. And yet, to integrate those varied perspectives across settings and cases, I decided to use four methodological tracks: two primary ones, and two supplemental. First, I conducted 110 semistructured interviews with members of key organizations in and around the three music festivals: attendees, organizers, founders, members of the chamber of commerce and visitors bureaus, headlining musicians, mayors, owners of local music venues, major record label executives, local media members, music promoters, and booking agents. (Anyone identified with a first and last name has not been given a pseudonym. For a list of respondents and a comment on using real names, see appendix A.) These interviews were done between June 2006 and August 2013, in a variety of locations and manners: at music venues, cafés, and convention centers, between sound checks and after late-night performances, in person and, in four instances where in-person interviews were not an option, on the phone. The second major technique was ethnographic. This methodology, also called participant observation, is a kind of data collection balancing on the line between being an objective spectator of social life and being fully immersed in it. I participated in a variety of ways: from performing onstage to listening in the audience, from gaining entrée as a low-level volunteer to being granted backstage media access.[12] I took a notebook everywhere, and wrote in the dark smoky honkytonks and bright convention halls, or immediately afterward if conditions limited my ability to write. In three situations—the above address by Austin's mayor and two public discussions about festivals—I digitally recorded the events and transcribed them. These two techniques of interviews and participant observation allowed me to match what people told me with what I saw myself across a range of different places. Throughout the book, there are sections like the descriptions of Borlänge and Austin that closely resemble what I wrote down at the time. Commonly called field notes, these sections provide a more visceral impression of these experiences, grounded in specific places and times: the sights and sounds from the sweaty front row to the air-conditioned offices of city hall, from a late-night performance with a bass guitar in hand to the dervishing mayhem of a closed-off street on a hot summer's day.[13]

I cross-referenced this information with historical accounts, media sources, biographies (when available), festival programs, and genre magazines (e.g., the folk magazine *Sing Out!* and the Country Music Association's *Close Up*) for a better understanding of the community, the history of the festivals, and the interrelationships between organizations and groups. Toward the end of the book, there is evidence from two additional methods, one unconventional and one more traditional. The first comes in chapter 5 as a set of strolls, or "walks with a purpose," as a way to compare places and investigate similarities and differences across these Music Cities and witness how economic development is experienced. I also administered a small survey to over 210 festival attendees to gain participants' perspectives on festivals for chapter 6: their engagement with these events, perceptions of city and corporate branding, and what they see as a close tie between the festivals and their cities.[14]

This multilayered approach seemed the best way to tackle such an odd social form across places and publics, connecting how these events are put together with how they are experienced, and the approach buffered me from both overly joyous and resoundingly pessimistic conclusions on the state of contemporary urban culture.

Understanding Festivalization: Four Resources and Three Patterns

The late German urbanist Hartmut Häussermann called the increasing presence of these events in cities *festivalization*.[15] I see festivalization as not just the general rise of festivals, but an ongoing organizational process wherein short-term events are used to develop, reinforce, and exploit an array of communal goods, churning out costs and benefits both near and far. Festivalization, then, is a *process* where cultural activity meets placemaking, but it is also a *cultural policy* that cities and communities can debate and adopt.

Although it did not occur to me at the time, Mayor Wynn's urban culture pep talk matched how I later viewed the relationship between these events and their communities, helping me identify just what those "communal goods" really are. His "three things to make Austin the Live Music Capital of the World"—music venues, musicians, and audiences spending money—turned out to be a great start. Mayor Wynn's speech unwittingly provided an outline of urban culture, allowing me to see how cities and their communities use festivals as ongoing mechanisms for investing in, using, and replenishing multiple kinds of resources, or capital—not unlike money in a bank.

Perhaps the easiest introduction to this way of thinking about festivalization (and really, urban culture more generally) is to focus first on the community asset closest to the metaphor of "capital": Mayor Wynn said audiences have to spend money to make his city a thriving one, and indeed, urban culture requires *economic resources*. There are financial benefits when outside spending exceeds a city's own local investment (e.g., municipal loans, waivers). Organizers and city officials often justify events to the local community in economic terms: direct visitor spending, hotel rooms booked, transportation taxes, tolls, parking fees, or indirect impact through local restaurant and other business growth. Although some festivals are run as not-for-profit organizations, music festivals are the most expensive type of festival to produce—due primarily to artist fees—and, therefore, they all need to garner revenue and some financial backing (perhaps from corporate sponsors looking to promote themselves through a particular event) to pay performers and secure event spaces.

Profit, however, is unlikely to be the sole justification, or the sole measure, of any urban cultural activity.[16] And the sociologist Henri Lefebvre noted that economics should not be the only resource for thinking about the relationship between culture and place. He believed that social, physical, and symbolic resources were additional "ingredients for" and the "potential beneficiaries of" such space-making, and these ideas—married to Mayor Wynn's speech—can help us come to a multi-dimensional understanding of how festivals draw out and reinforce the noneconomic costs and benefits for places as well.[17]

And so, following this recommendation, I also suggest a second resource of *physical* or *spatial resources.* Mayor Wynn spoke of these amenities in his speech too. He said Austin needs its clubs and music venues—not just that they should exist but that they should be geographically proximate: "We need venues . . . They gotta be in town. We gotta have a bunch of venues that are downtown, so that folks can walk to five or six or eight or ten or twelve venues in one night." It is a principle reminiscent of Count Basie's description of why Kansas City was a great place to perform: "Clubs, clubs, clubs, clubs, clubs, clubs, clubs, clubs . . . In fact, I thought that was all Kansas City was made up of."[18] Cities have a great number of these spatial resources for urban culture: both public spaces (convention centers, parks, streets, sidewalks, empty lots, and "ploaps"—places left over after planning) and private ones (concert halls, cafés, bars, honkytonks, and parking lots). When it comes to outdoor festivals, 71% use public plazas, parks, or streets.[19] The closer these resources cluster together, the greater their potential use for an event, and the limits of a festival's size can be attributed to the availability of such spaces as much as by money, local talent, or attendees.[20]

That brings up a third resource in Wynn's speech: people and their talents and skills. These are *social + cultural resources.* For simplicity's sake, this is a combination of two sociological terms from Pierre Bourdieu: the social capital of durable social ties of recognized interpersonal and group memberships, and the cultural capital of knowledge, skills, and education that reap benefits within certain related spheres of social life.[21] According to Mayor Wynn, the city needs to "support its musicians," but really, there are dozens of kinds of workers in and around a city's lively cultural scene: these are as varied as club owners, arts teachers, sound engineers, and members of the convention and visitors bureau. Festivals draw attendees, employees, and volunteers from near and far. This might mean particularly significant individuals (e.g., municipal bigwigs and industry hotshots from Los Angeles or New York) and collective community organizations that produce the event, or performing musicians.

Austin may already be home to thousands of musicians, but the example of Newport shows that local musicians are not required per se: unlike Austin and Nashville, the Rhode Island summer vacation town has a limited number of performers and little interest in fostering a local scene, and yet it hosts internationally known festivals regardless.

In addition to economic, spatial, and social + cultural resources, Mayor Wynn also referred to another resource, although indirectly, when he said that these three resources make Austin the "Live Music Capital of the World." This is not just an ad-libbed turn of phrase, but rather, the city's official motto. It originated with a local blues musician who, as she was driving home from a gig in Houston, reckoned the city needed a slogan and approached the city government with the idea of calling the municipality the "Music Capital of the USA." When research uncovered that Austin had more live-music venues per capita than Nashville, Los Angeles, or even New York City, they came up with the "Live Music Capital of the World." This kind of motto or slogan is a *symbolic resource*.[22] Symbolic resources are image- and idea-based goods that can be linked to, or promoted within, a city festival and the surrounding communities. The creation and manipulation of such symbolic goods could also be called *branding*, a remarkably flexible term used to describe marketing for anything from nations and ethnic groups to diet soda.[23] For cities, this level of brand promotion ties in with place and can be orchestrated via the coordinated efforts of convention and visitors bureaus (CVBs) and chambers of commerce. A Nashville CVB executive told me that the city's brand, "Music City, USA," is a recognizable resource they are "eager to use."

However, urban symbols and slogans, these mundane talismans of contemporary life, can also be organic and informal. They can be drawn from the shared local histories and regional identities that urbanist Gerald Suttles calls the *cumulative texture* of a city, which are then crystallized and promoted to a wider audience.[24] Folks call Austin "Weird City" on the radio, and country singers have long referred to Nashville as "Honkytonk Heaven." Sometimes an image unintentionally gets adopted as a city's trademark. For example, the graffitied image of an "alien frog" by infamous Austin indie singer-songwriter Daniel Johnston often serves as an icon for the city's informal and unofficial "Weird City" ethos. Of course, corporations can play the game of imprinting upon visual landscapes as well, from Boston's Citco Gas sign to Times Square itself (which people often forget was renamed in 1904 after a lobbying campaign by the *New York Times*).[25]

With regard to urban culture, festivals aren't the only sites for the use and exploitation of these kinds of resources. They are, however, a rarely examined one that can tell us something about how fleeting moments can set in motion a great many actors and assets for longer-term impact. They are another opportunity for some stakeholders to extract physical resources and economic benefits and impose branding. They might stoke revenue for local businesses and nonprofit institutions, nurture music scenes, and attract visitors and locals. Mayors and city stakeholders get a "signature" event, CVBs get something to promote for visitors, chambers of commerce get an influx of tourist dollars, musicians get to play to new audiences, local businesses get customers, residents may secure temporary employment, even police get paid time and a half. Festivals often make use of publicly held resources like parks and streets, but in the process, there is always the danger that these public resources are appropriated and coopted for the benefit of the few. At the same time, these events also provide opportunities for individuals and smaller groups to use these assets for their own, unofficial goals. There is, then, a lot going on.

The Newport, Nashville, and Austin festivals illustrate important differences in the availability of these reserves of community goods, and in the struggles over them, as the following chapters will explore in greater depth. Each shows the different ways festivalization can develop. The Newport Folk Festival, for example, began with the *economic* resources provided by local philanthropists, a network of stakeholders who used their financial resources to bring musicians to the small resort community and to finance production costs. However, high property values and taxes have limited the growth of much of a homegrown creative community despite the long-running festivals that bear the city's name. This smaller pool of social + cultural resources—aggravated by the city's smaller population and geographic area compared with Austin and Nashville—is balanced by the fact that, as the marketing director of Newport's CVB told me, the city actively promotes its events to gain tourist revenue from the "about 10 percent of the US population" that resides within a short, 200-mile drive.[26] And yet, there is a lack of live-music venues and thus a shortage of spatial resources. On the positive side, Newport has extensive symbolic resources generated by the prestige of its festival events—according to current festival producer Jay Sweet, "everywhere I go, when I say 'Newport,' people want to talk about the festivals"—and the festivals join other Rhode Island leisure activities as a key cultural offering.

The value of the name "Newport" echoes Mayor Wynn's description of Austin's large talent pool of musicians and a dense network of music venues as social and cultural and spatial resources that bolster its symbolic resource of being the "Live Music Capital of the World." This status then attracts more young, educated people to Austin. This can also be compared to the symbolic and economic strengths of Nashville's Country Music Association (CMA) Music Festival. The CMA Fest is firmly tied to the city's more extensive country music recording and marketing industries, and the CMA itself is a trade organization that aggressively uses corporate sponsors it feels match its audiences, just as Newport did with Ben and Jerry's ice cream. This is, of course, just the beginning of understanding how these festivals developed, and how they used their collective cultural goods.

Across all three cities, people from the municipal agencies, CVBs, and chambers of commerce reported seeing a steadily increasing level of concerted coordination to brand and promote their cities, a newfound emphasis on tying those images to their festivals, and a renewed interest in deploying these assets in the inter-city competition for more resources and visitors, new businesses and residents. In contrast with the massive mobilization of assets and organizations required to construct major museums, sports arenas, and tourist districts, festivalization offers a repeatable, adaptable, and potentially more responsive cultural form.

((( )))

This thumbnail sketch only hints at how these four resources are used. But each event is also oriented a little differently toward its communities, and its particular arrangements further highlight the relationship between event and city. These three cases offer three different patterns of cultural occasions—what social scientists, drawing from Max Weber, call *ideal types*: hypothetical frameworks for investigating real-life phenomena.[27] The following patterns are not proposed as perfect reflections of actual cases, but rather as good "tools to think with" because they allow us a sort of yardstick for comparing how resources flow through the different festivals.

Based in Fort Adams State Park, the Newport Folk Festival is a bit removed from the downtown area. The fortress spaces of the park made me think of calling it a *citadel pattern*: the festival is organized in a way that consolidates and isolates events within a single, bounded space,[28] similar to the Peace and Love Festival in the walled-off town center of Borlänge. This pattern benefits some restaurants and businesses but keeps others on the outside. When the festival is removed from the town center, as Newport's is, the citadel pattern likely requires that services (food trucks, facilities, first aid) be brought onto the grounds; at the same time, it allows organizers to carefully control the on-site activities. Seattle's Bumbershoot and Chicago's Lollapalooza festivals also demonstrate this kind of configuration.

The arrangement of Nashville's CMA Fest is noticeably different. The festival is situated around a centrally located set of downtown public and private spaces: a convention center, two sports stadiums, museums, and publicly accessible parks and streets. I thought of this as a *core pattern*, looser than the citadel one, where central facilities are utilized and passersby have mixed levels of admittance. Some events were free to anyone, while only ticket holders could access other activities. Nashville's restaurants and famed honkytonks, I will show in the coming chapters, are *not* an official part of the country music festival, but they are still integral to the experience for attendees. The sidewalks and many public spaces in and around the core have a jumble of festivalgoers and city dwellers concentrated into a relatively small area.

And then there is South by Southwest, which uses a great variety of locations in and around downtown Austin, like the Mohawk. This is similar to how Paris's Fête de la Musique (and the hundreds of cities around the world that replicate it) places musicians and bands at corners, alleys, and unconventional stages around the city. As Pop Montreal creative director Dan Seligman explained it to me, his festival follows this pattern too, engaging a wide array of places and organizations:

We try to really be part of the city and make the city kind of like the landscape for where the festival happens [using] venues you've never been in before and it's kind of like a creaky rickety old church or under a bridge and you're like "Wow this is amazing," and all of a sudden your senses are heightened and music starts and it's like it feels more like a real complete experience. That's something we try to do and it's something city administrators have really been helpful with—getting permits, and working with the fire department and the Festival and Cultural Event Office, and all those things—to like help make it happen.

Events like Pop Montreal, SXSW, and Fête de la Musique conform to what I would call the *confetti pattern*, which sprinkles festival events across a wide area, perhaps bringing together the widest array of actors, organizations, and experiences, but also involving the least amount of control over those activities.

These three festivals discussed in the following chapters only approximate the ideal types. SXSW is closest to a confetti pattern, and I will show that there is a measure of decreased control over the image and branding by festival organizers, while there are other aspects of the Austin story that do not fit so easily into that image. Furthermore, the spatial organization of each festival influences the distribution and use of resources: at the most general level, the more dispersed a festival is, the greater the potential struggles for controlling resources, and the wider the impact across a variety of local groups. A more confined and isolated festival is inclined to fewer struggles and more limited impact.

To say that these patterns and resources are good tools to "think with" is to indicate that using them is the start of analysis, not the end of it. These tools frame the expansive relationship of festivals, culture, and cities, shining a light on the individuals and groups that play a role in placemaking, examining how particular goals and ends are achieved, and noting those who work on the margins of these activities. As the upcoming chapters detail the lived experiences, on-the-ground interactions, varied perspectives, and tensions and challenges of these three different festivals, they do so in terms of these four resources. In conjunction, the three patterns are the "shape" of festivalization, from the physical organization of the events to the interactions and experiences around the music, which help us see how festivals fit within the larger systems of a city. These patterns are also critical in understanding how the festivals have changed in their relationship to city spaces and communities over time: I will show how, for example, the Newport Folk Festival moved from a core model of using downtown Newport to the citadel model, and how the CMA Fest moved from the downtown core, to a citadel pattern, and back to the core.

Conclusions: Festival as Music City

Festivals, as large moments of rather intense sociability, are another facet of urban life with costs and benefits in need of appraisal.[29] Urban policymakers, mayors, chambers of commerce, and local businesses are moving toward embracing urban branding with slogans like "Live Music Capital of the World" and "Music City, USA," promoting a kind of identity, and using festivalization to further their respective agendas. While there is legitimate concern over the privatization of public spaces—in the case of festivals using public space and economic resources for the benefit of corporate sponsors and the music industry and, in all three cases, finding different paths toward the successful annexation of their respective cities' spaces and urban branding—an understanding of the world around such developments ensures that one does not blind himself to their benefits. Musicians, fans, and creative communities participate in festivals, using them to their advantage and drawing out a measure of "pride of place." Festivals can also be the sites of unofficial participation and protest. The Music City is, if only temporarily, resplendent in crisp, bright experiences with lots of perspectives to tap, and lots of effects to trace out.

Understanding the process of festivalization requires a mapping of the key actors and institutions involved in the founding and managing of the events, but also the development over time into a rather unique and expansive organizational form.

((( )))

The trajectory of this book is as follows. The first chapter shows how historical trends in cities, music, and festivals create a moment of concentrated investment and participation in urban cultural activities by individuals and organizations. The next three chapters then provide the significant developments, experiences, key tensions, and intended and unintended consequences of three major music festivals. These more detailed chapters offer variations and nuances, and show different approaches to balancing competing agendas across city leaders, music fans, musicians, and corporate sponsors within three signature events. Critically, they identify the key players in these cities' festivalization— from Newport's wealthy benefactors to the union of Nashville's music industry and municipal growth organizations to Austin's countercultural scene—and critical moments in the process—from Newport's exile to the CMA's return to downtown to the Austin city government's embrace of South by Southwest. These chapters are ordered by their founding: from the Newport Folk Festival (since 1959), to Nashville's Country Music Association Music Festival (since 1972), and Austin's South by Southwest (since 1987). The chronology of these three chapters moves through the three patterns of citadel, core, and confetti and demonstrates a bit of a continuum, perhaps most easily differentiated by the decrease in the spatial consolidation and control of the aforementioned four resources. Chapters 5 and 6 build off these three chapters to compare across cases, analyzing the resulting costs and benefits to the different communities. The conclusion details the importance of festivalization as an urban cultural policy. An "encore" chapter reflects upon the findings of this book and uses Erving Goffman's call for a *sociology of occasions* to unpack how social scientists can see events as a more general sociological phenomenon, which situates this study and proposes a unique framework for analyzing mass social activity.

1

The Unlikely Rise in Importance of American Music Festivals

City, Song, and Symbol

Most of the early American music festivals were, ironically, showplaces for European music. There were classical music festivals highlighting Haydn, Handel, and the like in the late 1800s in places as scattered as Buffalo, Los Angeles, and Springfield, Massachusetts; perhaps the most successful was Aaron Copland's Yaddo Music Festival in upstate New York, a critical location for "serious" music from 1932 to 1952.[1]

The start of popular music festivals in the United States, however, could be traced to two people: Louis and Elaine Lorillard. The couple met in Italy during World War Two, fell in love, learned about jazz, and returned to their summer resort home in Newport, Rhode Island, resolute in their desire to add to the cultural fabric of their community. Rather than creating yet another festival in the European classical tradition, however, they decided to structure it around what is arguably the most distinctive of American cultural contributions: in 1954, they offered $20,000 to fund a jazz event. They reached out to George Wein, owner of the Boston jazz club Storyville, to manage and book acts. Five years later, with folksingers Pete Seeger, Oscar Brand, and Theodore Bikel and manager Albert Grossman, Wein cofounded the Newport Folk Festival to ride the growth of another distinctive American musical amalgamation: the mixture of blues, country, and pop that fueled the folk revival of the '50s and early '60s. Newport's twin events ushered in what music critic Leonard Feather called the *festival era* of large-scale, annual, outdoor events in the United States. Wein, who continued running the festivals for decades, came to be considered the patriarch of the American music festival.[2]

There followed a series of festivals that served as gatherings for, and the generators of, the American counterculture: the Philadelphia Folk Festival in 1962, the Monterey International Pop Music Festival in 1967, the Miami Pop Festival in 1968, the Woodstock Music and Art Fair in August 1969, and the Altamont Speedway Free Festival in December of that same year. Highlights from these events—the performances of Janis Joplin, Otis Redding, and Jimi Hendrix at Monterey; Richie Havens's improvised version of "Freedom" at Woodstock; and the descent into violence at Altamont—all serve as touchstones for a generation. These festivals served not just to promote particular artists and make money, but also to legitimate the countercultural music genres themselves.

Although the late 1960s and early '70s saw the founding of innumerable popular music festivals throughout the country, only a handful of them weathered the dramatic drop in attendance that took place in the 1980s and '90s: Milwaukee's Summerfest (established in 1968, a year before Woodstock), New Orleans's Jazz and Heritage Festival (1970), Seattle's Bumbershoot (1971), and Nashville's Fan Fair (1972). Austin's South by Southwest was founded during the dry spell in 1987, as was Chicago's Lollapalooza (1991–97, 2003, and 2005–present). By the 2000s, music festivals had started cropping up again, including the massive Coachella and Bonnaroo festivals (established in rural eastern California in 2001 and rural southern Tennessee in 2002, respectively), and bands themselves started organizing their own, smaller events. Phish periodically holds its own festival around the Northeast; Wilco runs the Solid Sound Festival in North Adams, Massachusetts; and Metallica briefly ran the Orion Music + More in Atlantic City in 2012 and in Detroit in 2013. And it's not only the number of festivals that is increasing—their attendance is growing as well. In 2012, 80,000 to 85,000 people attended each day of the Coachella Valley Music and Arts Festival; Bonnaroo, Lollapalooza, and Las Vegas's Electric Daisy Carnival all reached 100,000 attendees; 160,000 people attended Miami's Ultra electronic music festival; and even more attended Milwaukee's forty-fifth annual Summerfest. All were bigger than in years prior.

These alliances between art and commerce are reminders that the contemporary American music festival sits at the intersection of two major shifts in the broader cultural and economic context, a junction that serves as the core of this chapter. The first is the evolution of cities from being centers of production to centers of consumption. The second is the parallel change in the economics of music industry from the sale of durable products (records, cassettes, CDs) to the marketing of live music. Together, these trends further explain the relationship between these cultural events and the contemporary city.

Coketown to Circus City

In *Hard Times*, Charles Dickens describes the fictitious industrial city of Coketown in shades of black and gray, and fills his characters' ears with the shriek of the train and the wheeze of the steam engine. The book served as a critique of the rise of the modern city, as its characters struggled in the grip of a cold and practical world. Novelists weren't alone in criticizing the industrial city. Early sociologists matched Dickens's fears of the modern city as a center for factory and marketplace, increasingly dominated by bureaucracies and rationalization.[3]

This understanding presents the industrial city as a center for political and economic forces colluding for their growth-focused agendas, and envisions manufacturing as promoting development in other sectors, such as housing, retail, and public infrastructure. These coalitions of real estate investors, financial institutions, government agencies, civic institutions, and the media—what Harvey Molotch called a city's *growth machines*—shaped urban life by increasing land values.[4] This led to an increased privatization of public assets (mass transit systems, public utilities, etc.), which has placed limits on civic life. Although there are some differences of opinion on the relevance of the growth-machine theory, such mixtures of public and private holding of assets deeply affect the public culture found on the streets, parks, and sidewalks.[5]

Although this stage of urban development still exists within the United States and in many places around the world, new forces emerged toward the end of the last century. Trends in technology and communication led to increased globalization of banking, manufacturing, and management, while at the same time, US cities in the Midwest, Northeast, and Great Lakes regions were hit by deindustrialization, disinvestment, and capital flight. Jobs moved to suburbs or "Edge Cities," to the Sunbelt or out of the country altogether, deserting labor markets and emptying onetime bustling factories and mills.[6] In a few other places, however, cultural activities have moved into that vacuum.

New York City's Soho district often serves as a kind of classic case for understanding the shift from production to consumption. Light manufacturing abandoned the neighborhood in the 1960s, leaving behind large, empty, cheap spatial resources. Politicians developed a zoning plan in 1961 to deindustrialize Manhattan as a whole, and banks disinvested in the area by not offering mortgages.[7] Artists—often poor, young, and happy to occupy the big raw spaces for little to no rent—moved in, sometimes squatting. Instead of textiles, they made art. Sensing a scene developing, more artists relocated, and other institutions came along to cater to the burgeoning community that included artists whose work expanded to fill those big empty spaces, such as Donald Judd, Walter De Maria, and Gordon Matta-Clark; these spaces also influenced minimalist composers like Philip Glass. In the 1970s, there were first the bars, cafés, bodegas, and art galleries—not to mention the nearby music venues like CBGB's (founded to the east, on Bowery) and the Mudd Club (to the west, in Tribeca) that launched New Wave bands like Television, the Talking Heads, Blondie, and the Velvet Underground—then more stores and restaurants (even one, Food, that was operated by Matta-Clark). And soon, building off the hipness of the neighborhood, luxury lofts and higher-end boutiques arrived. The Guggenheim Museum opened a branch at Broadway and Prince Streets in 1992. Rather than growing up around traditional production and manufacturing, the neighborhood redeveloped through culture and consumption.

In the 1990s, scholars and municipal organizations alike learned the lesson that local art, music, and history can be valuable assets in other cities too, leading Richard Lloyd and Terry Nichols Clark to critique and amend Molotch's theory to suggest that "entertainment machines"— coalitions of finance, technology, and media workers—now excavate the more ephemeral element of culture as a resource.[8] In the face of suburbanization and disinvestment, the contemporary city-as-entertainment-machine attempts to churn out places for exciting consumption rather than material production. Luring corporate relocations, new residents, and tourists requires refashioning cities as appealing locales that can be marketed via strategic planning by additional quasi-governmental agencies like chambers of commerce (concentrating on promoting growth) and convention and visitors bureaus (focusing on enticing out-of-town visitors). Together, these efforts aim at packaging and selling an attention-grabbing set of amenities, services, and experiences.

The continued privatization of urban spaces and the rise of the city-as-entertainment-machine led to clusters of eateries, theaters, and bars as the new cauldrons of urban development. Gentrified neighborhoods like Chicago's Wicker Park, Brooklyn's Williamsburg, and East Nashville became home for new gentrifiers and businesses. Dormant manufacturing zones ("brownfields" like Pittsburgh's SouthSide Works and parts of Glasgow and Manchester, England) and even unique and unused places (like the spaces left over after the Berlin Wall or Manhattan's defunct elevated train trellis) are transformed into entertainment zones.[9] Where cities once used big industry and big projects to generate growth within those inner rings, they now looked for ways to utilize those same spatial resources of vacant mills and factories by combining them with the social + cultural resources of clusters of cultural activity. Under this new regime of cultural revitalization, this story played out in deindustrialized cities like London, Dublin, Newark, Boston, and San Francisco, where dormant smokestacks and mills became ironic symbols of industriousness rather than decaying reminders of a bygone production era.

Shortly after he left office in 2010, Austin Mayor Will Wynn provided a more detailed account of his view of the relationship between cities and culture—one that was grounded in exactly this historical context. In his words, the urban development model in the United States for the past century was to "build big stuff"—industries would colocate and construct harbors and airports and industrial parks, hoping employees and smaller businesses would follow. Manufacturing industries settled in cities in the Northeast and the Great Lakes area and exploited local resources, both physical and social. Chicago's iron deposits along Lake Superior and its large immigrant worker population, for example, gave it a competitive advantage against the steel companies in Pittsburgh.

Stating that people used to follow jobs, Wynn explained, "I'm proud of myself, that pretty early on I realized in this current century it's just the opposite: the jobs follow the people." Put another way, although using existing resources and attracting new ones remains at the heart of all city growth, today's cities draw as much—if not more—from their cultural resources as from their natural ones. Just as they once competed for heavy industries like automobile and steel manufacturing, US cities are now in a fierce contest for tourists, technology jobs, and service-industry businesses. Chicago today crafts its development strategy with a different ore, mining the rich historical and cultural traditions of the blues, signified by the Chicago's Department of Cultural Affairs and Special Events' free annual Blues Festival.[10] As cities transform into postindustrial centers, this view contends that culture can crystallize city identity and, conversely, a city's identity can crystallize its culture. This posits that municipalities like Austin need to develop their cultural assets: the physical resources (or amenities) of clubs and venues in close proximity, the social + cultural resources of local musicians (provided they are supported), and the economic resources of money spent by locals and visitors all reinforce the city's symbolic brand as the "Live Music Capital of the World." Having worked with dozens of colleagues through the US Conference of Mayors, Wynn is quick to legitimize his belief in the importance of creating an exciting city to attract the mobile social + cultural resources of young, educated people. Although this had always been, in his words, an "organic" and "imperfectly crafted process" in Austin, it grew into a more intentional policy over his time in office.

Wynn was not alone in this perspective. The mayor of Nashville, Karl Dean, echoed these positions on how he seeks to harness Nashville's creative community as part of his agenda. Only a few hours before he hit the stage to welcome tens of thousands of fans to his town's country music festival, Dean spoke happily about urban culture in his Nashville City

Hall office, flanked by a large signed poster of Neil Young on the wall and a crisp copy of Harvard economist Edward Glaeser's *Triumph of the City* on the coffee table. With the classic politician's combination of formality and warmth, Dean laid out his plan for Nashville in the coming decades, a vision that manages to combine the input of both the musician and the urbanist.

That mayors Dean and Wynn reached similar conclusions is no coincidence. Both have been energized by the thought of exploiting their cities' musical communities. While campaigning for mayor, Dean said he felt Nashville "really needed to do more to emphasize the city's music industry and to make sure they understood we want [businesses and musicians] to flourish here." Like Wynn, Dean felt that continuing to attract talent is crucial to Nashville's success. "Songwriters and musicians come in droves," Dean told me, "and their capital is their ability to write a song, their ability to play a song, their ability to produce a song." Perhaps thinking of his hero, Neil Young, he summed up his goals for Nashville by saying: "Artists and musicians. Those are the types of people we want to attract."

Both Wynn and Dean relied on this "jobs follow people" argument to explain why some places, like Detroit, fail, as others, like San Francisco, succeed: jobs in the new mobile age follow where people want to go. Richard Florida's *The Rise of the Creative Class* (and the battery of articles that followed) advanced the theory that urban growth in the postindustrial age requires attracting creative types and a professional managerial class. Dean's coffee-table book, Glaeser's *Triumph of the City*, follows the lead, in part, by championing the immense power of cities in their ability to foster growth and entrepreneurialism through face-to-face interactions and increasing density, something urbanists have embraced since Jane Jacobs's tribute to Lower Manhattan's neighborhoods, *The Death and Life of Great American Cities*. Glaeser calls cities our "greatest invention" for the job they do in improving social + cultural resources by providing good schools and then nurturing rich entertainment.[11] People, in other words, go to interesting places.

City power brokers embrace the "amenities/creative class" model when it suits them. Both Wynn and Dean cited it and talked to me about their intent to draw residents and tourists who are, in Florida's words, on a "passionate quest for experience."[12] And yet, places like Detroit, St. Louis, and Kansas City all have their rich cultural heritages too, from Motown to jazz. It is unlikely that becoming attractive locales alone will save places ravaged by deindustrialization and depopulation in ways that Sunbelt cities like Austin and Nashville were not. The "jobs follow people who go to interesting places" perspective is hardly generalizable, then. Even Florida himself has hedged on the creative-class argument, noting that not all cities can use his formula; the resulting growth he prophesied is often unevenly allocated among urban communities, and not all cities will benefit in the same fashion.[13] Economic geographer Michael Storper's book *Keys to the City* concedes that a certain measure of success relies on the "buzz" that face-to-face interaction generates and is what attracts many people to cities; Storper insists that cities are assuredly "workshops, not playgrounds" that must have a "minimum threshold" of employers that provide the kinds of networking for ideas and interactions that Florida promised.[14]

Rather than culture supplementing industry, culture is now interlocked with growth, and some see it as a marriage worth promoting.[15] One can now think of city leaders in government and members of quasi-government agencies, such as CVBs or chambers of commerce, realtors and property owners, as place professionals eager to brand and hype their economic, spatial, social + cultural, and symbolic resources to those desired ends. City branding and the promoting of locales is hardly a new strategy, of course. Pittsburgh was not the only town that manufactured steel, but it promoted itself as "Steel City." Rochester, New York, was not the only place producing flour, but it was "Flour City" (and then, after becoming a center for producing and packaging seeds, "Flower City").[16] Manufacturing-age branding was once used as a way to attract industry, and branding today has been adapted to developing *place character* as a strategy for attracting businesses, residents, and tourists.[17] Some city images arose organically, like the one contained in the slogan "Keep Austin Weird." Others were carefully crafted promotional tools, like New York City's 1970s "Big Apple" campaign in which the CVB resuscitated to great effect an image of unknown and confusing origin.[18] Although Providence is more like other former manufacturing cities than Austin or Nashville, it still attempts to align itself with these trends in hopes of attracting and retaining youthful residents: Mayor David N. Cicilline commissioned a study that resulted in rebranding Providence in 2009 from the Beehive of Industry to the Creative Capital. (Later chapters will show the mixed results of this endeavor.)

For Dickens, the circus serves as the thematic counterpoint to the rationalized industrial and educational machines of Coketown. In the opening pages of *Hard Times*, protagonists debate the allure of the "fancy" versus the colder, economical "fact." Certainly, cities have always balanced between these two poles, with fairs and carnivals mixing with the marketplace in the public sphere, and balladeers and clowns performing in European squares even through the modern industrial era. Today, however, the circus no longer serves as the contrast to the marketplace. Urban entertainment-based revitalization policies shape a new sort of industry town, filled with colorful lights and experiences quite unlike Dickens's Coketown factories. This kind of circus, as those who study culture know, is now big business.

"The Bowie Theory"

This move from the manufacturing of durable goods to the creation of memorable experiences finds its mirror in recent developments in the US music industry. Economists who study the music industry have found that live concerts have superseded album sales as the primary source of income for the industry. According to a 2005 study on "rockonomics," the ratio of touring income to record sales income was 7.5 to 1 for the top thirty-five performers in 2002, and these data, paired with a quote by David Bowie—"You'd better be prepared for doing a lot of touring, because that's really the only unique situation that's going to be left"— caused the authors of the study to dub the move to live music as "The Bowie Theory."[19] A survey of over 5,371 musicians by the Future of Music Coalition found that respondents received only 6% of their income from recorded music over the last year, with 66% of respondents saying they received *no* income from recorded music at all while, collectively, 28% of their income came from live performances.[20]

Of course, for the vast majority of human history, music meant live music. As the frontman for the seminal punk band the Pixies, Charles Thompson (aka Frank Black), mused:

> There's something ancient about gathering around a bonfire and someone getting up to tell a story, or lead the dance, or sing a song. Those kinds of things are very old, and very natural. Much more so than anything else we think is natural: iPhones, artificial light, and electricity.... Business changes, this goes away, that goes away.... But the live thing, it doesn't change, ever.

Yet, despite the unchanging appeal of what Thompson calls "the live thing," the changes in the business of music—the industry, scope, and technology that surround it—have had an enormous impact on how listeners receive and enjoy music since Edison's invention of the phonograph in 1877.

With the rise of the Edison, Victor, and Columbia music labels around 1900, the recorded-music industry was born, and it in turn spawned myriad small and large record companies over the next half century. By the 1950s, this cacophony had resolved into five major labels (Decca, RCA, Columbia, Capitol, and Mercury), but before long further changes—in the law (e.g., regarding copyrights), in technology (e.g., amplification and then electrified instruments, the rise of 45s and pocket transistor radios, etc.), in market demand (i.e., having radio stations cater to white and black audiences due to changes in migration), and in the organization of the music industry itself—opened space for greater diversity in content.[21] With the popularity of rock 'n' roll and the introduction of the album format at the end of the 1960s, dozens of labels popped up again. The 1980s brought the high-water mark for album sales, with eighty-four albums selling more than five million copies each, and nineteen albums selling over ten million each. Yet, by the end of the century, even more technological developments, like the compact disc in the 1980s and the MP3 in the 1990s, caused instability in the recorded-music market again, and there was another consolidation of labels.

More than any change since Edison's phonograph, the digitization of music has significantly altered how music is produced and consumed. On the one hand, programs like Pro Tools and Auto-Tune revolutionized audio recording and processing in the 1990s, eventually allowing sound engineers to reach into recordings and slightly adjust a guitarist's mistake or tweak an off-key performance to make even the most "pitchy" singer sound perfectly in tune.[22] For listeners, digitization of music made it easy to pass pirated songs from one person to another. File sharing (or "peer-to-peer" or "P2P") services and software like Napster quickly cropped up, making nearly all the world's music available to anyone with Internet access. Despite a significant rise in single-song sales, an overall decline in album sales started after 1999—the year Napster was launched, music industry personnel will point out—as piracy generated another wave of instability for major recording labels and altered the power dynamics in the industry further.[23] Online vendors iTunes and Amazon continued their ascent as premier sources for digital music (iTunes became the world's biggest music vendor in 2008, accounting for 25% of all digital and physical sales, and selling over ten billion songs by 2010). Traditional radio lost market share as satellite radio stations like SiriusXM and Internet streaming radio and, in 2013, Apple's iTunes Radio offered their music content either free with commercials or commercial free with a subscription.[24] These new forms of digital-music distribution and promotion eroded the Artist → Record Label → Radio → Record Store → Consumer model that had dominated for half a century. Internet music sites as a whole, for example, surpassed CDs as Americans' second source for discovering new and rediscovering old music, and they may soon eclipse radio as the primary source.[25] In 2014, only one artist's album achieved "platinum" status (selling over a million copies) for the first time since tracking in 1974: Taylor Swift (her earlier, more country persona appears in chapter 4) released a full-on pop transformation and chart domination with *1989*, an ascent that required pulling all her music from the streaming service Spotify and developing innovative marketing and packaging for her physical CD.

These changes greatly affected the position of the actual musicians within the recorded-music industry. Early record labels, with varying ability and success, would discover talent, record and promote music, and develop careers. Labels would often pay for the recording and production of a record (renting a studio, arranging and paying for backing musicians and engineers, etc.) and consider it an advance on future sales.[26] Over the last twenty years, however, better and cheaper technology has made it easier for musicians and bands both to make music and to produce and promote it outside the label system. Digitization allows even unsigned and self-produced music to be distributed to most corners of the earth.

As a touring musician and co-owner of a small label, Kristin Thomson realized by the early 2000s that emerging technologies and Internet-based platforms were leading to a "new age" in music creation and distribution, where "almost all the barriers to the marketplace had broken down." Simultaneously, she told me, the conversation about music and creativity had expanded to include "lawyers, tech people, and policy wonks."

With these rapid changes, Thomson felt that "musicians needed to be stakeholders in the discussions about rights and compensation. They also needed guides that could distill and translate information in a musician-friendly way." These were the core reasons she, along with bandmate Jenny Toomey, cofounded the nonprofit Future of Music Coalition in 2000, which advocates for musicians on the issues at the intersection of music, law, technology, and policy. "If there's a way to sum up what we're concerned about," she told me, "it's the challenge of the balance between art and commerce." Their group is one of several organizations helping musicians navigate this new landscape.[27]

Subscription-based music webcasting and streaming services like Pandora, Spotify, Rdio, Rhapsody, and Google Play now offer music fans a variety of ways to discover and listen to huge amounts of musical content online. Though the industry has vastly improved consumers' options, Kristin Thomson told me that this shift from an "ownership model" to an "access model" quickly altered traditional payment and compensation structures. These services negotiated deals with labels. In 2014, Spotify, for example, offered the four major labels an equity stake totaling around 20% and now can pay $0.005 per a single play of a song to songwriters and publishers—a rate that is adjusted based upon factors like the region it is played in and the kind of listener or subscriber.[28]

Many musicians have balked at these changes. The frontman of indie rock band Galaxie 500, Damon Krukowski, broke down his earnings in the rare and "best case" position of a band retaining all its royalties and rights. One of their songs, "Tugboat," was played (or "streamed")

7,800 times on Pandora in three months, for which the three members earned twenty-one cents—or seven cents each—in songwriting royalties. In comparison, "Pressing 1,000 singles in 1988 gave us the earning potential of more than 13 million streams in 2012. (And people say the Internet is a bonanza for young bands...)"[29] Although others claim that independent artists like Krukowski misconstrue the intricacies of compensation from these new digital sources as severely damaging to music careers, artists who have seen a measure of success—such as Chan Marshall of Cat Power, JD Samson of Le Tigre and MEN, David Lowery of Camper Van Beethoven and Cracker, and the band Grizzly Bear—have penned articles or blogs or have been quoted in interviews stating that they don't have health insurance and are, essentially, poor because of these changes.[30]

And yet, just as in the early part of the last century, these technological changes did not diminish live music. As the *recorded*-music industry struggles—July 2013 marked the lowest album sales since Nielsen began tracking them in 1991—the live-music industry carries on.[31] A study of concert data from 200,000 performances by 12,000 artists from 1995 to 2004 and album sales data from over 1,800 bands finds a sharp rise in the number of concerts occurring at the same time as a steep drop in album sales.[32]

According to Nashville rock musician Jack White, the proliferation of digital music only heightens the importance of live performance. In an interview, he said that he wasn't "anti-Internet" but instead "pro-real experiences" of face-to-face performances.[33] White's perspective is echoed by an aspiring musician named Sam that I interviewed at Austin's SXSW. "The performance *means* something. To be *here* means something to these folks," he said as he looked out onto the crowds walking down Austin's Sixth Street Entertainment District. "I mean," he continued, "there may have been historic moments in recorded-music history, but could they possibly compare to the heat generated by the Beatles live on the Ed Sullivan show in '64, Dylan at Newport, Hendrix at Woodstock, or Queen at Live Aid in '85?" Like Sam, many musicians feel that the relevance of live performance is only heightened in the age of digital media, in both experiential and financial terms. With fewer labels making less money and a diminished ability to support new bands and nurture mid-career ones, artists I spoke with talked about the value of the live concert.[34] Newport Folk Festival alumnus Erin McKeown told me that gigging is the major focus for mid-career, established-yet-not-superstar-level artists, as "the most important way for us to make any money." According to a Nashville-based manager of top-selling artists, only the top 10% of artists make money selling records, and everyone else goes on tour;[35] however, Fred, the manager for another major household-name artist, states that live touring for even very established musicians like his client is "the most lucrative part of the business, where it wasn't the case twenty years ago." Talking Heads frontman David Byrne, in his book *How Music Works*, writes that the idea that musicians lose money on a tour is an "old lie… that really doesn't hold true anymore."[36] Touring used to be a part of the marketing for an album, as a way to generate press and build an audience. For many, it is now the primary focus.

Not that tour money comes easy. The live-music experience serves as a more direct economic exchange between an artist and her audience, with its own difficulties. Musicians who aren't at the same level as Byrne have a starker perspective. After paying for recording, publishing, publicity, lawyers, agents, and management, performing still requires funding for transportation, gas, lodging, a tour manager (or doing it yourself), and paying music publishers for the recorded material sold. Then ticket sales and distribution companies (e.g., Ticketmaster, Brown Paper Tickets) get their percentage of the price.

The most straightforward profits on tour come from selling merchandise, or "merch." A musician told me: "I feel like I'm a T-shirt business with a band on the side." "If you ever want to help out a band like mine," another told me, "buy a shirt at our table." In like fashion, 2013 Newport Folk Festival singer Father John Misty's website humorously shouts:

T-SHIRTS ARE CHIEFLY HOW THE MODERN MUSICAL ARTIST DIVERSIFIES HIS INCOME. THERE'S QUITE A BIT OF OVERHEAD INVOLVED IN TOURING. GAS, HOTELS, PURE CUT COCAINE, PITA, HUMMUS, CARROT STICKS, CHERRY TOMATOES, ETC. AS YOU CAN IMAGINE, IT ALL ADDS UP! SO HOW DO I GET YOU TO PART WITH YOUR HARD EARNED DOLLARS, WHEN MUSIC IS FREE ON YOUTUBE?

And even then the profits are reduced: the music venues usually get a cut of the band's in-house sales, and the musicians usually have to coordinate and compensate someone to hold down the merch table.

Mention of Ticketmaster should not be missed, as it is itself a major player in the music business that demonstrates how, just as the recorded-music industry consolidated, so too did the live-music industry. Many local concert promoters coalesced into SFX Entertainment, which was then bought by Clear Channel. Clear Channel then sold its concert arm in 2005, becoming Live Nation. Live Nation branded itself as Live Nation Entertainment when it purchased Ticketmaster in 2010, which sells tickets for over 80% of major venues (the next closest competitor was under 4%), and over a hundred concert venues like the House of Blues, which it acquired in 2006.[37] The company is expanding further, pulling musicians like U2, the Rolling Stones, Madonna, and Jay Z (to the tune of $10 million each for three albums) away from conventional record labels by signing them to "360° deals" offering a full-service combination of artist management, promotion, ticketing, and events production. As live music takes primacy as the centerpiece of a musician's fiscal foundation, and in a time of losses in the recorded-music industry, concert revenues have ballooned: in 2000, concert revenues were $1.7 billion, and despite an economic downturn they reached $4.4 billion in 2009, up 10% from the previous year.[38] The ascent of Live Nation was, in fact, one of the brighter spots in the music business.

In the digital age, live music is a force.

Festivals as Collective Activity

With this sense of urban placemaking dovetailing with the rise of importance of music performances, these larger cultural and economic forces must be understood in terms of the festival as a collective activity: the product of groups that create, maintain, legitimize, promote, and challenge these large-scale events.

Festivals depend upon this vast network of people. In the words of Dom Flemons, whose Grammy Award–winning string trio the Carolina Chocolate Drops has performed at dozens of festivals of bluegrass, Celtic, blues, jazz, folk, Americana, classical, and rock, these events are "a whole bunch of people coming together—musicians, fans, producers, media people—but there are a whole lot of *other* people and groups that are there long before and a long time after I've packed up and left." That communality of cultural work makes it important to flag what groups play their parts: (a) *cultural individuals and organizations* (e.g., arts patrons, people from the recorded- and live-music industry, media, entrepreneurs, etc.), (b) *musicians*, (c) *government* (e.g., municipal, state and local, fire and police, etc.) and/or *quasi-governmental entities* (e.g., convention and visitors bureaus), (d) *for-profit entities* (e.g., local or major corporate sponsors, vendors, venue owners, etc.), (e) *audiences*, and (f) *local communities*.[39]

Although I suppose one could say that there could be no music festival without musicians, these groups all rely upon one another and organize differently in different cases. Some festivals are created by local arts groups, and others are founded by city officials. Local communities serve to promote these events, but they can also challenge them. Connections among these groups determine expansion and contraction, valorization and contestation. These relations make what estimable music scholar Simon Frith described as a series of "interminable negotiations" over any number of topics, including "who will appear and in what size type on the posters, who will perform when and for how long on which stage; on detailed arrangements with local fire and police services; on calculated logistics of sewage, food and first aid."[40] Appreciating these events means understanding the relationships within this social ecology—the festival's social + cultural resources, if you will—but also with an eye to how these relationships shape the festivals themselves.

First, there are the cultural individuals and organizations. Although the Lorillards used significant economic resources to found their Newport Jazz Festival, they also relied on a board of directors that included corporate sponsors and media advisors who were able to marshal resources and positive coverage of those early festivals. Austin's South by Southwest was born of friendships between people who worked at the city's alternative newspaper, the *Austin Chronicle*, and folks working in local music venues.[41]

Second, there are the musicians themselves, who have to be attracted to perform at events, too. Festivals often pay a "guarantee," a set payment that could be sizable for more established acts, as compared with the smaller gigs in venues, where musicians could be paid a percentage of the ticket sales instead. Fred, the aforementioned manager for a major artist, described to me how festivals work as a part of the overall business but also serve as "anchor points" for a tour. "They pay pretty good," he told me, "particularly during the peak summer festival season, and work out well for everybody." Erin McKeown echoed the idea that festivals are "an anchor you build a tour around," but also notes that they serve an additional, critical function: "they allow you to play for people who already know your music and allow you to find new audiences too." Festivals are "great for both" for McKeown because they introduce artists to different audiences with slightly different tastes.

Third, there are the aforementioned municipal governments producing, supporting and, at times, limiting the festivals. Although locals believe Seattle's music culture grew in the '80s and '90s in spite of the municipal government's help, the Bumbershoot festival, for example, was founded by the mayor's office in 1971 as "The Mayor's Arts Festival" and was intended to boost a local economy still reeling from its aerospace industry's near collapse.[42] It is of note, actually, that each festival in this book began with little official blessing or recognition of its local government, thrived despite the lack of support—or in the case of Newport, being kicked out!—only to eventually be embraced. As festivals found success (individually, but also collectively around the United States), many city agencies came to recognize the importance of culture.[43] Around 44% of music festivals receive funds from city government, for example, in order to keep police and firefighters on hand, although it is support that pales in comparison with European and Canadian festivals, which have far greater financial backing from government agencies and cultural ministries.[44] (More on the comparison with other countries in chapter 7.) Even with public funding, festival producers still need money to hire staff (festival organizations themselves may be staffed by a handful of people throughout the year, but balloon to hundreds of temporary staff and volunteers during the festival), pay musicians, promote events, and secure venue space.[45] And in the absence of, and often in conjunction with, these public economic resources, for-profit entities can fill that gap.

Fourth, sponsors held an early presence at each of the festivals in this book. The local Narragansett Brewing Company, for example, sponsored the early Newport festivals. For the better part of the past two decades, US festivals have increasingly relied upon "headlining" corporate underwriting. Whereas Narragansett had an ad in festival programs, Dunkin' Donuts sponsored the entire Newport Festival to get top billing over the city name itself. Today, 72% of today's outdoor festivals have at least some corporate sponsors.[46] This kind of marquee-level sponsorship is often needed to bring major headlining acts to the festival stage. For artists like Charles Thompson of the Pixies, who has performed at countless festivals over his career, the money pouring into festivals was "getting fucking ridiculous." "If you get in the upper slots, you get paid *a lot* of money. And the money got bigger and bigger and bigger, starting twenty-five years ago." When asked how much, he shook his head and said, "For a headlining slot? You were getting half a million to a million dollars and for some of the big big bands? One five." Even though he has remained wary of commercialism from the earliest stages of his career—he embarrassingly recalls even saying "no" to write the theme song for *Bill Nye the Science Guy*—he described how festival commercialization is made palatable by being funneled through the event itself, never compelling the artists to deal directly with sponsors. But Thompson also described changing perceptions of commercialism in music, and the festival's role in it:

> People's comfort level with branding changed, whether it's the artist or just people in general. The world of advertising and branding whatever, it has become more a part of our life. *They* [the festivals] spent the money. *They're* branding the shit out of everything. And all the artists, we took the money. Happily. Because there's no ostracization now. You're up there performing. You're not necessarily in a TV ad. I'm not representing Heineken, I'm just playing my songs.

Corporate interest may increase the money for the artists, or alter the visual landscape and experiences of the festivals. Behind the scenes, it can even influence the lineups themselves. At a SXSW 2012 music panel on festivals, David Silbaugh, talent buyer for Milwaukee's large Summerfest music festival, talked about receiving "wish lists" and band names they don't want from sponsors, as well as requests to run the lineup past sponsors before finalizing their contracts. In response to a question from the audience, Silbaugh was unwilling to say he feels "pressure" but did say the "massive jigsaw puzzle" of booking a festival includes keeping sponsors happy: "Sometimes sponsors will be disappointed because a band they want isn't on a certain stage, but ultimately the decision is ours." The overall slowdown in the global economy, however, led to a significant drop in corporate sponsorship available for festivals after 2007.[47]

Chambers of commerce, powerful players in city operations, were slow to embrace festivals as meaningful expenditures for promoting their local business community. Although Nashville's festival has existed since 1972, the president and CEO of Nashville's chamber of commerce, Mike Neal, told me that strong ties between the mayor's office, the chamber of commerce, and the CVB have only solidified over the last few years through a series of music-based "Blue Ribbon committees" (an informal term for appointed government-advising panels). Sitting a few blocks from Nashville's famous strip of honkytonks on Lower Broadway, he told me that the committees were focused around the Country Music Association (the industry trade organization, or "CMA") and were designed to "advance the relationships between the country music industry, represented by the CMA, the city, and the local business community," not necessarily the wider public. As these groups combined interests, he recalled, the festival became the logical focus for collaboration. In 2012, Mayor Dean verified the continuation of this mission, telling me that the chamber of commerce and the mayor's office often invite businesses to the festival and awards shows as part of their entertainment during their visit, so executives can "get a feeling of how exciting Nashville can be." Assuredly, not all cities seek such strong linkages between culture and their municipal identities, but such legitimation could trigger greater governmental support.

Fifth, there are the attendees, both local and from out of town. According to the National Endowment for the Arts, American festival attendance surpasses any other cultural activity short of movie attendance, and audiences tend to be white and between thirty-five and fifty-four years of age, with slightly more women than men—this is representative of the US population as a whole, although with slightly less representation of

Nashville's "Lower Broad" closed off to traffic and opened to booths and activities, looking east toward Riverfront Park.

Hispanics.[48] A 2012 *Rolling Stone* article notes that live-music revenues have doubled since 2000 due to the growth in attendance of summer music festivals, and quotes Charles Attal (coproducer of Chicago's Lollapalooza), who states: "All the major [festivals] that have been established for a while sold out faster than they've ever sold out."[49] In recent years, many US festivals sold out before the lineups were even announced.

Finally, however, festival audiences don't necessarily jibe with the last group: the local population. Sometimes these two communities have a positive relationship, but they often have a more contentious one. Long-brewing tensions between the festivals and their local communities exist at all three festivals studied here. The checkered relationship between Newport and festivalgoers, for example, has been marked by a number of tensions. Early festival lineups included African American artists and countercultural figures playing to audiences with a large number of beatniks and college students. None of these groups fit with the more tony elites of the Newport set, nor with the town's very large naval population. Wein's move in the late 1960s to incorporate more rock-oriented performers resulted in much larger and rowdier audiences and, when crowds overwhelmed the small police force in a 1971 riot, he relocated the event to New York City for the next ten years. George Wein often expresses surprise that he and his festivals are embraced today. "I never would have thought," he said in an interview, "that we'd be so warmly welcomed by the Newport community as we have been since we returned." Today, these festivals are mostly appreciated as sources of attention and visitor spending for Newport residents. The festivals are no longer seen as oppositional because both they and the jazz and folk music they promote have become more mainstream.

Festivals originated from varied interactions between these groups, and those activities produced different results. Some festivals were sponsored by wealthy impresarios (as was the case in Newport), some were founded by alliances between local industries and the city's power elite (as I will show with Nashville's CMA Fest), and some came out of a city's subcultural music scenes that also linked up with the larger music industry (as I will show with Austin's South by Southwest). The group relations forged in any event's founding place a lasting impression on its future activities, what sociologists call *organizational imprinting*.[50] This is certainly true of each of the three festivals to be discussed in this book.

The early maneuverings of these groups—the behind-the-scenes influence of the sponsors, the role assumed by chamber of commerce members, the struggle of festival organizers to stay economically viable, the influx of attendees looking for a good time, and the participation of local business owners hoping for new customers—make an imprint on these events, sometimes even years later. These complex, complementary, *and* contentious negotiations determine the shape and feel of the festivals, and sit at the center of place marketing and urban culture today.

Conclusions: Experiences and Communities

Rituals play a significant role in binding communities together and in communicating complicated systems of values and beliefs to both participants and outsiders. They are, according to Émile Durkheim's *The*

Elementary Forms of Religious Life, critical because they are what he calls *collective representations*: they channel complex ideas about the community, ideas that are forged in an ongoing collective process that is not the creation of any single individual or group.[51] Inspired by Durkheim, W. Lloyd Warner's ambitious community study of Newburyport, Massachusetts, showed how residents used their small town's tercentennial festival and parade to "collectively state what they believe themselves to be."[52] It is now clear that religious and secular occasions can reflect cultural values and help define community identity via coordinated social activity.

Today, as cultural events like festivals grow in scope and vitality, these rituals might have a more beneficial impact than any other kind of planned event in contemporary culture—for example, in comparison with the high-stakes strategies of building permanent theme parks, destination museums, retail zones, sporting arenas, and tourist-targeting open-air entertainment districts (some notable examples include New York's South Street Seaport, Baltimore's Inner Harbor, San Antonio's River Walk, Dallas's Victory Park, and LA's Universal CityWalk). With varying degrees of success and failure, these places have been criticized for their crass commercialization and indifference to local communities' needs. A troubling study by the University of Chicago's Cultural Policy Center offers this relevant metric: 725 arts and cultural facilities were built between 1994 and 2008 (on par with or even surpassing education and healthcare facilities), costing over $15 billion but outpacing demand and straining public resources.[53] Even the Guggenheim's attempt to capitalize on Soho's emerging cool fizzled; the museum closed its downtown outpost in 2001 due to high operating costs and low attendance. Research on these "heavy" urban cultural moves has rightly criticized the exploitation and commercialization of public places and culture.[54] Festivals seem to offer cities a different option.

And yet, collective representations like festivals are also struggled over and, of course, do not sync up so perfectly with their communities. The resources festivals use and produce are contested. The way that festivals are lashed together with strategies of urban branding and become significant landmarks in these three cities is part of the story that lies ahead— but so too are the numerous ways that people actually act and use these gatherings for their own purposes. Festivals are powerful forces for shaping urban and cultural landscapes—but so too should they be understood as shaping and being shaped by people's individual experiences.

As an urban cultural policy—when city agencies and organizations explicitly direct rituals as components of a city's planning, alongside other amenities like parks, museums, and waterfronts—festivalization may be an effective tool for branding and promotion in the postindustrial, experience-focused economy.[55] And when thought of as places for people's enjoyment and work, festivals can also be understood as the settings for individual action and meaning making. As increasing numbers of attendees come to see and interact with musicians, more musicians can use festivals in their attempts to build careers. As some urban players hope to hitch themselves to the successes of festivals, others choose to reject—or at least challenge—these representations of their communities.

The remainder of this book builds off four points made so far:

First: Contemporary festivals are often situated within a context of strategic urban placemaking and the increased importance of live performances for the music industries.

Second: Festivals are the result of collective action by participants with a variety of experiences and sometimes competing, sometimes cooperative, motivations, whether it is to build a career, promote a city or business, have fun, or forge a community identity.

Third: Festivalization is a process of using these temporary, reproducible, and malleable social occasions, which can be understood according to three distinctive patterns, and their relative costs and benefits depend upon the management and use of economic, spatial, social + cultural, and symbolic resources.

Fourth: Festivalization is also an emerging urban cultural policy wherein groups attempt to develop, use, and exploit these resources to a variety of ends.

The next steps look at these three cases, the relationships behind them, and the lived experiences around them to see how different arrangements create different outcomes. Chapter 2 highlights how the partially isolated Newport Folk Festival looked to a nearby, relatively inexpensive, and loosely affiliated network of musicians at a point when it was having a simultaneous economic and identity crisis. Chapter 3 traces the success of a music trade organization in its use of a downtown core of institutions and images to label Nashville as "Music City, USA," while fans eagerly enjoy a branded landscape of scripted interactions and activities. Chapter 4 shows how the confetti-like organization of the hybrid music conference/music festival of South by Southwest, with its wide array of official and unofficial events that create many indistinct roles for participants, collectively ensures the commercialization of festival spaces as much as the city's weird subcultural status.

2

Music in Ruins
The Newport Folk Festival

We have searched the world over to find you
And now that we have found you, you have changed
We are still the same crew of berserkers
That you knew, but maybe just a little more strange
—"MABEL GREY," BROWN BIRD

Like a Graceland Adrift

The approach to the 2007 festival is arduous but beautiful—it runs south through the center of the town and then east along the water's edge to Fort Adams State Park, a walled enclosure sitting on a narrow peninsula jutting into the harbor opposite the town. The bumper-to-bumper summertime traffic, exacerbated by the sudden increase of festivalgoers, braids slowly through a row of rather large homes with four-car garages, a series of brick walls and gatehouses, until it eventually ends at the park. This year's sponsor, Dunkin' Donuts, has designated the various parking areas with the name of their different beverages; I pull into the Coolatta lot, where a shuttle bus picks me up to cover the last stretch to the fort itself. People talk excitedly about the lineup. Exiting the bus, I hang my pink, orange, and brown pass around my neck and walk under a pink, orange, and brown gate into the enclosed grounds of the Dunkin' Donuts Newport Folk Festival. The spatial isolation reminded me of Borlänge's Peace and Love Festival, except that Newport is positioned outside the city's main business district.

I walk along the outer border of the event for an overview of the surroundings. I pass the small Waterside stage with white folding chairs lined up in front of it, and just beyond it, a mid-sized tent for a few hundred seats but only a few dozen people settling in. Further along is an arcade of thirty tents selling all sorts of items, mostly from New England artists, giving the look of a home-spun and appropriately eco-conscious, liberal-leaning event: handmade bags from recycled goods, cigar box banjos, dulcimers and lap harps, handmade sandals, and lanterns made from used cans. There are tents with Mayan, Balinese, and Ecuadorean crafts. Separated from town, these vendors have an exclusive and captive clientele.

I continue walking and make my way to the main stage to catch the opening act. From afar I see the Carolina Chocolate Drops, a trio of twenty-something African Americans, dwarfed by the huge stage and speaker system. The band leaps into some old-time banjo and fiddle music, starting with "Trouble in Your Mind":

> Back home in the country,
> When a storm blows in,
> Where it feels like heaven,
> When that water hits my skin,
> We live in a downpour,
> But it's just not the same,
> Nothin' washes my soul clean,
> Like that Carolina Rain.

The predominantly white crowd claps along to the upbeat jig. Egging the audience on during a rendition of the century-old folk song "Salty Dog," singer Rhiannon Giddens puts down her banjo, grabs the straw porkpie hat off the head of jug player Dom Flemons, and dances the Charleston to much applause. Between songs Dom talks about learning to play the jug from watching *Festival!*, a documentary about the 1963 to '66

The Carolina Chocolate Drops onstage in 2007. Note the sign language interpreter in the middle-right of the picture.

Newport festivals. Looking out through his round sunglasses and reaching for the jug placed at his feet, he says, "The very first scene has the Kweskin Jug Band, and that's where I got my basics and I made it up after that." The audience claps. "It's like a circle," Rhiannon adds.

It's only 11:30 a.m. For the first time in the history of the festival, there is a cordoned-off VIP section directly in front of the main stage, but only its first two rows hold a smattering of seated attendees, as a sea of more than twenty rows of mostly empty black plastic chairs bake in the ninety-degree heat. Beyond is the rest of the audience. The crowd stretches out over the main lawn with picnic blankets and folding chairs, surrounding the VIP area. It's like a circle too, or a doughnut.

The band displays their wide repertoire of musical styles with a folksy cover of Blu Cantrell's 2001 R&B hit "Hit 'Em Up Style," and then ends with a traditional song, asking the audience to join in when they sing "Hi-ho diddle-eye day." As the group heads offstage, an MC announces: "You can see them at 2:30 p.m. for a CD signing at the Borders booth."

The Gibson Guitars open mic.

Against the fort wall is a small open-mic tent, sponsored by Gibson Guitars, and about ten feet from that is an air-conditioned truck with twenty or so guitars that anyone can sit and play. A man with a gray goatee, red sleeveless T-shirt, sunglasses, and a heavily curled cowboy hat offers a laidback soliloquy about wars in Iraq and Afghanistan between his two original songs. People pass, rarely waiting for a song to begin or end, and there is a twenty-foot gap between him and a crowd of ten or twelve people. To his left there's a signup sheet with ten names on it.

Two park rangers take in the music while scanning the crowd through reflective sunglasses. The officers, one in his thirties and the other in his fifties, tell me how much they love working the festivals. "We basically listen to music and walk around," says one with a smile. "We actually have *less* to do than usual, because the festival staff take care of a lot." His partner adds: "We don't expect any trouble at these kinds of events anymore." The audience is, indeed, pretty tame: a woman whose long, straight gray hair rises up in the wind spins her Hula-Hoop over a multicolored dress; a few people dance. A whiff of marijuana comes from the crowd, but the faces of the two rangers remain unchanged. Like a sustained chord at the end of a song, the sweet smell drifts and fades with the Atlantic breeze.

Later in the day, the main stage hosts Amos Lee, a similarly genre-blending artist, playing a subdued acoustic set. The size of the stage seems to correspond to the broadening definition of folk music: the bigger the acts and the broader the audience appeal, the larger the stage. I look out at the crowds soaking in the sun and tapping their feet. I sit next to a couple that grouses over the Allman Brothers Band's headlining set the night before. They feel the 1970s southern blues/rock group wasn't an appropriate fit for the festival. Katy, a Bostonian in her early fifties who is attending with her husband, Thomas, at their fifth Newport Folk Festival in ten years, tells me: "I guess you can't have the Indigo Girls here every year." She spreads sunscreen on her arms, and the smell of coconut fills the air. We look up and watch Lee. Over the speaker stacks on either side of the stage hangs a fifteen-by-fifteen-foot sign with a "DD" in orange and pink and, above that, a "Newport Grooves on Dunkin'" banner. I ask about the corporate sponsors, and Katy agrees with many of the attendees I speak with that Ben and Jerry's was a better sponsor because it was a closer match to the overall feel of the event. Although mostly silent, Thomas chimes in at this point and says, "I guess Dunkin' Donuts is more local as compared to Vermont," contrasting the corporate homes of Ben and Jerry's and Dunkin' Donuts' nearby Massachusetts headquarters. He continues, however, emphatically punctuating each word: "and I wouldn't mind it so much if it weren't on every. Single. Thing. I. See," pointing to signs in his visual field as he speaks. He finishes by gesturing to a large trailer truck serving Dunkin' Donuts coffee at the back of the grounds, and I say my good-byes to check it out.

The large truck looks like an emergency mobile caffeine dispensary, and features a sign stating that all of the proceeds are being donated to the Rhode Island State Firefighters' League, indicating an attempt to make a connection to the area's nonprofits. As Emmylou Harris runs through a set of mostly cover songs, I look past the truck. Out in the water is a ribbon of boats that dropped anchor just offshore, close enough

The Dunkin' Donuts tractor-trailer café.

to see the large video screens near the stage. Maybe a hundred rowboats, kayaks, and sloops are bobbing in the water, with people lounging and enjoying the music for free.

((( )))

My experience in 2007 showed a walled-off and heavily branded festival, contrasting the images of the 1950s folk revival I had in my mind, when old Woody Guthrie and Lead Belly songs were taught to earnest young college kids with banjos over their shoulders, and of the 1960s, when Dylan "plugged in" and changed music history. The Newport Folk Festival seemed to be in deep contradiction as it struggled to balance its identity as the paragon of folk music while at the same time using corporate branding to stay viable as an economic enterprise. The people I spoke with on the festival grounds were mostly ambivalent. They offered comments like "It is just a mix of mellow-sounding music," and "Sure, there are some singer-songwriters, but it just doesn't feel very authentic anymore." Even musicians I spoke with felt the festival was in the midst of an identity crisis. The festival seemed unmoored, they said, didn't offer anything new, while also losing its connection to its past, and had little relationship with the region's music community or Newport itself. I was not particularly enthused about returning.

Later in my research, however, I began hearing that the folk festival had undergone some interesting changes since 2007. David Wax—whose band, the David Wax Museum, gave a breakout performance of their uncommon mix of Mexican and American folk music at the 2010 Newport Festival and then returned to play the main stage the following year—echoed some of the same feelings I had originally held. Sitting at a café, with his ice-blue eyes and a messy mop of reddish hair, he told me, "I knew Newport was where Dylan and Baez were introduced to a national audience, and it held an aura as an important musical place, like a Graceland . . . but it was a place that had lost its way." And yet, he continued, the festival had recently managed to transform itself, and he was again very excited to be onstage at such a relevant and unique event. Perceptions seemed to have changed.

Looking into the festival with newfound curiosity, I found a story similar to many of the old folk songs themselves: one of redemption, reclamation, and even rebirth. It was a tale of how economics had reshaped the iconic American event, but in a way that had allowed organizers to slough off aggressive corporate branding, to recapture some of the festival's earlier symbolic value, and to reconnect and bolster a local music community. It was also a story of how a group of musicians from a nearby music scene had seized the opportunity to hitch their rising fortunes to the growing appreciation of the festival. If it were once "like a Graceland" adrift, it was now hoping to chart a course toward prominence again, with a stronger focus on the region.

The Beginnings of Newport

Locals are fond of talking about Newport's literally and figuratively rich history. Founded in 1639 upon the ideals of religious freedom, it was the fifth-largest city in the United States before the Revolutionary War, and it still holds more historic colonial houses than New York, Philadelphia, and Boston combined. During the Gilded Age, this harbor town became a summer resort for northeastern and southern elite families like the Vanderbilts and Astors, desperate for cool summertime breezes; the city still holds a stunning collection of mansions.

In the '90s the Newport Convention and Visitors Bureau claimed Newport was "America's first resort," and called it a "city of firsts" in promotional materials. Both phrases serve to wrap existing cultural resources into the sort of coherent package that tourism scholar Dean MacCannell calls a *tourism set*, which works to frame a visitor's expectations (e.g., San Francisco's combination of Coit Tower, the Golden Gate Bridge, the Presidio, the wharf, etc.). In Newport's case, the city boasts the nation's oldest synagogue, the oldest state house in Rhode Island and the fourth oldest in the nation, the nation's first church steeple, the oldest lending library, the oldest continually operating tavern, and even the nation's first gas streetlights. Picturesque natural assets along the eastern Atlantic cliffs and the harbor along the western Narragansett Bay side of the city further enhance this cultural and historical nexus. The city was the site for the America's Cup regatta from 1930 to 1983, and situated between the mansions and the harbor is the International Tennis Hall of Fame. These sites and sights comprise the city's tourism set, a package city officials hope to promote. Such a collection allows for placemakers to craft a set of spatial and symbolic resources.

Locals describe their community as a seasonal ebb and flow of a few very different groups. There are those who inhabit Newport year-round, who own businesses or work at the Naval War College, at Salve Regina University, or in the shipbuilding industry. Then there is what one longtime resident called "the summer colony": the elites who come to live in their summer homes. Then there are the tourists.

With such elite residents, it is no surprise that the festival's impresarios came from their ranks. Elaine and Louis Lorillard were Newport fixtures and initially pitched the idea of the Jazz Festival in Providence, not Newport, but the city government refused assistance.[1] As their daughter, Didi Lorillard, pointed out in an interview, they initially funded the events and massaged their social networks to "grease the community's wheels." The first Newport Folk Festival was held in 1959 at Newport's Freebody Park, behind the Newport Casino on Bellevue Avenue and close to the elite row of mansions. There were twenty acts, including an eighteen-year-old Joan Baez. Though the first two festivals were a success with music fans and musicians, there was not a financial windfall. In 1960, thousands of college kids arrived for the sold-out Newport Jazz Festival and, during a Ray Charles performance on July 2, things got out of control. Newport had gained an image of a hip destination (thanks to the festivals and films like *Jazz on a Summer's Day*), and the town's police force, only a hundred strong, was overwhelmed by thousands of festivalgoers. "You have to remember," Didi Lorillard explained, "that the force was built for the fifty-five *non*festival weeks of the year, not the two weekends of these festivals." The National Guard, tear gas, and fire hoses were used to disperse the crowd. The next day, as out-of-towners were forcibly bused out of Newport, the city council voted four to three to cancel the rest of the festival, and neither the jazz nor the folk festival was held in 1961.[2]

The festivals returned in 1962 and '63, replacing the Lorillards with a board of directors that served as the organizing nexus for a for-profit venture: Wein, Albert Grossman (manager of Odetta, Dylan, and many others, and the owner of Chicago's folk club Gate of Horn), and folksingers Theodore Bikel, Oscar Brand, and Pete Seeger. Seeger and his wife, Toshi, pushed for a Newport Folk Foundation in an attempt to avoid the commercialization of the festivals (the booking of the Kingston Trio had led to concerns over selling out from the very start) and of folk music in general by earmarking any profits for the maintenance of the festival and its workshops, as well as distributing money for field-research grants, instruments for musicians, and recording equipment for university folklore departments. The board agreed that all performers would be paid the same amount: fifty dollars plus room, board, and travel expenses.

By 1963, the folk revival was in full swing, and the festivals took off. Wein wholly controlled the festivals, as a for-profit called Festival Productions, Inc.[3] In 1964, there were over 46,000 attendees. As a result, the city council decided to ban the use of Freebody Park, Wein moved the event a few miles north, and attendance increased to 76,000. *New York Times* music critic Jon Pareles describes the folk festival's ethos at the time:

Most of the performers...weren't telling their own stories or singing their own songs; their material is by Traditional, Anonymous and half-remembered blues and gospel sources. They presented themselves as preservers and disciples of venerable styles, holding on to music that was homemade and proud of its distance from the machinations of commercial pop. Performers certainly had egos, but they were careful to preach their humility and loyalty to roots.[4]

There was, early on, a strong back-and-forth between musician and attendee: hours-long workshops on dulcimer and autoharp playing and panels on topics like "Ballads," "Whither Folk Music," and "Topical Songs," and later—indicating a diversification of the tastes in the genres of folk music—"Bluesville: The South" and "Bluesville: The City."[5] All sorts, from the headlining musicians to ex-convicts from Texas, led workshops through the 1960s, and attendees would come with guitars in their hands and sleeping bags on their backs.

Perhaps the most famous story from Newport is when folk icon Bob Dylan went electric in 1965. With Dylan's (reportedly) spontaneous decision to "plug in," chaos erupted both in the audience and backstage. It's been argued just how much the crowd booed and whether or not a fight broke out in the wings, with Pete Seeger allegedly wielding an axe to hack the audio cables. Jim Gillis, who reported on the fiftieth anniversary of the event for the *Newport Daily News*, told me that Seeger claimed he was only unhappy about the sound quality, while Baez maintained that Seeger was now backtracking. "Pete," Jim told me, "has been consistent about his story."[6]

Although it is a tale musicians have commonly cited in interviews, it is one that overshadows other internal tensions within the organizing community and fans over the idea of what folk music should be that played out in the festival's politics. On the one hand were the older folk traditionalists, who resented newer acts pushing boundaries within the genre, but there had been concerns over maintaining "authenticity" as early as the second festival. Notably, Seeger and musicologist and fellow Newport Folk board member Alan Lomax grumbled about the increasing commercialism and "slickness" of the events.[7] Advertisements were there early on at the folk festival, but the presence of ads for record labels, guitar manufacturers, and a local beer were rather muted in the original program.[8] The concerns over cooptation, however, did not reside just in the pages of the program. The lineups mattered more. Bands were not just noncommercial, but were explicitly anticommercial and political, offering union songs like "Which Side Are You On?" and Guthrie's "Union Maid." They contrasted with parts of the 1960s folk revival, like the Kingston Trio, that popularized folk music to the urban and college-aged crowds through their slick (as evidenced by their overproduced reworking of standard murder ballad "Tom Dooley"), commercial (they copyrighted old folk songs in the public domain), and apolitical (they were concerned, not altogether unreasonably, about McCarthy-era blacklists) style. Recognizing dissent in his ranks, Wein called for a committee of musicians to help book the event as a way to appease concerned parties in 1963.

There were external tensions, too. Though the small arts community enjoyed the events, according to one business owner, "There was some resistance [because] locals didn't like all the traffic. They didn't like all the commotion." In the words of one early festivalgoer, Newport was a "twenty-four-hour festival for us, with singing and pickin' in parks and on street corners." Another festivalgoer, attending his thirteenth Newport Folk Festival, admitted that in the old days, "We drank too much, we slept on the beach, we sang songs too loud. We were young." Arts reporter Jim Gillis (whose first apartment in Newport was rented from Elaine Lorillard) added: "Elaine and Louie used to have parties at their estate with the musicians over until all hours and people in the neighborhood didn't like that too much."[9] The presence of the city's naval population didn't help matters. There were only so many watering holes in town, and some of them were notorious sailor dives hostile to the beatniks and hippies trying to get a drink after the night's final set. The relationship between the festivals and Newport's communities was a chilly one.

The Kingston Trio notwithstanding, the events were energized by political activism as well. Many festival musicians were African American, and the festivals became more than symbolically linked with civil rights.[10] The Student Nonviolent Coordinating Committee, with Joan Baez, marched through Newport's streets, and the Congress of Racial Equality was invited to attend in those early days, pushing tensions even further. High-society folk fretted over the African American performers in hushed tones—Gillis suspects there was a "hidden racial aspect" to the antagonism too—and made a public case against the festivals based on the crowds of young college kids singing around campfires on beaches at night (since every hotel was booked) and clogging the streets by day. In his autobiography, Wein insists that he pleaded with the chamber of commerce and city hall to assist in enforcement and control during and after the events, only to be rebuffed.[11] And when people "raided" the jazz festival in 1971—ironically, due in part to growing interest in the afore-mentioned Allman Brothers—demanding free admittance and forcing the cancellation of two concerts, the city council decided again to inter-vene, and again revoked the folk festival's license.

From there, the festivals and the Newport name—copyrighted brands owned by Festival Productions, Inc.—hit the road, in exile from their original locale. Wein held the Newport Jazz Festival–New York, Newport Jazz Festival–Saratoga, and a Newport Jazz Festival in Japan, as well as the New Orleans Jazz Festival. He started searching for corporate spon-sors, and produced a twenty-city tour called Schlitz Salute to Jazz, and then, in a confused merging of corporate and place branding, the KOOL Newport Jazz Festival–New York (the sponsorship of a cigarette com-pany, combined with the existence of a competing cigarette company, led him to drop Newport's name after the founding year).[12]

Eventually, the festivals came back to Newport again: the jazz festival in 1981 and the folk festival in 1985, after the city council developed a newfound interest in tourist revenue, asking Wein to return. This time, however, the events would be at a new location across Newport Harbor, at Fort Adams State Park, a largely underused asset. Newport City Man-ager Ed Lavallee was in the police department at the time and remem-bered the rationale for the selection of the fort in this second era. There were some real concerns over the "rabble" from the festivals causing problems again, and the major issue for the city was to isolate the impact of the event, capping the attendance at 10,000 (a fraction of the high-water marks of the 1960s) and making the promoters responsible for safeguards, from controlling ticket scalping to forbidding alcohol. "Ever since then," Lavallee told me of its present citadel location, "it's worked out just fine."

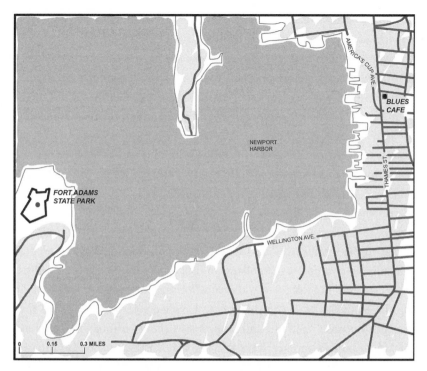

Fort Adams on the left side; on the right, across the harbor in Newport's downtown, is the
Newport Blues Café.

Despite the change in venue, there were efforts to keep a tie to the
past. Wein's coproducer Bob Jones wanted to bring back the artists
signed to perform at the cancelled 1971 event. And then, in the late
1980s and '90s, there was a move toward more female-fronted folk, rid-
ing the popularity of the Indigo Girls (who played ten times between
1990 and 2001), Shawn Colvin, Ani DiFranco, Dar Williams, and Su-
zanne Vega; the festival seemed to have been lulled into an uncertain
identity in the early 2000s.

When I visited Newport in 2007, it was a small city (24,672 in the
2010 Census) with a well-established node on the map of American
cultural significance. Walking near the intersection of America's Cup
Avenue and Thames Street, the heart of Newport's walkable shops, restaurants, and bars, I watched as tourists flipped through postcards of
the Tennis Hall of Fame and the Breakers as buses rumbled by on their

way to the mansions or the Cliff Walk. Seasonal employees talked about how their employment opportunities tripled in the summer months. An art gallery owner told me: "Look. Every summer weekend is precious. If you get a bad or slow one. . . . You know, two summers ago we had record rainfall and it killed business. The festivals, like 'em or not, bring in money." Newport County Chamber of Commerce Executive Director Jody Sullivan described the interest of the business community she represents: historically and culturally inclined travelers stay longer and spend more, and that's something the city tries to foster. When I asked Ed Lavallee about the seasonality of business, he concurred. Retailers in the downtown area, he explained, make a large amount of their yearly profits in the summer months, and then shorten hours or close altogether in the winter. He explained that "the wisdom of previous elected officials" was to nurture a collection of summer events to which those businesses could look forward because of the potential for profits. Noting the festivals' return in the 1980s, Lavallee said that he is glad they are back because, "like the tall ships visits, the mansions, the sailboats, they're an important part of the culture here." The city's civic groups are eager to capitalize on Newport's heritage; its cultural, nature, and adventure tourism; as well as special events like the festivals to maintain its position as a tourist destination.[13]

The festival, however, is geographically separate from the business strip, behind the citadel walls, where the crafting of image and culture continues somewhat separate from the city itself. The arrangement is telling; from its origins to its return, the festival has an arm's-length relationship with Newport itself.

Rebirth and Transformation

It was easy to see the commercialized symbolism at the 2007 Newport Festival: the Gibson Guitars truck and open-mic tent, a Borders music tent and autograph queue, and, as festivalgoers noted, few vistas were left untouched by the orange, pink, and brown color palette of Dunkin' Donuts. After my first visit, I felt I had a good sense of a simple story: the festival as a cultural event was a rather hazy mix of questions about what folk music is onstage and a struggle backstage with the realities of corporate sponsorship. But this simple story was more complicated than I had realized, and unseen internal maneuverings led to a much stronger tie to the region in a variety of ways.

Seven months prior to my first visit, eighty-two-year-old George Wein sold his festival business (which included jazz and folk festivals in Paris, New Orleans, and Newport) to Festival Network LLC. The new CEO, thirty-six-year-old Chris Shields, stated that his goal was to create and maintain "destination" music festivals like Newport, with careful attention to other second- and third-tier cities.[14] This global plan for corporations to sponsor over seventeen events, from Newport to Mali, ran afoul of the 2008 recession. As the global economy slowed, major sponsors tightened their budgets. Even with some initial financial backing, Festival Network ran into further trouble when cash-strapped fans didn't buy tickets at projected rates. The 2008 festivals limped along while the company lost millions and cancelled events. Because the company could not pay its fees from 2008, the Rhode Island Department of Environmental Management terminated Festival Network's license to use the fort the following summer.[15]

By March 2009, nothing was set for the late July festivals and Wein grew fearful that the events he had worked on for most of his life would implode.[16] Distrusting Shields and his company, Wein established the Newport Festivals Foundation, a 501(c)(3) organization with the mission of maintaining the festivals in Newport and also developing arts and music education in New England. This newly formed organization took over running the festival as the Festival Network fell into bankruptcy. Wein was able to secure contracts and licenses, benefiting from years of connections and goodwill, but he also promoted someone from within the Festival Network to help run the folk event: Jay Sweet, a cultural tastemaker as editor-at-large of *Paste Magazine* and cofounder of a company that uses music to brand corporations. Aside from these cultural bona fides, Sweet also attended high school in Newport and still lives nearby, solidifying his investment in the festival's success. Reporter Jim Gillis expressed happiness in seeing his city and the nonprofit bound together with the festival, which now costs about $3 million to run. Asked about the brief period when Festival Network controlled the event, he notes, "Nobody's going to remember them." He was careful to add that if

Wein had not returned and wielded his influence to corral sponsors, secure permits, and attract musicians within a very limited time frame, "the company's downfall could've been the end of the festivals altogether."[17] Changes in funding were not the only factors involved in the festival's new incarnation, but also the growth of a network of Rhode Island musicians.

With limited resources and a search for legitimacy and footing, Sweet started building off the emerging and hip scene in and around New England that embraces Americana—a contemporary musical genre that blends roots, blues, rock, and folk music. In a story told to me by a number of musicians and reporters, this rise of local Americana at Newport began with a ragtag bunch of Brown University students who volunteered to pick up trash and recycling at the 2008 festival. Having gained access to the grounds, they passed around CDs of their sparse, "low-fi" self-produced album under the name the Low Anthem. Their homemade package made its way into Jay Sweet's hands. In 2009—the year Wein wrestled back control of the festival—they were invited to perform on the small stage and to distribute their album, which had been rereleased on Warner Music Group's Nonesuch label. They appeared again in 2010, this time on the main stage, launching a critically acclaimed career. The band gained notoriety from their music as much as from their strong filial connection with Providence and the press's description of their breakthrough story at Newport. When the festival announced a newly founded board of advisors, band member Ben Knox Miller joined more established artists—the Decemberists frontman Colin Meloy, My Morning Jacket frontman Jim James, Gillian Welch, and Woody Guthrie protégé Ramblin' Jack Elliott—to help steer the ship.

David Wax, whose success was another a feel-good story—his band won a contest to perform at the festival in 2010—told me that he paid close attention to how the Low Anthem was able to "weave a compelling narrative that benefited them and Newport [Folk Festival] to be associated with each other." As an artist seeking his own story and how it tied with the newfound relevance of the festival, he reflected on how these acts breathe new life into what he sees as folk music. When asked to name the next new act to "break," he cited a Providence duo called Brown Bird.

Brown Bird's David Lamb and MorganEve Swain certainly hoped for the bump in prestige and attention in launching careers that the media sometimes calls the Newport Effect. Lamb lived in Maine and Seattle before meeting Swain on tour, and the two decided within days to join forces. The duo's performances usually consisted of Lamb picking the guitar or banjo while using one foot to thump a beat on a kick drum and the other to hit a series of pedals activating a woodblock or tambourine as Swain played the cello, double bass, or fiddle. As the son of a preacher, Lamb often painted his lyrics in the colors of moral ambiguity and fire-and-brimstone spirituality, matched with the ethos of hard work.

I interviewed Lamb and Swain a few weeks before their appearance at the 2011 festival, and they told me they were still juggling workaday jobs while touring and recording music. Lamb was working at a Rhode Island shipyard installing electrical systems on boats. Over beers, we started by talking about their many tattoos. Swain wore bangs that swooped low and a nose ring; Lamb had a long beard and dark, soulful eyes.

Speaking of her friends in Providence, Swain said many were surprised that Newport was becoming a destination for acts like theirs. Despite the short distance, "there was never any reason for our friends to go to Newport." Lamb told me how he saw the new connection between the festival and the region's music community:

> There are more and more Americana/folk/roots-oriented groups coming out of Providence, maybe somebody—maybe Jay [Sweet]—saw what was happening to the state of music festivals and wanted to help it out, make it something less corporate again. And realized: "Now we have more local groups doing something that would fit into the whole idea of what Newport was and should be."

Given that they played in and were friends with bands in the Providence scene, and that Ben Knox Miller was on the advisory board, Lamb and Swain told me they weren't altogether surprised to receive an invitation.[18] Festival producer Sweet corroborated this story, bringing up Brown Bird specifically. "I asked the board, 'Who do we bring in from Rhode Island?' and everyone said Brown Bird. That counts more than some random press release or email link." Sweet insisted that he "100 percent trusts the board," and "If those bands testified for them, I listened to them and they were great." Brown Bird was in.

The growing Providence-based social ties continued with Brown Bird's friend Joe Fletcher. Like Lamb and Swain, Fletcher lived in Warren, Rhode Island, a onetime whaling community between Providence and Newport. With an Ernest Tubb Record Shop baseball cap hiding a loose pompadour, and a plaid shirt with the sleeves rolled up to reveal a few tattoos of his own, Fletcher strolled around his neighborhood with me, reluctantly answering questions about the relation of place to music, and how his seafaring surroundings might inspire him to write lyrics like "I never would've gotten on this boat if I'd known it was gonna take me home." Musicians dislike being pigeonholed, and Fletcher was no different.

He claimed he's "more honkytonk than sea shanty," with a mix of rock and folk that's similar to Hank Williams's style, although he admitted that the anchor tattoos on his finger and his left forearm may contradict the point. Still, he was raised in Rhode Island, and was pleased the festival spotlight was shining on this loosely affiliated group. In his thirties, he described his imagined version of those early festival years as being "very, very significant," but like Swain, he saw its 1985 return to Newport as an event he and his fellow Providence musicians "didn't really care about. . . . it was just like this dead vessel." Although there were certainly those who enjoyed the festivals in those days, for him and his community, "[i]t wasn't," he continued, "something we were going to spend sixty dollars to go to just to relive something that's not happening anymore." The festival eventually did catch his attention, though. It was hard not to notice when his local musician friends started getting booked.

When Fletcher was starting his music career in Providence, he recalls, he saw a local rock band called Deer Tick perform, and remembers that the singer, John McCauley, was "just magnetic." Fletcher told me he "just wanted to hang out with them, play shows with them as much as possible." Eventually these musicians grew closer, and when Deer Tick and the Low Anthem played the newly refashioned folk festival, Fletcher felt it was "big news" for his network of musicians. He saw a potential opening just down the road. He worked as Brown Bird's roadie at the festival first, happily following the Low Anthem's cue by distributing his self-produced CDs as he walked around the grounds. Laughing, he described it as "almost infiltrating" the festival.

What the artists and the media call the Newport Effect has to do with the reception of these artists as they gain exposure. What remain less visible, however, are the social networks of these musicians. One act following another, and then another, resembles the process of immigration that sociologists call *chain migration*. In terms of understanding cultural workers and their careers, sociologists are starting to study how certain kinds of *reputational work* are key in these processes. Reputation ties tend to facilitate trust, and this chain of artists follows a reputational line: drawn through a regional social network, linking culture, place, and an event as they reinforce each other.[19]

What's more, these reputation-based relationships also shape what is now considered to be folk music as presented at the festival. Being from the same city and playing at the festival, according to Fletcher, drew two unlikely bands, the subdued the Low Anthem and the raucous party band Deer Tick, closer together:

> This is where I grew up, this is where all the guys in Deer Tick grew up. The Low Anthem and Deer Tick broke around the same time as far as like national attention, going on *Letterman* and things like that. I mean those are two really sort of almost unrelated bands. I mean *now* they're buddies.

"Now," he said, "they're tied together under a big umbrella called folk music." Fletcher told me it was a stretch to say everyone in Providence hangs out, but "if you're talking about Brown Bird and Deer Tick, yeah, those are pretty good friends of mine." Producer Sweet described the music community as "a Venn diagram [with] a lot of overlap." And David Wax, leading a Boston-based band looking only slightly outside, teased out the symbiotic relationship between the event and the bands from the region, commending them for "embracing being from Providence, trumpeting that fact, making that part of their identity, and then forming strategic connections with other bands with Providence connections." Sure enough, Fletcher made it to the second-largest stage in 2012 and hosted his own four-hour honkytonk set of performers, named "Nashville to

Newport" (after Chet Atkins's song on the 1960 album *After the Riot at Newport*), in 2013.

Providence residence is not the only path toward entrance, however. Advisory board members also strengthened the lineup *outside* the Providence scene by working their social ties. As Fletcher said, "There's a somewhat strong social infrastructure as far as having artists like Jim James, John McCauley of Deer Tick, and Gillian Welch as good advocates saying: 'Come play with us, because it's going to be fucking fun!'" Jay Sweet told me these wider reputational networks not only build prestige but also help bring in better bands than the festival could otherwise afford. And, in preparation for the 2013 event, the Newport Folk Festival did something a little more notable: they asked their Facebook followers to recommend bands on their page. They received over 900 comments for the request. This was far removed from when Alan Lomax convinced the Newport Foundation to hire someone to travel 12,000 miles through the United States and Canada to seek out traditional folk music fifty years ago.[20] The festival also has to consider bands in their career trajectory. Speaking about the era prior to Sweet's direction, impresario George Wein said in a radio interview, "we get them on the way up, and on the way down."[21]

Even though there are booking concerns that are common across festivals, the distinctive element here is the burgeoning and improbable connection between the festival and the Providence scene. The financial turmoil of 2008 and these network ties led to the unintended consequence of matching culture and place: musicians like Deer Tick, Brown Bird, the Low Anthem, and Joe Fletcher all make their claims to folk music, and all see that, through the embrace of this local resource of a music scene, there was a refashioning of what folk music is on the stage. Perhaps without intending it, the organizational change from for-profit corporate event to nonprofit local event had reshaped artist investment and audience experience of the festival. These musicians, as a group, served to lend legitimacy to the event.

These changes meant that I had to return to Newport over the consecutive summers of 2011 and 2012 to find what these efforts to exploit these networks looked like, as musicians and festival organizers sought to connect with old traditions and establish new ones.

Reinventing Tradition in a "Living Museum"

I get in early as a volunteer for the Convention and Visitors Bureau Information Booth. As the crowds outside swell around the gate, the Providence-based What Cheer? Brigade, a dozen-member troupe named after the city's motto, position themselves to welcome everyone as they come through. My boss for the day, CVB Vice President of Marketing Kathryn Farrington, and I stand with a stack of maps for the grounds. She tells me, "This is what I call 'the running of the bulls.'" The band kicks up, and people begin rushing straight to the main stage, hoping to stake out a good spot. Our task is to pass out maps to the crowd, repeating, "Thank you for walking," "Thank you for walking," "Thank you for walking."

I look at the map to field a question about a new area called the Fort stage and notice that a whole other area inside the walls of the fort itself has opened up. Previously the stages were all outside the fort walls, but this year the citadel itself—an area once used as a backstage for the artists, separating them from the audience spaces—has been opened to the event. Inside the granite and shale walls in the six-and-a-half-acre Parade Field—used for occasional Civil War reenactments of battles and encampments—are a new fourth stage and a large media tent, positioned between the artist accommodations in the fort's old officer quarters and the large stage. Entrance is through a dark, cool tunnel, with flows of people streaming in both directions, opening onto Parade Field, where the media tent and the stage occupy center ground, surrounded by an outer ring of smaller tents and food carts. The festival has expanded within its own citadel pattern.

Inside the media tent, four white couches encircle a live video feed from the main stage. To the side, a massage therapist is working over someone's lower back. There's a bar dispensing free Magic Hat beer. On a long table at the back are three computers for the media, but most people I see are sitting at tables, furiously tapping on laptops or cell phones. The ninety-two-year-old Pete Seeger is flanked by two reporters who are interviewing him between his many appearances throughout the event. Whereas the new Providence bands lend their hip credibility, Seeger lends his historical relevancy.

Emerson College–based WERS Radio Promotions Director Cady Drell tells a similar story to what I had gathered from the musicians—the rejuvenated festival is connected with the region, but she also talks about the angle for the festival she's most interested in: the mixture of homecomings for festival veterans (Mavis Staples, Ramblin' Jack Elliott), the emphasis on diversifying what defines a folk musician (rockers Elvis Costello, Tegan and Sara), and the inclusion of young, hip Americana acts from near and far. A WERS intern asks about my interests, and I tell her I'm looking forward to seeing the Decemberists, the Oregon-based rock-folk band who were recently nominated for best rock song at the Grammy Awards. "Their career," she says, "is moving more in sync with the festival." She relates a story about how frontman (and festival advisory board member) Colin Meloy stopped their 2009 show mid-set to reenact the Dylan-going-electric story, including pantomiming Seeger cutting the cables with an axe. The album the Decemberists are currently promoting, *The King Is Dead*, the intern explains, was inspired by seeing Pete Seeger here in 2009, and features Meloy's fellow advisory board member Gillian Welch on two tracks. The artists shape the festival and, in a way, have been shaped by it as well.

((( )))

Whereas my 2011 visit widened my view of how traditions were reinforced, my trip in 2012 further deepened my understanding of how the festival started to bolster itself as a tradition unto itself, and to really develop interactions between acts and across the musicians and fans.

((( )))

At the 2012 Newport Folk Festival, Brown Bird is opening the events on the main stage, having graduating from the smaller stage, just as the Carolina Chocolate Drops had the year before. This year, the VIP section I saw back in 2007 is gone, replaced by an open walkway between the front row and the stage—a "pit" where media photographers can get a clear angle of the performers. There are certainly photographers with large professional cameras, but also one or two regular folk, taking pictures with their iPhones. When I ask a security guard if I can pass, he just moves aside. It's a striking difference from watching from a few hundred

Brown Bird on the main stage, from the photography pit, July 2012.

feet away; I take advantage of this spatial reorganization to take a few pictures on my own phone. Turning around, I see the audience lounging in the noontime sun, settling in for their long day.

Brown Bird plays "Bilgewater," a song Lamb wrote while working as a marine electrician, and "Fingers to the Bone." Both songs are about working hard and being servants to the ebbs and flows of weather and water, to straw bosses and other "lords of labor." I linger with four other lay photographers, then exit to wander back through the crowd. I use the shared experience to ask Josh, a thirtysomething music fan from Philadelphia who is also leaving the pit, what he thinks of folk music. "It isn't easy to categorize," he says, then adds rhetorically: "What's a genre mean anyway?" Pressed on the point of what makes folk music "folk," he acknowledges that "it's far too white as a category from the crowds I see, but there's reverence for the blues, and there's some diversity onstage." We join his wife, Melissa, on a nearby blanket and talk about the bands they are interested in. I ask about an upcoming act, the Alabama Shakes, whose African American frontwoman is twenty-three-year-old Brittany

Howard. Josh tells me that a lot of the African American performers at the festival—Gary Clark Jr., Mavis Staples, the Carolina Chocolate Drops—all share the roots of American music, "but these guys are pretty Americana-rootsy too." From the stage, David Lamb announces: "We would like to end with a cover, in the spirit of the festival and to honor those who came before us"; Brown Bird closes their set with Johnny and June Carter Cash's "Jackson."

Afterward, Josh tells me I "need to check out" a man named Frank Fairfield: "He looks and sounds like he stepped out of the Appalachian foothills." Fairfield is performing on a very small stage in a small building that was, until recently, the Newport Museum of Yachting. The packed room listens attentively as Fairfield fiddles out a folk standard, "Rye Whiskey," singing: "If the ocean was whiskey and I was a duck, I'd dive to the bottom and never come up." I only have a partial view, watching through a glass display case that once held a replica yacht; listening quietly, I look down at the placard still sitting at the bottom of the dusty box. Only a few moments later the feeling of historical curation is evoked again when a band called Spirit Family Reunion dedicates a song, "Green Rocky Road," to the recently departed folksinger Karen Dalton. One of them says: "We owe a lot to the artists who played here before us for the past five decades. . . . The Newport Folk Festival is a living museum." The audience cheers as the band strikes up the tune.

This year's festival has offered a number of new opportunities for interactions between the musicians and the fans; the new photo line in front of the main stage is only one unexpected innovation. Another is the Ruins—a series of short, more intimate performances cosponsored by Jay Sweet's magazine, *Paste*, and an audio equipment company, Sennheiser. In an old cannon turret, Brown Bird sets up for a three-song set. Festivalgoers grab wireless headphones and crowd the space to see this more intimate set.

Yet another, more informal interaction comes in the appearance of the Boston-based Berklee City Music Gospel Choir. As the What Cheer? Brigade did in 2011, the choir is tasked with wandering the grounds, giving impromptu performances between the more formal sets onstage. These more intimate events craft closer connections between festivalgoers and performers. Yet, paradoxically, this sort of intimacy gradually becomes less possible for musicians as they develop their fan base. As Dom Flemons of the Carolina Chocolate Drops told me, between his band's successful performance in 2007 and his visit in 2011, more intimate connections with audiences became harder: "It's gotten trickier to go around the crowd because everybody means well, but it takes forty minutes just to walk around." Because festival producers still want to nurture those kinds of interactions, however, they contract lesser-known bands like the What Cheer? Brigade, a busker named Jonah Tolchin, and the choir to provide spontaneous events to loosen the format and fill in the blanks.

Since the early days of the festival, there has always been a place for political and nonprofit groups at Newport, and around the edges of the Parade Field, mixed with jewelry and henna-tattoo tents, there are tents to sign up to donate bone marrow, to volunteer for Clean Water Action, to learn about the dangers of moving firewood, or to attend the John C. Campbell Folk School in Brasstown, North Carolina. In the tent for the New England Folk Music Archives, I sit down with its founder, Betsy Siggins, who was also a founding member of Club 47, a '60s hotspot for Cambridge's folk scene. As Joe Fletcher plays his honkytonk set in the background, Siggins tells me about people in the Boston scene "back in the day," like her freshman dorm roommate Joan Baez, and her experiences at Newport. Looking out over the grounds, she explains how the college dorms, the club, and the sidewalks were her education, and the festival "was like our summer school." She's attended Newport steadily since 1959, "save for a few," and tells me she hopes the festival's transition back to a nonprofit will bring new opportunities for organizations like hers. Undeterred by the loud music in the background, she goes on to say that this year reminds her of the early festivals more than any she's been to in years: "The breadth of artists is so wide," she says. "You know, in the early days there used to be workshops all set up around the outer rim of the grounds and you could go from world blues to city blues to Cajun blues to Detroit blues. . . . There's a variety of artists this year that reminds me of that." Asked if it is just the variety, she answers, "No, no, it's more dynamic than it's been in years. There are all these buskers." She listens for a few moments to Fletcher again, and says that he would have "fit right in."

Back at the main stage, the day is ending in a storm. Advisory board member Jim James's band, My Morning Jacket, leans into the wind blowing from over the harbor. As the sky darkens, the better prepared in the crowd unfold ponchos and I wrap my phone in a plastic bag. Brittany Howard from the Alabama Shakes returns to the stage to join them for the Band's "It Makes No Difference" and its familiar refrain: "And the sun don't shine anymore . . . and the rains fall down on my door." When James gestures out from the stage, whether he is pointing to the soggy crowd or to the sleepy town across the bay, to the coming thunderheads or to his own rock fame waiting out there in the gray mist, one cannot be certain. The downpour intensifies, and Sweet is forced to cut off the show. Standing onstage, James calls to the crowd as we head for the exit: "Thanks so much for sticking with us in the rain. . . . It's an honor for us to be playing on this holy ground."

Resource Mobilization into Site Sacralization

Betsy Siggins's conclusion—that the festival's musicians are more like they were "back in the old days"—is a kind of rhetorical legitimization I heard often, as folks like her talked about the festival's self-conscious ties to its own history. Siggins's comment echoed Joe Fletcher's description of the festival's backstage, where "they put up all these old pictures of the festival to give us a sense of the tradition." The 2011 and 2012 festivals featured a variety of traditions, crafted both on- and offstage.

Historian Eric Hobsbawm coined the phrase *invented traditions*: "a set of practices, normally governed by overtly or tacitly accepted rules and of a ritual or symbolic nature, which seek to inculcate certain values and norms of behaviour or repetition."[22] He was interested in how nations actively create and refashion their pasts for present-day political purposes. Not dissimilar to the symbolic set of tourist locations comprising Newport's brand image as a leisure destination (the mansions, the Cliff Walk, the Tennis Hall of Fame), the experiences I witnessed worked in similar ways. Like watching Frank Fairfield play his fiddle through an empty glass case in the repurposed yachting museum, the vessels in which these events were staged served to authenticate and legitimate the event and the genre. One can understand such a transformation as a cultural process.

If the organizers aimed to craft a sacred site, Pete Seeger was the priest doing the benedictions as he moved from stage to stage, connecting past and present. Such symbolic tethering of meaning and place is what anthropologist Dean MacCannell called *sight sacralization*, but here it could also be *site* sacralization.[23] The first stage, of course, is identifying a cultural good as an object for refashioning, and the Newport Festival was a valuable commodity in economic and identity crises. The festival's use of Fort Adams's old, weather-worn walls and artillery fortifications—paradoxical, given the antiwar tradition of the 1960s folk revival—as well as the stunning views of the harbor lent a blend of historicity and beauty to create a kind of consecrated space. The ritual and the location were already set.

After key stakeholders identify a cultural good for touristic sacralization, it can develop through stages of what MacCannell calls *framing and elevation* and *enshrinement*, in which the goods are displayed, enhanced, and venerated. Artists performed traditional songs like "Rye Whiskey," popular country songs like Johnny and June Carter Cash's "Jackson," unearthed Woody Guthrie songs, and also "classic-ified" newer songs, like the Carolina Chocolate Drops' folk rendering of the R&B "Hit 'Em Up Style." With each pronouncement, these bands weaved in the past and historicized the festival's present. But then musicians also attempted to elevate the event explicitly, with their declarations of the festival's specialness: that it is "like a Graceland," a "living museum," or "holy ground"—despite the fact that all the original, mythical festival events actually occurred across the bay and not at the fort. At the same time, the festival transformed itself into a nonprofit for economic reasons, which resulted in a limited amount of corporate branding and a less commercialized symbolic landscape, further cleansing its stature. And the festival established additional places for environmentally, socially, and historically conscious vendors and groups that continued to bolster its emotional and political soul. Each activity served to enhance and elevate the event.

The fourth phase is *mechanical reproduction*, wherein the media engage in the process. The festival provided a great deal of physical space and access to local (WERS and WUMB Boston's Folk Music radio), national (Bob Boilen from NPR's *All Songs Considered*), and social media. Inventions of tradition need conduits, and the media's broadcast and promotion of these experiences and rituals raised the profile of the festival as a whole, and created a "Newport Effect" for some artists. For example, the David Wax Museum's performance in 2010 brought them national exposure; that they were dubbed "NPR darlings" was possible only due to the increased presence of NPR's coverage of the event. The station hosted live streams of performances but also offered downloadable archives for the majority of the acts at the festival.

MacCannell's final stage of the process is *social reproduction*, through which these values and symbols are reproduced through ritual. This was accomplished both onstage and off. Festival producers booked key acts—both new artists who, in David Wax's words, "have an eye on the past," and festival veterans, like Seeger and Elliott—who served to connect to and revere the festival's earlier incarnations. These social networks of artists worked to further reinforce the sacralization with artistic collaborations occurring both onstage—guest appearances happened in nearly every set—and over the course of these artists' careers (as with Gillian Welch's appearance on the Decemberists' album). These social connections are also used to bring new acts into the fold, and these offstage interactions spill back over onto the stage as artists who return make surprise guest appearances during each other's sets. And then there are spaces for audience members to participate in the reproduction too: as they perform at the open-mic tent, they can say that they performed at Newport. The new incarnation of the festival created supplementary places for interaction between musicians and the audience—from the new photography pit to buskers interacting with the crowds to smaller-scale performances in the museum and the Ruins—that allowed for a greater intimacy.

In general, the process of cultural legitimacy is a constant struggle over what is deemed worthy or canonical, and tastemakers like Jay Sweet and NPR are critical for lending such acceptability, sitting in a privileged social position with the ability to marshal resources to confer status.[24] In Sweet's case, as the editor of the music magazine *Paste* and producer of the most celebrated folk festival in country, he plays a major role in revitalizing the festival and shaping the genre. As he acknowledges, he is not alone: the advisory board, a team of producers, and a recurring cast of local musicians also play a part.

However, each of these tradition-inventing practices—booking artists, limiting commercialism, promoting alternative organizations, creating intimacy, and crafting sacred spaces—could not work without the collective "buy-in." These rituals and practices lend legitimacy for an event struggling to emerge out of—in the eyes of the musicians I spoke with—its earlier sins of commercialization. The transformation, or sacralization, of the event from the Dunkin' Donuts Newport Folk Festival to a nonprofit organization, and the reorientation of the brand toward being a more place-based cultural product, has not gone unnoticed by the musicians. Dom Flemons admitted to being "disappointed" when the festival was sponsored by Dunkin' Donuts because "it wasn't the Newport that I had in my mind, but just kinda like any other festival." Joe Fletcher credits Jay Sweet for turning the festival around: "He's done a good job rebranding the whole thing, from the T-shirts and all the design stuff to giving it more of a Rhode Island identity." Sweet aimed both to associate the festival's brand with the region and with regional musicians, and to have those musicians themselves bond with the festival in return. He acknowledged being thrilled when performers mention themselves as "Newport artists": "I mean, what's a 'Bonnaroo artist'? They have 120 slots for musicians. South by Southwest has thousands. There are only twenty-five touring bands that *don't* play those festivals, and that's how many slots we have."[25] And once bands are in, they are part of a history, and Sweet would have you believe they are part of a family. "Yes, there are some brands that we've used to make ends meet, but I've said this before: I don't want the festival run by *brands*, I want it to be run by *bands*." Getting his invitation to be a part of the few bands playing Newport is, in his estimation, a validation for those acts.

There were still other changes in the relationship between the festival and Newport since my 2007 visit to the harbor front community. These changes are somewhat surprising considering the awkward history between the festival and the town itself, but they also show how the citadel-like pattern of festival activity cannot truly limit other cultural action.

Back in Town: After-Parties,
the Newport Nightcap, and BridgeFest

As the rains continue to pour, scuttling the performance by My Morning Jacket, I inch back through the traffic along America's Cup Avenue, past the Newport Blues Café, where there is a large banner: DEER TICK TONIGHT. The festival is at the fort, and this place is an outpost—the Deer Tick after-party unfolds to a packed house every night once the festival concludes. According to Joe Fletcher, these gatherings sold out in eighteen minutes. "Even I had a hard time getting in," he said, "and I was performing!"

Several activities begin to demonstrate how groups at the edges of the festival negotiate their places in and around the festivalized city.

((( )))

A few days later, on the Wednesday after the 2012 festival concludes, I walk around the city for the fourth annual BridgeFest. On swanky Bellevue Avenue, in the reading room of the Redwood Library and Athenaeum (the nation's oldest community library), there is a quartet performing to thirty-two people. The pianist, Lois Vaughan, is presenting a history of jazz through a series of songs, including standards by Brubeck, Davis, and Hancock. She is also the founder and impresario of the week-long event.

Originating in 2009, BridgeFest set out to create a series of musical performances to "make a bridge between the jazz and folk festivals . . . ten whole days of music in Newport." Vaughan approached the nonprofit Arts and Cultural Alliance of Newport County, and within two months they included twelve venues in the program and promoted it in the newspaper. Newport Arts and Cultural Alliance members Cris Offenberg and John Hirschboeck, along with Vaughan, all maintain that the event is not designed to take away from the Newport festivals, but rather to add to them with free local music and events. According to Offenberg, the Arts and Cultural Alliance delegates the booking of the music to the venues, and concentrates only on promotion. Vaughan's use of an array of different venues, including the historical library, is born of economic demand, though she acknowledges that the incorporation of a wider set of Newport locales is a benefit: "As a nonprofit we can't rent out spaces, especially during the height of the tourist season," she tells me, "so we rely on alternative places, like the library, Salve Regina University, or Greenvale vineyards, rather than traditional clubs and bars." BridgeFest contacts the venues and offers to promote anything under their logo, so long as it fits their theme of live local music.

Afterward, I see two events on the BridgeFest schedule: a reggae band and a "Conversation on the State of the Festivals" with George Wein and longtime festival producer Bob Jones, moderated by local arts reporter Jim Gillis. I head to the latter. A jazz trio opens the proceedings as the audience settles in under a crisp white tent on a pier. First off, Gillis asks Wein about the historically rocky relationship between the city and the festival, and Wein answers:

> The festival was too big for the town. The town didn't recognize that, and we didn't recognize that. We were just putting on a festival; we had to learn about the relationship between the festival and the community. And the community had to learn how important the festival could be for the community. And that's where we are now. The relationship between the festivals and the town could not be better. I'm really happy. It's taken us fifty-eight years to get here but I think we've arrived.

The audience applauds at the joke. When Gillis asks about Wein's own stature among the community, he says, "I've outlived my opponents."

Newport Arts and Cultural Alliance member John Hirschboeck is in the back, shaking hands. I remember that he characterized a conversation with Wein about BridgeFest as supportive: "George told me this was something he wanted to do all along, but could never get it going." Organizers feel that, as a nonprofit, their event is more clearly partnered with the community, and are eager to build local social + cultural resources through it. They have developed free composition workshops and educational programming as a part of their schedule, adding something that the newly formed Newport Festivals Foundation has only begun to roll out as central to its mission. "That's where," Vaughan explained, "we can really contribute something to the festivals, we're here, we're local, and we can help foster those connections." She told me they are hoping the

NFF and BridgeFest will coordinate and that the international and national acts don't overshadow the local-music orientation.

From the festival's perspective, BridgeFest is a good idea, to be improved upon with better coordination. Jay Sweet told me that he's willing to lend BridgeFest some of their marketing and advertising resources. He told me that the foundation would like to have more control of the event, still describing the relationship as "very unofficial," "very cordial," and "non-confrontational." If the Newport festivals and BridgeFest are going to work together, Sweet wants it on his terms: "We've said, 'If you allow us to do it, we'll work with you. But you've got to allow us to do it because it's our brand, and we know the best way to reach out to our audience.'" He told me he suspects and hopes there will be more coordination moving forward.

When an audience member asks why nighttime shows are limited, Wein answers, "I don't like, and the town doesn't like, 10,000 fans disgorging after the festival into the streets. Newport, even on a Saturday night, is a quiet town." As I walk off to the last BridgeFest event, I think about the Deer Tick after-parties, and their limited encroachment on this quiet resort town.

I walk through a neighborhood filled with one of the largest concentrations of eighteenth-century colonial homes, to a bar and restaurant called the Rhumbline, where Lois Vaughan and her bass player, Tom Pasquarelli, are playing for the early dinner crowd at the last music event of the day. The Rhumbline is what Lois calls her "anchor": her standing weekend performance that she then can supplement with her other gigs. She admits that it's pretty challenging to put together a career as a musician in Newport—"If I had ever known how hard it would be to be a professional musician . . . I wouldn't have done it"—but she tells me there are a few Newport musicians who can build a career. In addition to this gig, Lois also works at weddings, corporate events, private parties, funerals, church jobs, and concerts. These jobs "come and go." She says she would love to see Newport as a "thriving music destination," including having buskers on the streets even though she knows the community "isn't ready for it" and still maintains prohibitive noise ordinances. Live music is a tough sell in Newport, where, she says, "noise is a constant issue." But at the Rhumbline, she is inside, playing songs for a subdued crowd of diners who clap politely after each song.

((( )))

A month after that, I return to the Newport Blues Café to speak with owner Jim Quinn. The venue has been open since 1995, and Quinn has owned it for seven years. Born and raised in Newport, Quinn has fond childhood memories of the festivals, and talks about the musicians he and his friends met—almost always referred to as "friends of Pete Seeger"—as they crashed on people's couches across town. Like City Manager Ed Lavallee, Quinn is retired from the police department but is still active in shaping the community.

He explains that operating the venue has been his most challenging and rewarding endeavor. "It's not easy to operate a live-music venue year-round in a seasonal town," he says. He relies on good relationships with the hotel and bed-and-breakfast owners, and he says that a lot of tourists are directed to his place because of it. He's proud of being "Newport's best live venue" for over twenty years, and says that it's a passion. Sitting in his empty bar, he describes his clientele as "people looking for some-thing to do on the weekend while visiting Newport; looking for a place to go where they can have a good time, dance, listen to some great music—not necessarily a national act." As I listen, I notice his thick eastern New England, broad-A accent: "Newport" is "Noopaht" and "after-party" is "afta-pahty."

Since 2011, the Blues Café has served as the venue for the official Newport Folk Festival after-party, a benefit for the Newport Festivals Foundation hosted by Providence-based John McCauley and his band, Deer Tick. Quinn describes the proceedings as having a "family reunion" atmosphere, explaining that it is typical for many of the musicians from the festival to come over at night, hang out, and jump on and off the stage: "You never know who's going to show up." Just as the festival's board of advisors work to convince acts to join them at the festival, it's been Deer Tick's job to cajole friends playing the festival to join them onstage later at the café. For $10 the first year and $20 the second, festi-valgoers can extend the festival experience and, as the only really sizable music venue in town, the Blues Café is a hot ticket. I was finally able to get a ticket in 2013, and the show was as described: a late night filled with boozy performances by the host band and a running chorus of festival performers from the day.

Jay Sweet approached Quinn about doing an affiliated event at the café, but the deal fell through when Quinn asked for, in Sweet's estimation, an "astronomical" price. Now that the festivals are nonprofits, Sweet believes "everyone's on the same page" and that the arrangement is a "win-win": the festival gets nighttime programming and the café gets a three-night after-party, a packed house, and good money coming in from the bar tab.[26]

The Deer Tick shows weren't the only after-parties. In 2011, the Newport Nightcap was an unofficial lineup of bands performing at the Gas Lamp Grille 500 feet away for only a $5 entry. "The festival ends very early," David Wax tells me, "and I have friends who put on an after-party with bands that were not quite ready to play the festival but, I think, could one day get there." Organizer Scott Pingeton says that he has been to the festival a few times and really enjoyed it, and thinks that Sweet and his team do a "fantastic job." He says after the festival ends, "it's still light out, yet there's not a hell of a lot to do after the festival ends." Because of these limitations—and thinking about festivals like SXSW, Coachella, and Bonnaroo—Pingeton and his friends decided that they would "try to cultivate a culture where everyone congregates in downtown Newport after the festival," noting that there might not be proper music venues but there were "plenty of bars" that could be filled, "sort of SXSW style [with] local bands that we thought fit the vibe of the festival." There was no specific backlash from their rogue event. The Newport Festivals Foundation continued to develop after-parties in the following years, and, as David Wax predicted, one of the Nightcap bands was invited to the 2013 festival.

Pingeton tells me that the Nightcap was never explicitly about making a profit, admitting they lost money on the endeavor, but that he felt he was successful in "making the Newport Folk Festival experience that much richer." For official and unofficial event organizers, the drive to make the Newport experience "richer" is limited due to the small crop of live-music venues, the disconnect between the festival and the downtown area, the small talent base of local performers, and some reservations from the Newport community regarding noise. These official and unofficial after-parties and the burgeoning BridgeFest offer slight reconfigurations of both community and event, but are rather modest when compared with what I will show in the following chapters.

Conclusions: Fortress Folk

From the stage, musicians have a wonderful view: the audience, then the boats rocking on the water, and behind them, Newport's harbor. For David Wax, the fort is a "perfect," "unique," and "impressive" location, but one that "feels different from SXSW because it feels very divorced from the town." The city has "quite a sense of luxury and privilege around it," and that "contrasts with the festival."

The view from across the harbor is a reminder that, although the aforementioned three patterns of festivals are intended to be a more metaphorical way to understand the relationship between space and culture, Fort Adams is, quite literally, a citadel, as compared with the core and confetti patterns. The selection of the disconnected site, as former police officer and city manager Ed Lavallee indicated, was a decision based on policing strategy. "The performance is along a back wall and that wasn't by happenstance, but by design." The wall, in his words, "wouldn't be violated," and if they had to, he said, laughing, they "could drive everybody into the water." Community safety wasn't the only logistical consideration. The citadel pattern makes sense because there just aren't that many spaces for 10,000 people to congregate in a town with a population of around 25,000, and keeping the two populations separate avoids the headache of having Newport's population increase by 50% if the festival were located downtown. It was a resolution with ramifications for activities inside the event and for the communities outside it.

From the perspective of the locals, the consensus these days seems to be that there's less griping about the events. For the city, the folk festival and its sister jazz festival (and even BridgeFest) are parts of a wider effort to be a tourist destination. Newport's city manager, Ed Lavallee, finds the balance of a variety of events a good way to promote Newport's resort-community image, even if the folk festival is an imperfect match.

"It shows the city's a good place for special events... from the mansions to America's Cup to the Tennis Hall of Fame to the festivals. When you look at branding, the festivals put Newport on the map as a destination with the other things we do." This echoes much of what I heard from the city's business community: they want the festivals' success to not come at the expense of their city's very small tourism set.

Organizers from the jazz and folk festivals are slowly building stronger connections with the city, from the after-parties to lending support to BridgeFest. They hope their cautious embrace is returned in kind. Producer Sweet has been on the frontlines of the criticism and praise, and told me that the relationship has improved now that residents see the financial and cultural benefits: "It's become part of their identity now and people are able to say, 'Oh, I live in Newport, where the festivals are,' in their everyday lives." He is astonished at how many promotional materials from the Convention and Visitors Bureau and the Rhode Island Tourism Division are for the city's wedding industry, or boating, or the mansions, and not the festivals. "I mean, everywhere I go, the people I speak with know about the festivals. We're in the smallest city in the smallest state in the union, and why wouldn't Newport be ready to jump on its tag as one of the musical capitals of the US?" Jim Gillis notes that the twin festivals might be "landmark events in terms of the history," but whatever prominence the festivals have in the wider music community, here they are "part of the whole."

As such, this relationship, disconnected in some ways and connected in others, is constantly negotiated through a variety of forces. Although a more detailed analysis of the economic, spatial, social + cultural, and symbolic resources will be discussed in chapters 5 and 6, there are a few points that not only summarize, but serve as points of connection to consider alongside the following chapters on Nashville and Austin: (a) unlike the other festivals, the 2008 global economic downturn necessitated an organizational shift at Newport that led to a redefinition of the folk music genre and an unlikely opportunity for new connections with its region; (b) that reworking also opened up the opportunity for musicians themselves to help bolster the social + cultural resources within the festival by building social networks; (c) musicians, festival organizers, and fans collectively sacralized the venue and event by limiting its commercial content; and (d) the citadel model required new activities to be developed within it (e.g., from buskers to smaller bands performing among the crowds), which affected the festivalization of Newport itself, as new activities emerged outside, even as the business and political community refused to see Newport Folk (and Jazz) as the city's signature events.

In contrast to massive music festivals with fewer spatial limitations like Bonnaroo and Coachella, Newport is restricted and even reserved. According to Joe Fletcher, this isn't an altogether bad thing. The folks he speaks with behind the scenes insist that "everybody's passionate about not making it bigger or moving it somewhere." The festival has a special quality being where it is, he says, and "it looks great, especially now that there's no Dunkin' Donuts signs in the background." Physically separated yet symbolically tied to the city itself, the Newport Festival's geographic position is a reminder of the importance of place and culture, and culture in place.

3 "When Country Comes to Town"
Nashville's Country Music Festival

Well I don't give a dang about nothing
I'm singing and bling-blinging
While the girls are drinking
Longnecks down!
And I wouldn't trade ol' Leroy
Or my Chevrolet for your Escalade
Or your freak parade
I'm the only John Wayne left in this town
—"SAVE A HORSE (RIDE A COWBOY)," BIG AND RICH

Kickoff Parade

Crowds pack the sidewalks of Broadway for the 2006 Country Music Association's CMA Kickoff Parade. The commencement of Nashville's big event begins with a high school marching band, followed by a series of six or seven floats pulled by tractors, a few pickup trucks, a race car, and several convertibles with celebrities in the backseats. Many in the audience staked out spots with their lawn chairs. "I got here at 8 a.m. to see everyone come by," Vicki from South Carolina tells me. "It's a real show." In a neon-pink Old Navy T-shirt, she grabs a Grand Ole Opry church fan (essentially a piece of heavy stock paper mounted on a stick, in recent years used as a promotional device) that a twentysomething distributes to the crowd.[1] Someone else circulates "VIP Party" tickets.

Music blooms from the open Chevy truck beds like thick summer pollen. Convertibles are loaded with country singers, professional anglers, and NASCAR drivers, concluding with an uncomfortable-looking yet grinning Taylor Swift in a strapless white dress atop a red Corvette, a tiara shy from being Nashville's homecoming queen.

The parade wraps tightly around a core set of Music City institutions: it rolls by the old Nashville Convention Center and the famous Ryman Auditorium, then the strip of famed Nashville honkytonks, turns a corner by the nearly complete Schermerhorn Symphony Center, and then turns again to pass the Country Music Hall of Fame and Museum, and finally doubles back toward Broadway at the hockey arena. There the parade ends, but the show continues at the Chevy All Access Music Tour Stage Block Party with well-known country bands like the Grascals, Povertyneck Hillbillies, and Little Big Town performing. The host is the African American country "hick-hop" singer Cowboy Troy. Toward the end of the lineup, surprise guests Big and Rich join Cowboy Troy to play the single off Troy's *Billboard* #2 country-charting album: "I Play Chicken with the Train":

> Hold 'em up! Here we go!
> All the hicks and chicks feel the flow,
> Big black train comin' 'round the bend,
> Go on kinfolk tell ya mam an' them,
> Chug-a-lugga, chug-a-lugga, chug-a-lugga who?
> The big blackneck comin' through to you.

Big and Rich then power through their rock-country hit "Save a Horse (Ride a Cowboy)" and really get the crowd jumping. The self-styled country outlaws William Kenneth "Big Kenny" Alphin and John Rich mix hip-hop slang like "bling-blinging" with iconic country figures and imagery. Listening to them on the Chevy stage, I think about their super-slick video, which has its own parade—with Cowboy Troy leading a marching band, a gaggle of scantily clad secretaries busting out of their business wear, and friends they call their "Muzik Mafia"—while the duo rides in the back of a Cadillac convertible slowly rolling into town. Creating a powerful mixture of homespun values and urban marketing, the symbolism of country artists parading into the city of Nashville atop Chevrolet vehicles in the music video foreshadowed the 2006 CMA Parade and Block Party.[2] This ain't your grandma's country music.

((( )))

During my stay in Nashville, I was lucky enough to meet Buddy Killen, onetime Grand Ole Opry bassist, legendary songwriter and producer, and Nashville music pioneer, during a celebration for another musician's album release. When asked about the relationship between the music industry and the city, he talked about how there used to be "two societies" in Nashville: the Belle Meade folks, meaning the social elite, generally located in the suburb of that name, and the music society, meaning the music-recording industry, located down on a strip known as Music Row. Describing the city's duality, he said it's a place "you can get down or you can get up." In his mind, these communities grew closer over the years, and yet the twofold quality is characteristic of the city's dynamic nature.

Walking around the downtown districts of Nashville as they crank into gear for its festival, I think of that meeting as I see and hear country music reverberate out windows and from around corners along Broadway. Killen's comments on the city's communities in relation to music get to the heart of the matter. If the story of Newport is about a cautious connection between culture and city, with a problematic history, Nashville displays a stronger tie between the community and the music, with the former hoping to brand itself on the distinctive culture of the latter. And yet, it is a brand that binds together and masks different communities and their oftentimes-competing visions for the city. Where the Newport story illuminated how both the festival and Providence musicians were able to coalesce around the idea of Americana music, this chapter illustrates, first, the rise of country music in Nashville and its relationship with a core set of organizations around the city, and second, how the festival grafts corporate branding onto a variety of experiences while mixing country values with more cosmopolitan flair. And, as historical and political maneuverings led to Newport's festivals being spatially isolated and viewed as two of many events at the resort destination, the CMA Fest has woven itself into the fabric of Nashville with significant "buy-in" from municipal and business elites.

Nashville to Cashville

Because of the twenty-one universities and colleges in its municipality, its emphasis on the arts, and a grouping of Greek-revival buildings like the State Capitol, Nashville was once called the Athens of the South. After the 1897 state Centennial Exposition, which included a pyramid, a Sphinx, and other international cultural reproductions, only the full-scale reproduction of the Parthenon remained, due to its harmony with the city's nickname. These are a few of the symbols that locals often associate the city with when speaking of its more refined culture. Killen continued to tease out how the tension developed over the years, as those from the more "sophisticated" Belle Meade society had to grapple with the rising prominence of the music scene. He said country music "gives us a personality that you can think of when you think of the name 'Nashville.'" As he described it:

> Why should anyone be ashamed of one of the biggest industries in the world? And believe me, it's a lot more sophisticated than they think it is. When I came to Nashville it was more traditional, you had a lot of people who were out of the country, they weren't that sophisticated because they weren't that educated, they just came in on their talent. Somehow it didn't sit very well with some of the people in Nashville, in some sections, but over a period of time that all changed.

He continued by saying that there's a "coalescing going on" among people in town. And, as he spoke of this tighter interweaving, he spoke of his own experiences, proudly recalling how he brought singers like Johnny Cash and Chet Atkins in the 1970s to play at the exclusive annual Swan Ball benefit for the Cheekwood Botanical Garden and Museum of Art.

From the country music side of things, there are five organizations serving as the major interlocking gears of the city's cultural infrastructure. They were, in fact, partially encircled by the 2006 Kickoff Parade. Each playing their part along the way, these businesses and associations started in the early part of the twentieth century and developed over the course of the second half of the century to transform the more sophisticated Athens of the South image—so well liked by the social elites—into what Killen noted as the city's coming together around the idea of Music City, USA. First and perhaps most important was WSM-AM radio, founded in 1925 as National Life and Accident's radio station (WSM stood for "We Shield Millions"). Dubbed the Air Castle of the South, WSM to this day still finds talent, broadcasts musicians and programming to a wide audience, and trains producers, sound engineers, and music entrepreneurs for Nashville and beyond, functioning as the on-air home for country music.[3] In the 1920s, when rural folk were fleeing the countryside because of depressed prices for their crops, WSM provided a link between the urban experience and rural nostalgia.[4] The second component of the entertainment machine is WSM's most famous radio program, the Grand Ole Opry: first broadcast as the WSM Barn Dance, and then renamed in 1927, the show is one of the longest running in media history, and its cast members include country music legends Hank Williams, the Carter Family, Patsy Cline, Garth Brooks, the Dixie Chicks, and Brad Paisley. The third is the Ryman Auditorium (once the Union Gospel Tabernacle, built in 1892), which housed the Opry from 1943 to 1974 and is dubbed the "Mother Church of Country Music" (in 1974, the Opry itself moved ten miles away to a theme park and mall complex called Opryland). Fourth is Music Row, the nexus of country music recording studios (e.g., RCA's historic Studio B, called Home of a Thousand Hits for helping define the more polished and pop-oriented Nashville Sound), record labels (e.g., Warner Brothers, Curb Records), and business offices (e.g., EMI Publishing, BMI, ASCAP) a mile away from the Ryman. WSM spawned more Nashville recording and publishing businesses than just the Opry.[5] Then, at a 1958 meeting at National Life's WSM facilities, a group of music industry insiders established the Country Music Association as a trade organization to promote the music genre with a board of directors comprising over sixty volunteers.[6] One of the early WSM program managers and key figures in the development of country music, Jack Stapp, gave a speech on the newly chartered CMA, insisting that its major function should be to "educate people behind closed doors" about the appeal of the genre because it could not rely solely on "the tastes of [its] loyal followers."[7] And fifth, there are the downtown honkytonks around the corner from the Ryman and the Country Music Hall of Fame, which served as venues for both performances and networking among local musicians and music industry personnel. As a cluster of physical buildings, social-cultural organizations, and events, these five cultural forms (three of which are currently owned by Gaylord Entertainment) represent country music in a very real and tangible fashion.[8]

In contrast to the somewhat tortured efforts to make Fort Adams a "sacred" space for folk music, the strip of Broadway leading down to the Cumberland River and the Metro Riverside Park, where I watched the CMA festival's Kickoff Parade, is as close to a symbolic and geographic hub for this entertainment machine as Las Vegas's old Fremont Street is for the city's gaming industry, or Bourbon Street is for New Orleans jazz. Lower Broad was once a port, as barges would float goods along the Cumberland, and the major commerce artery was what is now Second Avenue, two blocks west of and parallel to the riverbank. When the Opry moved to the Ryman in 1943, a nexus of record stores, bars, and honky-tonks popped up along this area of Broadway. Every Saturday the Ryman hosted the Opry, broadcast live over WSM, and artists would make their way out the back door and across the alley to the back room of Tootsie's Orchid Lounge. This honkytonk (originally named "Mom's," until Hattie Louise "Tootsie" Bess bought it in 1960) served as a kind of private club for Opry musicians for years and is the site of much Nashville lore.[9] In the late 1960s and early '70s, Kris Kristofferson and Willie Nelson haunted the place.

But the area wasn't always a continuous source of live music. Hall of Fame singer and songwriter Tom T. Hall has spoken about his 1964 arrival in Nashville and his realization that there was little in the way of live music: "You know, being in the country music business, I got here and I said, 'Where can I go hear some pickin'?' They said, 'You can't.'"[10] When the Opry left the Ryman for the suburban Opryland in 1974, National Life and Accident (owners of WSM) planned to demolish the building until *New York Times* architecture critic Ada Louise Huxtable—perhaps still smarting from the destruction of Penn Station—stepped in.[11] Hattie Bess passed away in 1978, and in 1987 five honkytonks were bulldozed to make way for the convention center a block west of Tootsie's. The area fell on hard times, with pawnshops, liquor stores, peep shows, and porn shops operating through the 1980s. Steve Smith, who bought Tootsie's in the early 1990s, described the area to the local alternative newspaper: "There was homeless people living in the street on Lower Broad. There was prostitutes and drug dealers everywhere."[12]

And then came the national chains—the NASCAR Cafe, Planet Hollywood, Fuddruckers, Hooters—a few of which tore down some historical buildings. Except for the Hard Rock Café, most of those themed restaurants have folded, while a few local businesses like Tootsie's, Robert's Western World (home of the Sho-Bud Steel Guitar company), Hatch Show Print (where iconic concert posters of Cash and Nelson are still printed on letterpress), and Ernest Tubb Record Shop labored on.[13] (Ironically, as theme restaurants landed downtown, the Opryland theme park, which had once drawn tourists away from Lower Broad, closed in 1997, though the Grand Ole Opry continues to broadcast part of the year from its suburban location.) Office spaces were vacant at the turn of the century, reaching 40% of what they were in the 1990s. By 2000, major downtown employers were downsizing, scarce and costly parking dissuaded locals from visiting, and the Lower Broad area was in trouble.[14]

A wave of redevelopment brought new million-dollar institutions to Lower Broad, solidifying the city's existing symbolic and geographic set of culture-based resources: the Schermerhorn Symphony Center (home to the Nashville Symphony), the Gaylord Entertainment Center (now called Bridgestone Arena and current home of the NHL team the Nashville Predators), LP Field (the home of the NFL Tennessee Titans since 1998), and the $37 million Country Music Hall of Fame and Museum (operated by the nonprofit Country Music Foundation, which moved in 2001 from Music Row to a new downtown building a block off Lower Broad, across the street from the hockey arena, and will be connected with a new sixteen-acre, 1.2-million-square-foot convention center, the Music City Center).

These new and old Nashville institutions, alongside common metropolitan organizations like the chamber of commerce, city hall, and the convention and visitors bureau, create a downtown core of institutions and organizations.[15] The visitor can see all these gears of the machine click and grind together as they serve as the resources for the CMA festival's programming. The festival, in turn, bolsters these institutions.

The music festival is not the only event that makes these components spin—indeed, I will show later how they work together for the development of economic and social + cultural resources—but it is perhaps the most spectacular. As with the Newport Folk Festival, I will show how this relationship developed, and how and why the pattern of activity changed over time.

As in Newport, Nashville's elites held their local music world at arm's length. Unlike Newport, however, Nashville has a far more robust entertainment machine, now matched with a nexus of music-oriented destination attractions. The "coalescing going on" that Killen spoke of is largely due to the city's newfound recognition of country as, according to *Fortune*, "a surprise profit center for the music business," leading to businesspeople across the United States calling the town Cashville.[16] The transformation—the rise of the festival and the country music industry and its pairing with the city's image—is not necessarily a perfect fit. One high-ranking city employee, who has interacted with the festival in one way or another since 1972, told me that in the early days there was a "clear disconnect" between locals and the music festival. Over and over, I heard people inside and outside the Nashville music industry talk about the locals' response to the festival attendees. No anecdote was more common than that of the non-country radio DJs. "They would trash [the festival] on the radio every morning," one local told me, "then the TV morning news shows would say 'Well, the invasion of Fan Fair is back again.'" A longtime local, who moved to town because of his interest in country music and the festival, told me that the community "resented the crowds, they resented the strain at restaurants, they resented what the crowd did to traffic, and they just kind of looked down on that social class, I think." Reinforcing culture- and class-based distinctions, locals would peg the out-of-towners with pejorative labels: "squirrels" for their rural and untamed qualities, and "lobsters" for their sunburned and overweight bodies. Local radio stations used to feature "fannypack counts."[17] It appeared the city wanted the benefits from the festival, just not all that came with it.

The next section shows how Nashville was able to take the uncomfortable relationship between city and festival—so similar to Newport's relationship with its festivals—and navigate the city's Janus-faced identity. The next section traces just how downtown Nashville became festivalized, showing a real difference when compared with Newport's fort-like arrangement.

From Family Reunion to Honkytonk Heaven

Unlike Newport's festival, which arose out of the financial backing and social networking of impresarios Elaine and Louis Lorillard (and then George Wein), the CMA Fest was the product of careful organizational maneuvering between the municipal government, and the aforementioned gears that comprise the city's music culture.

WSM initially wanted to host a birthday celebration for the Opry, and this turned into an annual Country Music Disc Jockey Association convention by the end of the 1950s. The music labels courted DJs with free food and booze, and performances with musicians in hopes of getting their acts radio airplay. The Opry had a booking agency that took 15% of the profits, and had a vested interest in getting their artists airplay to get them out on the road between Opry productions. These annual conventions, by all accounts, were a wild time for the rowdy group of DJs—so much so that fans recognized the convention as a way to meet stars and get free merchandise as well. Rather than excluding fans, organizers sought to redirect their enthusiasm. Local radio and television pioneer and then-president of WSM Irving Waugh convinced the CMA and the Opry to develop a fan-centered festival called Fan Fair, and to reschedule the business meetings, now called the Country Radio Seminar, for later in the year.

The first Fan Fair was held in 1972 at the downtown Nashville Municipal Auditorium, a few blocks north of Lower Broadway. The plan was to provide fans with a lot of entertainment at a reasonable price. Events were organized around music labels (e.g., Capitol Nashville, Asylum, Arista, Curb, Mercury), but there were also independent artist showcases and sets that mixed up acts, and then there were pairings of established and new artists, fiddling contests, and "Honkytonk Finales." CMA and industry personnel often mention how artists always volunteered their time for the event, although they admit that labels periodically had to cajole their artists into performing.[18] Five thousand attendees came the first year, and when the organizers moved the event from April to June the following year, attendance doubled.

Sitting in the Special Collections section of the Nashville Public Library, Ronnie Pugh, one of the better-known members of the Nashville music community, reflected on those early decisions to hold the festival. He said that the organization originally kept pushing fans away from the DJ convention, and "it took them about fifteen years to realize 'Hmm, why are we pushing away the fans? Let's do something for them!' You would think it wouldn't have taken that long, but it did." He looks back fondly upon that choice, since he headed to the second Fan Fair, taking the Greyhound bus from his home in Marshall, Texas, to be "one of the few twenty-year-olds" at those early festivals. As he described the experience:

> [The festival was] down here at the Municipal Auditorium, and of course we were able to do a little of the tourist thing. I'm sure we went to the Ernest Tubb Record Shop. [I saw] two Opry shows that week. The shows, of course, were all sponsored by the record labels, and they were almost around the clock. And the artists had their booths up on the exhibit space [in the convention center].

He built his vacations around the festival for an annual pilgrimage. He told me about the family-like feel among the "salt of the earth, working class," "typical country fans" who were southerners or transplanted southerners, but also between the fans and the musicians, too: "You really felt close to the artists. I know I still have the autograph book that I filled up that week, and I remember very well getting Dolly Parton's." Later, Pugh moved to Nashville and authored a well-received biography on Ernest Tubb.[19]

By 1982, Fan Fair had moved from downtown to the Tennessee State Fairgrounds, three miles south. The single location provided for two stages under white and red striped awnings, exhibition spaces, and parking for people who arrived in RVs and camped for the week. Admission included entrance to the Opryland Amusement Park and the old Hall of Fame, and two tickets for Texas-style BBQ fare at the Odessa Chuck Wagon Gang, served by men in big white Stetson hats, kerchiefs, and long white aprons.[20] The festival grew more. In the 1980s, there was a spike of popularity that industry personnel often refer to as the *Urban Cowboy* years, after the Travolta film, wherein country moved to a pop sound, attracting a wider audience with acts like Barbara Mandrell, Kenny Rogers, and even Olivia Newton-John. And then the Garth Brooks years in the late 1980s and '90s paved the way to even wider popularity. The facilities couldn't match the growing interest—the grandstands, for example, could only hold 18,000—and Fan Fair had to cap their attendance at 24,000. Despite the fact that the fairgrounds offered all the control and benefits of hosting an event in a gated-off location, like Newport, the buildings were old, hot, and dirty. The CMA started looking for a new venue.

Ed Benson, CMA executive director from 1992 to 2005 and chief strategic officer from 2005 to 2008, was at Fan Fair in 1980, and watched the transition from the downtown coliseum to the fairgrounds; he then oversaw its next big move. He told me how the fairgrounds management board approached the CMA with plans to redevelop the site, construct new buildings, add to the capacity, and expand the footprint of the facilities, all in hopes of getting the CMA to commit to a long-term occupancy arrangement. The fairgrounds, however, were struggling with funding, with their long-term relationship with the Nashville Metropolitan County Council, and with their neighbors over the acquisition of adjacent property.

At that time, a few concurrent events changed the city. First, two new facilities opened: in the mid-1990s, a superspeedway was constructed in nearby Wilson County,[21] and the city built a new stadium across the river from downtown to accommodate the relocated Houston Oilers NFL team. The speedway group approached the CMA about moving Fan Fair to their facilities. At this critical juncture, the new mayor, Bill Purcell, grew concerned at the notion of the festival moving outside the city limits. The mayor brought in the speedway management and, according to Benson, "put the fear of God in them." Members of the CMA felt ambivalent about both options: going to the speedway and getting new facilities but leaving Nashville's city limits, or moving downtown to expand the overall operation and align better with the internal demographics that indicated a growing young and urbane audience, but losing the family-reunion feel nurtured at the fairgrounds. The mayor's nudge, however, led to negotiations with the CVB and the chamber as intermediaries for a return to downtown. Benson described it as a "collaborative process."

The CVB presented the festival with a commitment from city hall for rent-free use of the convention center, the football stadium, and Riverfront Park, as well as accommodations for police for traffic and security, and for keeping firefighters on duty. The CMA, according to Benson, realized that the range of daytime activities made "all the downtown hotel and restaurant guys and merchants in that Lower Broadway area really, really happy. They didn't know how happy they were going to be." Benson, CVB CEO Mike Neal, and others expressed gratitude for how the city stepped in to underwrite fire and law enforcement for the event.

Finally, the letter of intent was signed, and the festival made the move in 2001. Mayor Purcell released a statement that was included in that year's program, trumpeting that downtown core:

> This year Fan Fair® returns to Downtown Nashville—its birthplace and, I am convinced, the place where it belongs. Country Music is a treasure that is truly Nashville's own, and Fan Fair's return to downtown allows us to give this unique festival the showcase it deserves. All over downtown—at Adelphia Coliseum, the Gaylord Entertainment Center, Riverfront Park and the Nashville Convention Center—doors will be opening for Fan Fair. What's more, you'll also be among the first to experience our brand new Country Music Hall of Fame, the Frist Center for the Visual Arts and our new downtown Public Library. It's only right that a bright, new Fan Fair should be coming to a bright, new Nashville. In planning Fan Fair 2001, the CMA has had our city's full resources at its disposal.

Despite the mayor's positive attitude, many old-time fans complained. Benson described being accosted by eight older women who walked up to him to complain about the change in setting and vehemently declared that they would never return. The lament was not about the fairgrounds as mere backdrop, but rather the loss of the family-get-together, county-fair feel.

In 2004, the CMA put their brand up front, calling the event the CMA Music Festival. Whereas those early festivals cost folks like Ronnie Pugh

$20 for four days, a four-day pass now costs anywhere from $125 to $260. The ticket provides access to a dozen venues, including the signature and photograph event in the convention center's Exhibit Hall (which is now called Fan Fair), the Riverfront stage where bands play from ten in the morning to six o'clock daily, and the spectacular nighttime shows at the football stadium.

((( )))

It was a triumphant return, almost as if it were narrated by Toby Keith's 2000 hit "When Country Comes to Town." Still, some fans expressed feeling a loss of family and community with the downtown move. "Oh, I still miss it," said one sixty-year-old fan, pining for the hot summer days at Fan Fair even while enjoying the air-conditioning of the convention center: "I liked meeting up with people I'd seen every year who also brought their RVs. It was a real community and I'm still in touch with some of 'em." According to Benson, though, most people have come around: the same women who accosted him in 2001 approached him again the following year to admit that after they had gone home, they realized they had an even better time with Fan Fair's relocation. This move to a country music urbanism sparked new growth for the festival. From those first 5,000 attendees, the 2014 events attracted 80,000 daily festivalgoers for both ticketed and open-to-the-public events, up 13% from 2012.

There is another way of thinking about the CMA festival, too, one that gets at the deeper foundations of this "country meets city" idea. The story of Newport in the last chapter showed how changes in the festival organization—from a for-profit entity back to a nonprofit one—shaped the event, as old traditions were founded and new ones were fashioned. With the CMA festival, the expressly commercial organizational relationships influence the overall tone of the event. The concept of organizational imprinting, discussed in chapter 1, makes the simple but useful point that, as an organization is established, its initial logics continue well after their founding.[22] It provides a significant contribution for understanding festivals, because it implies that the institution's initial founding informs the perpetuation of particular practices (like cultural events) and corresponding relationships. An understanding of traditions as well as this melding of *country* and *city*, in fact, relies upon an appraisal of these organizational logics. Just as changes in the festival organization reoriented the content at Newport toward a nearby music scene, this quick history of the Fan Fair/CMA Fest shows how its tenor changed when it moved from the fairgrounds to the city. Its more commercial- and fan-directed agenda has left an organizational imprint throughout the activities of the festival, as well as making a mark on the city itself. This understanding also requires, however, an emphasis on how place is used; the pattern of the event moved from downtown core, to the citadel of the fairgrounds, back to the core. Its latest move brings the event into proximity with old and new downtown cultural institutions, synching as critical cogs in the Nashville entertainment machine to make the Music City imprint.

The festival, in this light, serves as a temporary apparatus designed for the promotion of a narrowly defined version of a music genre via close fan interactions and a symbolic mix of city and country. This imprint is omnipresent on the street level, as one walks through the event.

A Walk through the Fair

I park my car at the municipal buildings and walk to Riverfront Park, a tiered amphitheater dropping down to the second-largest CMA stage, which sits atop a barge on the Cumberland River. I pass through the security checkpoint and walk along a line of food tents offering hot dogs, beer, lemonade, and battered alligator-on-a-stick to see hundreds of sun-washed country fans. From the stage, the singer says: "On a day like this, when you come into town, when you come once a year for a festival like this, you'll see we all got a little redneck in us." As the music plays on, I turn to chat with Jay and Bill, two college students from rural Georgia, shirtless on the lawn. Jay proclaims: "We drove eight hours to lay here, listen to music, and flirt with girls!" They bought tickets for the night's shows and plan to stay tonight with a college friend who lives nearby. As I spoke with them, I thought of Ronnie Pugh as a twenty-year-old at the early Fan Fairs, but he said he was one of the few younger folks back then.

"We don't plan on moving all afternoon, until the show at LP Field tonight," Bill chimes in. "We've got beers and food." Asked what their

Riverfront Park and a stage on a barge on the Cumberland River.

favorite part of Nashville is, Jay adds, "Last night we went out to the downtown bars late, and we're ready to do it all over again." While some people bring beach chairs or blankets to spend the day, they are just sitting on the grass, flip-flops kicked off. When I ask about the lineup, they say they don't care too much about who is playing until the nighttime shows.

Meandering through the crowd, I am handed a few church fans, one advertising an unofficial after-hours party at Jimmy Buffett's Margaritaville, sponsored by Sony Music. A new singer shouts to the crowds from the stage:

> I know you all are just like me—You get up in the morning and you turn
> on the radio.... And you hear a country song and you think "That's about
> me too." Or "That could've happened to my father," or "That could've
> happened to my ma," or "That could've happened to my grandfather,"
> or "That could've happened to my grandma." And that's the thing about
> country music: it's about real live people.

I make my way over to Broadway, thinking about how country stars on-stage communicate their connections to the fans with their lyrics and banter.

On the corner of Second Avenue and closed-to-traffic Broadway, a band is playing on an outdoor stage in front of the Hard Rock Café to my right, and there's a giant BBQ grill designed to look like a train engine for the History Channel's *Cross-Country Cookout* show to my left. A river of bodies flows around tents set up in the center of Lower Broad like water rolling around rocks. Walking upstream, I can pick up a coupon for Peak anti-freeze, play a game on a Sony PlayStation 3, or receive free markers from Sharpie, free razors from Gillette, free Pepsi, free ice cream, free candy, free guitar picks, free Jack in the Box, free T-shirts, and even free dog food. The ABC television tent is promoting their new one-hour drama, *Nashville*, set in and around the city's music scene, and the stars are stopping by. There are also caricaturists selling portraits, and a man selling pictures with his pet monkey for ten dollars. Someone is selling small, pink souvenir guitars—fans buy these guitars not to play, but to have them signed. Some of them are already signed by country music stars: Loretta Lynn ($300), the Dixie Chicks ($350), and Keith Urban ($150).

Even at 11 a.m., the windows to the bars are open, bands and singers are playing, and people are sitting on stools drinking beer and eating food. Like an elaborate street fair, anyone can walk through this area, and the festival organizers see this as a way to "give something back" to the city. Music and laughter spill down from open windows and onto the street. Further west, toward the Ryman, on the block between Fourth and Fifth Streets is Merchants, a onetime hotel for Ryman musicians like Patsy Cline and Hank Williams, then a flophouse front for downtown prostitution, and then in 2010 a fancy restaurant that serves "Johnny Cash's Iron Pot Chili" for $7. There's a knot of venues on the other side of the street, including Robert's Western World, Layla's Bluegrass Inn, the Second Fiddle, Tootsie's Orchid Lounge, and, farthest west, Legends Corner.

Past the honkytonks is the convention center, with its Exhibit Hall hosting what is now Fan Fair, where labels, talent, and sponsors set up booths, and fans get to cycle around in the cool air-conditioning. The Exhibit Hall offers a host of little experiences. I wade in the mob around

Lower Broad area looking west toward the honkytonks and the Bridgestone hockey arena's twenty-two-story tower.

CMA Fest venues, June 2006.

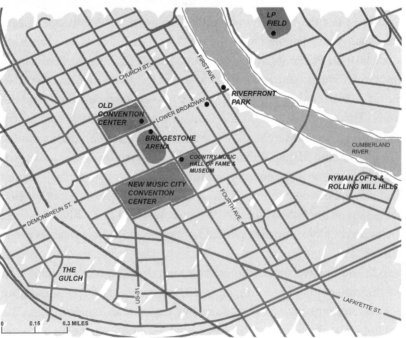

American Idol star Carrie Underwood. I notice lots of American flag T-shirts and one that says "WWWD?: What Would Waylon Do?" Younger women wear jean shorts or sundresses with their cowboy boots; men tend toward T-shirts and frayed baseball caps. Although there are stories of the old days—when Garth Brooks signed autographs for twenty-three hours straight, for example—superstars like Underwood might only put in an hour or so these days, if any time at all. Sometimes B-list stars will host a booth for a television channel or a record label.

Booths used to be built and run by the stars' fan clubs, as can be seen by flipping through old copies of the 1972 and '73 CMA magazine, whose title, *Up Close*, reinforces that personal connection between country music fans and musicians. The organization handed out awards like "Most Original" booth. As a onetime Music Row office manager, country music reporter, coiner of the "outlaw" label for a group including Johnny Cash, Waylon Jennings, Willie Nelson, Merle Haggard, and Kris Kristofferson, winner of the CMA's Media Achievement Award, and longtime Country Music Television host, Hazel Smith has credibility when providing an overview of the changes in the interactions between artists and fans at the festival. The "mother hen" of country music told me: "When you would see an artist out there with a hammer and a nail, it was really special." She continues, "It was the camaraderie between the star and their fans, which was a special thing." As the CMA became more professionalized, and moved away from the family-reunion feel, the booths became more professional looking as well. When that happened, she says, "It took a whole lot out of it, as far as I'm concerned." Smith's fandom and advocacy for the genre is near bulletproof. She believes Fan Fair keeps its tradition of close fan-musician interactions, maintaining, "I still think it's special." She points to the aspiring stars and the ones who've been around a long time, who log longer hours at the "howdy and shake" to meet fans, take photos, and sign autographs.

At one end of the Exhibit Hall, past the racks of clothes and luggage from Reba McEntire's collection for Dillard's and a Wrangler Jeans fashion show, WSM broadcasts live from their own stage (sponsored this year by Durango Jeans). Balladeer Doug Stone plays his 1990 Epic Records hit "I'd Be Better Off (in a Pine Box)," getting good cheers at the start, the chorus, and the end of the song. A middle-aged woman, who introduces herself as Sarah, has been singing along through most of his songs, and she beams when asked about the signatures on her straw hat. She takes it off and rotates it in her hands as she scans the different people she's met over her six CMA Fests: "I've got seventeen autographs so far." She also shows me a bracelet with charms on it—one is a guitar, another an eighth note, and another spells out "Country Girl." She smiles as she waits in line to add Stone's signature to the collection on her hat, while the person behind her is holding one of the pink guitars being sold on the street, already covered in signatures. Stone's booth is simple, with a big banner in white with red lettering hanging behind it. When Sarah finally gets her chance, she shakes Stone's hand and effuses, "I just loved your set!" Thanking her, he looks into her eyes and asks if she's had "a great Fan Fair," calling the festival by its old name. Instinctually, he uncaps his Sharpie marker and signs her hat, but noticing the camera in her hand he asks, "Would you like to get a picture together?" She hands the camera to her husband, standing off to the side, and Sarah and Stone both smile at the count of three.

Fewer single men seem to be getting autographs, and none of them seem to be carrying an autographed hat or guitar. A quick count of the different queues suggests that close to 75–80% of the people in the signature lines are female. The men get photographs with the singers more often than autographs. Pete, a forty-two-year-old man at his fourth CMA festival, tells me, "I don't know what I'd do with an autograph, but I do like to shake their hand and get a picture." He shows off a series of photos on the screen of his point-and-shoot digital camera as he narrates his experiences:

> Usually, I haven't heard of them before, which is kinda dumb but.... Like, here's my picture with Sarah Darling, and I don't know who she is. Standing here, I can see she seems real nice.... I'll get a picture with someone and *then* I'll go home and find their music online. If I like it, I'll buy the music. It's a way to get to know new musicians.

This echoes others, who know these lesser-known acts are more eager to meet folks.

TV personalities and country music VJs hold an even stronger presence in 2012. Back in 2006, Carrie Underwood had just won *American Idol*, but now even less successful contestants from television get the all-star treatment.

((( )))

At night the crowds head to the shows at the NFL stadium, flowing over one of the two bridges that cross the Cumberland River and bookend Riverfront Park. As the sun sets to the crowd's backs, festivalgoers hoot and laugh, eager to catch the headlining acts. Since 2006, these nights at the football stadium have become more and more successful.

In 2012, ten minutes before the eight o'clock start, people are queuing up for the Photo Line. A long-standing tradition at the festival, it is the same setup as my last time at Newport, only strictly organized and on a much grander scale: a space has been established between the front row and the stage to allow regular folks to see the big stars on the big stage for a few minutes before cycling back to their seats. There are separate lines for each of the first acts of the evening—the lines are backed up for hotter new acts, but I slide right into the empty queue for Glen Campbell. I wind my way down the stadium steps and join a few dozen folks grouped in front of the massive stage. Traci, a fifty-three-year-old fan attending her seventh CMA Fest, echoes my surprise at the short line for the country legend: "I just walked past hundreds of folks waiting for Miranda!" Asked what it means for her to be in the Photo Line, she spins around to view the audience. "Look," she says, "I've done Fan Fair time and time again—my first one was in 1985—and these crowds get bigger and bigger. I'm happy I can get so close to some of the big stars without having to pay the big prices."

After a welcome from Mayor Karl Dean, the Nashville School of the Arts choir is introduced as beneficiaries of the $6.1 million raised for music education through the Keep the Music Playing Program, and they sing a song. But when Glen Campbell kicks off the evening's performances, Traci and the fifty others in line perk up and cheer. She starts clicking her camera, flashing over and over. Campbell suffers from Alzheimer's and is on his farewell tour. Wearing a traditional country shirt

Glen Campbell seen from the Photo Line, LP Field.

and faded blue jeans and looking a little lost, he is pointed to the mic by the band. He smiles as the band has to play the intro to "Try a Little Kindness" twice for him to start on the right note. Though he drops in and out of the lyrics of the song, he plays his old guitar licks without hesitation. "Oh," Traci says to herself, "he's still got it!"

As Campbell complains about the keyboard in the monitor, the security guards start waving to us to move on. Our time is up. Traci isn't done, and I see her being cajoled by the yellow-polo-shirted crew. I hear security ask five times before Traci slowly starts shuffling her feet sideways, still taking photographs.

As we head up to the stands on stage right, I ask Traci what she's thinking. "Oh," she begins, "it's such a thrill. My heart races every time. I got to see him in real life and that's just great, great, great." While many line up to see the younger generation of artists, fewer and older folks thrill over seeing legends like Campbell and Kenny Rogers. Still, it is a bittersweet performance: Campbell tries to leave the stage after the first song, forcing the band to turn him around; he comes back to the mic to say, "OK. I guess we're going to do another one." Later, after "Southern Nights," he tells the audience, "I'm glad to be here, but at my age, I'm glad to be anywhere."

In sharp contrast, the fiery Miranda Lambert opens the next set with her rocking single "Baggage Claim" on a matching hot-pink electric guitar and mic. The stadium is full now. "This is still surreal to me," Lambert tells the audience. "I started way up there at the top with my head against the wall and I moved my way down every year. The last year I came as a fan, I was in the twelfth row. I can't tell you how much this means to me." After that, the show rolls out crowd-pleasing hits. Jason Aldean plays his "high on country living" songs: "Hicktown," "Big Green Tractor," "Fly over States," "Dirt Road Anthem," and "She's Country."[23] Two *American Idol* alumni, Kellie Pickler and Lauren Alaina, play too. Big names cycle through after that: Lady Antebellum plays their pop ballads; the Zac Brown Band plays country rock that includes a cover of "The Devil Went Down to Georgia"; Brad Paisley closes out the night with "This Is Country Music" and "I'm Gonna Get Drunk and Play Hank Williams" along with Hank Williams Jr. himself.

Staging Intimacy

A common element of contemporary music and sports fandom is an attempt to nurture close contact, or at least the illusion of connection, between stars and fans. In the case of the CMA Fest, a great deal of energy is put into creating spaces for intimate experiences to occur, from Fan Fair to the Photo Line to booking acts at the different stages set in the downtown core. And yet, the move back downtown opened the event to other, unscripted interactions too.

The Photo Line is one of the most enduring and endearing rituals of the festival, where all of these relations come into sharp focus: the fans play the part of "checking to see if they're real," the organization creates spaces cultivating proximity, and the musicians embrace their role by continually reinforcing that they are just like their fans. For CMA Executive Director Ed Benson, the Fan Fair in the Exhibit Hall is "the keystone of the event, and that's the unique interaction opportunities with the fans and the artists." The perspectives of festivalgoers Traci, Jay, Bill, Pete, and Sarah highlight the pains the CMA goes through to assure a spatial proximity that allows for a feeling of connection with the stars, and a breadth of experiences through their own set of traditions. Organizers control many of these activities, but with the move downtown, there are official and unofficial occasions and interactions that do not jibe as easily.

Most of the festivalgoers I spoke with knew little about all the careful, behind-the-scenes efforts by music industry professionals and organizers that are required to produce what appears to be such a seamless event. CMA Fest shows are orchestrated down to the minute. For some understanding of the intense coordination, Martina McBride told *USA Today* that her 2006 set was under strict rules: "I'm on for thirty-four minutes.... Not thirty, not thirty-five, but thirty-four."[24]

Record labels once played a prominent role in arranging acts into Fan Fair showcases. Labels would get together and divide two-hour blocks of showcases for their acts, from 8 a.m. to 8 p.m. The 2001 downtown move changed that. The big media companies no longer get top billing and, instead, the sets emphasize the artists themselves and the CMA as a whole.

As an explanation, Joe Galante, who is the chairman of Sony BMG Nashville and has over forty years of experience in the industry, including an active role in the production of Fan Fair since its earliest incarnations, stated that today, "people don't buy *labels*, they buy *artists*.... The consumer never looks at the record label and goes, 'Oh, it's on Arista, it must be great.'" Saying that one of his artists could walk onstage with the wrong music label logo behind him and no one would know the difference, he pointed out that music differs from most consumer goods because the business involves building the artist's brand, not the label's. Further, he noted that the emphasis at the festival is on both artists *and* the wider CMA organization: "The fact is, the brand is CMA, not the RCA label group show, or the Sony/BMG show." Effectively, the label is undercut twice.

For Galante, the festival has never been a direct revenue source for his labels. "The city is making out really well, and CMA's doing well," he continued, "but the labels are not." Positioning artists and label staff around the festival events and arranging transportation and logistics is a big investment of time and money by the labels. "It's great to see an artist's picture in the paper locally," he said, but "I'll look at this week in terms of sales and it was up 2%."

Why, then, do the labels participate at all? Jim Foglesong is a 2004 Country Music Hall of Fame inductee and longtime Music Row executive (he has served as president at Dot Records—a country label that folded in 1977—as well as at ABC, MCA, and Capitol Records, and has signed stars like Barbara Mandrell, Garth Brooks, George Strait, and Reba McEntire). As an active participant in the early years of the festival, he echoed Galante's hypothesis that people are more interested in artists than labels and, therefore, believes that artist participation is important for "establishing relationships with the fans, hopefully long-term." This mutual appreciation between fans and musicians serves as the best explanation for the labels' participation in the festival, especially in the early days. "I heard other labels saying they had trouble getting their stars to perform, [but] all of our stars would," he shrugged. "I had to tell some people they *couldn't* do it." He believed that it has something to do with how many country musicians grew up in poverty. "Even though they're millionaires now, they love to talk about how poor they were, what little they had to eat and all that," he said.[25] While Galante could not think of any major artist at his label that has *not* played the festival, he did mention that some—especially more recent superstars—occasionally need to be convinced. There is what he described as a "constant give and take" when it comes to these kinds of commitments. He had to "use a chip" to get Kenny Chesney to perform, and had to make a personal call to get Martina McBride to perform, too.

The move to downtown and the shift away from the label-centered showcases also has created new opportunities for more acts in different kinds of places, and a new host of programing challenges. On the front lines of making the scheduling work is Jeff Walker, CEO and president of AristoMedia Group and CMA board member since 1994, who arranged talent for the Riverfront shows from 2005 to 2009. He told me his strategy aimed to include "as many quality acts as we can" in the time between 10 a.m. and 6 p.m. He described the whole Riverfront lineup as a "sampling." Save for the opening and closing bands, each gets fifteen minutes.

There are some guidelines. To play the Riverfront stage, a band has to have had at least one top-fifty record in the previous year. Walker uses the Music Row charts rather than wider industry measures like *Billboard* magazine's rankings because they are kinder to "up-and-coming" acts. Although major labels dominated the old Fan Fair, there was always an independent showcase. "It's a sort of starter chart," he said, that gives "equal balance to independent labels as to the majors." While the bigger acts are on the LP Field stage, Walker described the value of the daytime shows to new and mid-career musicians:

> It's a chance to get in front of the fans. Your fans come here, over the four days we have 40,000 fans, at Riverfront 10,000 fans on average. They come down, they probably have a membership in your fan club, they want to see you. You have an opportunity to perform. If they're true fans they'll buy a ticket and plunk their money down and see you on the road.

In addition to balancing smaller and major label artists, Walker also talked about matching more experienced artists, who perhaps have not had a hit in a few years, with newer acts.

Unsigned performers could still crack the lineup. If Walker saw an act he liked, and felt they had a strong manager and booking agent advocating for them, as well as a willingness to promote themselves, he would be willing "to push the envelope a little bit" and include them on the Riverfront stage. Sometimes, he acknowledged, acts are upset about not being on a bigger stage—since none of the performers are paid—but he says he is careful to point out to them that even if they do not get on ABC's hour-long recap of the festival (musicians are paid if their performances are broadcast), there are other media outlets, and "it's still an opportunity." There are, he reinforced, "a lot of little extracurricular things that go on," with lots of chances for artists and fans to interact. And amid the small backstage army of sound and lighting engineers, stage crew, volunteers, CMA officials, catering services, security, and band managers, there are also booking agents, label scouts for an artist to shake hands with, or someone from a radio station doing interviews. The production side is arranged and paid for by the CMA. For the artists, they just "show up and plug in," according to Walker.

Then, finally, the festivalgoer gets to see the artists perform. For Joe Galante, although some new acts might need coaching on a set, once they reach a certain status his musicians know how to work the crowd. From his perspective as label head, he told me:

> I think we have the conversation about the single, but for the most part with the headliners they've got a good sense of what they got to get done, they're running a show, they probably try to bring in something new but for the most part [they] all have a good sense. At least our artists do.... Kenny [Chesney] came in and kept it up, he knew that he had fifteen minutes to basically go in there; to do a ballad would not be the right thing. He just hit the stage and it was bam, bam, bam, bam, and he was off and people were just "Whoa!" It was perfect.

((( )))

The experience of seeing an act onstage is only one part of the CMA festival, of course. Another of those opportunities is at Fan Fair. For years, there was a tradition of enthusiastic fans camping overnight on the side-walk, waiting for the chance to meet the artists at Fan Fair's "howdy and shake." Starting in 2012, however, a new policy for the signature lines was introduced: an online lottery replaced camping in place in the sig-nature line. This generated a lot of confusion and hurt feelings, although few likely miss sleeping on the sidewalk.

Country musicians will often hold their own "meet and greets" with their fan clubs on the road, as well as off-site during the CMA. Fans join the club for a few dollars and in return receive a signed photo, membership card, and maybe a newsletter. Alan Mayor, a photographer with many, many years of experience at the CMA Fest, described "meet and greets" as often offering a chance for fans to connect with the musicians backstage before a show. Mayor described these events as "almost like a stealth thing going on underground, but if you were a fan you'd know," and said the official Fan Fair experience was really "younger artists" getting "their first taste [of attention] before they get a fan club going." Running concurrent with the festival, these events are an important experience for many fans.

Even early on, there were enough of these peripheral events to keep a subset of country fans from attending the festival itself. Ronnie Pugh said that these happenings didn't exist when he first started coming to Fan Fair, but he did mention a friend who would bring his family on vacation without attending the official festival. "For years I'd ask them, 'Well, did you register this year?' [and they would say] 'No, we're just up here, Bill Anderson's fan club is doing this . . . so-and-so's club is doing this, and then there's the midnight jamboree, you can always go to that for free.'" Nowadays, the fans I spoke with seemed content enough with all the free activities provided by the festival that they did not wish to join a fan club.

There are still talked-about events, however, serving as narratives that reinforce the belief that musicians are committed to close interactions with fans. Echoing Brooks's epic twenty-three-hour autograph session, Taylor Swift held a thirteen-hour fan event in 2012. One woman, Karen, brought her preteen daughter after winning a raffle for tickets. She told me, "Taylor just sat and signed autographs all day long. She took a break and played three or four songs." She said that Swift was "*so nice*. . . . She asked my daughter how old she was and if she wanted to be a singer when she grew up." She described the moment: "It was quick, maybe a minute or two, but [my daughter] will remember it forever." Swift has such a strong following that she held her "meet and greet" in the hockey arena for hundreds of fans like Karen and her daughter. Others, even superstars like Blake Shelton, hold their fan events at local bars and restaurants. Some of these events serve as fund-raisers for an organization of the artist's choosing.

((( )))

It's not just interactions between artists and fans. Placing the event downtown provided an opportunity to incorporate that nexus of available city spaces. Despite the CMA's concerted efforts to attract locals, including a media blitz and the introduction of single-day tickets, it was a challenge to find a local who wasn't tending bar or strumming a tune or otherwise working the activities downtown. This fact wasn't lost on even the highest CMA officials. Benson talked with me about how the relocation offered a chance to establish events for locals, too: "All of those 'zones,' the Chevy stage, all that stuff is free, not only to the people who are registered and have bought a four-day ticket to the event, but to any Nashvillians." In my experiences, this mostly amounted to packs of college-aged coeds drinking beer and singing classics like Garth Brooks's "Friends in Low Places" at top volume along with the house band.

The move to the downtown core also opened the event to unsolicited participants, and organizers now feel compelled to manage public spaces in a way they did not have to at the fortressed fairgrounds. At key intersections, sidewalk signs notify pedestrians that they are entering the CMA festival's footprint, that "THE SALE OF ANY NON-AUTHORIZED ITEMS IS STRICTLY PROHIBITED," and that the festival benefits music education in the city, compelling passersby to support only approved vendors. Counterfeit merchandise has been a major concern. Musicians Eric Church and Taylor Swift filed lawsuits in federal court against individuals selling unauthorized T-shirts, and in May 2012, a US District Court Judge ruled in their favor.[26] During the 2012 fest, I saw no evidence of illegal activity, not even a panhandler. Still, use of the downtown core offers plenty of opportunities for less choreographed activities.

One notable example of these unscripted moments was a man named Kerrigan Skelly, who stood outside the Bridgestone Arena in 2012, equipped with a megaphone and dressed in a bright orange T-shirt stating "FEAR GOD." He was alternating between quoting the Bible and engaging with passersby: "I've never seen as many immodestly dressed people in all my life!" and "You are going to stumble into hell because of your drunkenness." He also critiqued country music itself, describing it as "filthy music that encourages fornication, drunkenness, and worshipping false idols." Although many walked right by, he and his two companions (one with a camera, another with a sign that read "DON'T GO TO HELL REPENT AND BELIEVE THE GOSPEL OF JESUS CHRIST") were so contrary to the usual experience of the festival that they gathered a crowd. One of the companions handed me a Bible tract. On the front were pictures of Toby Keith and Tim McGraw, the 2012 CMA Music Festival logo, and the question "IS THERE LIFE AFTER DEATH?" in bright blue letters. On the back was text that pitched the gospel to the country music fan:

> Toby Keith has a song titled, "Die With Your Boots On." In this song he says things like, "sometimes you beat that devil sometimes you don't" and "till the good Lord calls us home." In his song, "Live Like You Were Dying," Tim McGraw talks about the things one would do if they really believed that they were going to die soon. The fact is that we are ALL living to die. We will ALL die someday! It is a guaranteed fact! The Big Question: Is There Life After Death? Will it make a difference if you "die with your boots on" or not? The Bible says that you will either go to the Kingdom of Heaven or to Hell. Which place will it be for you? Let's find out: Have you ever lied? Stolen? Had sex out of marriage? Gotten drunk? Hated someone? If you have done these things, then you are a liar, a thief, a fornicator, a drunkard and a murderer (1 John 3:15). The Bible makes it clear that you will not enter the Kingdom of Heaven (1 Cor. 6:9–10, Rev. 21:8). You are on your way to Hell, and it looks like "the devil is beating you!" You need to "live like you were dying" and get right with God today! God sent His only begotten Son, Jesus Christ, to be a sacrifice for your sins. Jesus lived a sinless life, shed His blood on the cross and rose from the grave on the 3rd day. Now, He commands all men, everywhere, to Repent of their sins (forsake them), Trust in Him and Follow Him! Turn to the Lord Jesus and SURRENDER ALL to Him TODAY! He is GOOD!" Think you are a Christian?: www.ChristianTest.org Not?: www.Heaven-Or-Hell.us

This was Skelly's fourth year at the CMA, and he described his experiences as "pretty smooth." He said he does his best to minimize confrontations by aiming to educate police officers and security guards about his rights, and part of his talk mentions that "even if people don't like what I say, the First Amendment is there to protect unpopular speech." Asked about any confrontations at the CMA Fest, he described a moment when Bridgestone Arena security guards encouraged him to leave:

> I called their bluff. I told them to call the cops. And when they did, the police showed up and told security that as long as we stood on the sidewalk and used proper amplification, that we have freedom of speech. I told police, respectfully, "Thank you for your service."

The CMA is not his only stop. Based in Kentucky, Skelly runs a circuit of different locales, including hockey games, country BBQs, and college campuses, adapting his pitch as needed. He tailors his material to his audiences, hoping to gain their interest. One of his tactics is changing the 4¼ x 2¾ glossy Bible tracts depending on the venue. These are most effective, he claimed, to "get the message out" when he works in public places. "Someone will grab it and, later on when they are alone, they'll pull it out of their pocket. They'll read it. Maybe they'll pass it to their friend or their son or daughter.... Who knows where it will go, but the whole point is to get the Word of God in people's hands." The festival, by using the downtown area, is open to such intrusions. Similar to the push to control counterfeit goods and buskers, the CVB campaigned for a sound ordinance that would have limited street preaching, but the motion failed on free-speech grounds.

However, it is not just the buskers and street preachers that create disharmony with the more scripted events of the CMA. The Lower Broad honkytonks themselves—so physically central to the events downtown and such a strong symbol of Nashville's music scene, and a component of the overall festival experience—still offer moments of contrast. As country music moves toward more contemporary rock styles, the honkytonks maintain their usual lineups of local talent. As festivalgoers find out as they wander in for a beer, these acts remain better suited for live barroom performances than for the radio.

At Robert's Western World, for example, the Travis Mann Band played a set of what Mann described as "an evil mix of rockabilly and country" that seemed to be a sharp detour from the polished acts on the River-front stage. Between the first few songs, someone shouted a request. "You wanna hear 'Folsom Prison Blues'?" he asked without making eye contact. "We must have played that eighty-seven times in the last few days." Hair slicked back, deeply grooved and shiny like a 45, Mann led the band in the Johnny Cash classic. In an interview after his show, Mann described what it is like being an everyday musician on Lower Broad: "There's a lot of history down here. I see us as being a part of all this down here, because I think Lower Broadway is really a pretty cool, neat place. There's a pretty good vibe.... It's like a big family, everybody that plays down here hangs out." He was wary of the CMA crowd, how-ever—he was not offended by someone calling out a classic Johnny Cash song, but rather by people asking for a more contemporary one—from people like Kenny Chesney or Tim McGraw—who are then "pissed off" when he does not do it. For Mann, there is a disconnection between the expectations of these fans and the songs he is interested in playing.

"There's obviously a lot of tourists in here," Mann sighed, expressing surprise that no one was tipping him. "This is the first time I've played Fan Fair," he told me. "I was looking forward to making a shitload of money." He suspected that festivalgoers passing through the honky-tonks did not recognize the difference between the CMA musicians at the festival and the working musicians in places like Legends, Tootsie's, and Layla's. As the musicians outside offer their services gratis for the good of the festival, the musicians inside play for tips. Mann said that fes-tivalgoers seemed offended when he asked them to put a few bucks in his tip jar. When the audiences' expectations for more contemporary coun-try music clash with these musicians' performances—in Mann's case, more original rockabilly—musicians have to learn a few crowd-pleasers or stick to their own material.[27] Even though many of the workaday mu-sicians have little chance to hit the big stages at the CMA, what is inter-esting is that most don't want to.

Farther up Broadway, kitty-corner from the big Chevy Block Party stage, was Legends Corner. Like the other honkytonks, the bar had a stage in front, with big windows and an open door to attract passersby. Old album sleeves lined the walls, along with a few old instruments hung high as ornamentation. Concert posters by Hatch Show Print adorned the walls, and 45s were embedded into the bar. The bartender said, "It's good to see you again," and put a Bud at my stool. It wasn't my first visit here, but it might just be her common greeting. Skip Towne, a middle-aged singer with tight jeans, a silver belt buckle, and a mustache, was crooning to a fully packed house of half-interested visitors from Japan, Germany, Australia, and Western Tennessee. After a rendition of George Jones's "White Lightning," he added, "If you don't clap, I'll play it again," which earned a few cheers and chuckles.

Between his songs, the sounds of Little Big Town, playing onstage across the street, drifted into the bar. The polished two-boy, two-girl group looked more like catalogue models than country musicians as they sang their hit "Boondocks." The song reinforces the ever-present "when country comes to town" and "it's where you're from" country and city spirit:[28]

> I feel no shame, I'm proud of where I came from
> I was born an' raised in the boondocks.
> One thing I know, no matter where I go
> I keep my heart and soul in the boondocks.

The rockin' guitars and harmonized vocals overwhelmed Skip's Merle Haggard cover at times. By the end of his song, he turned around and watched the goings-on across the street. After a few long seconds, he turned and sighed into the mic, "I remember when country music wasn't rock 'n' roll," and started a song about how he likes his country "straight up." Little Big Town's fresh young image and pop-rock sound are braced by claims of authentic down-home values. The two stages contrasted strikingly. One hosted all the trappings of a slick contemporary rock production, and the other beheld a singer-songwriter alone on a barstool like a quaint curio on a mantle.

Markers and the Industry's Imprint

George Wein certainly pioneered branding with the Newport festivals, ramping up branding with Ben and Jerry's ice cream but then regaining some status by going nonprofit and avoiding marquee-level branding. The CMA's commercial ties are at another level. The music business is a *business*, and country music is no exception. Of course, WSM radio, the crown jewel of country music, was a commercial investment for its corporate owners, a way to promote their brand. The country format was profitable in the early years as corporations lined up to sponsor music radio programs with familiar brand names like the *Maxwell House Hour*, the *Palmolive Hour*, the *General Motors Family Party*, the *Wrigley Review*, and so on.[29] As an extension of WSM, the Opry, and the Country Music Association, the festival is a way to package business interests with a shiny bow. (The Opry, now owned by Gaylord Entertainment, signed over their rights to the event to the nonprofit CMA in the 1980s.) Music Row executive Jim Foglesong reminisced over Wrangler, Marlboro, and Ford as CMA sponsors, but also thought of the example of Loretta Lynn advertising Crisco in her Fan Fair booth early on, mirroring the look and feel of the TV commercials she made for the company in the 1970s. The interest here is not that there is commercialization, of course, but how it is kneaded into so many of the experiences at the CMA Fest.

Ed Benson told me the CMA was the first music organization to strategically visit corporate headquarters and advertising agencies to make a pitch about country music, starting in 1988. He explained to me that the safe, wholesome, and family-friendly atmosphere of the festival "fits the imagery for a lot of corporations." The CMA's push for developing corporate support coincided with the move downtown, which facilitated a bigger event that necessitated corporate sponsorships to help reduce costs. The organization tasked a strategic marketing team and a vice president, Rick Murray, to integrate existing corporate sponsors and cultivate new relationships. Benson said that they "work very hard to integrate corporate sponsors [by] linking some of them up with artists and tour sponsorships and deals and endorsements and commercial use." He underscored the point that the automotive category was crucial. Ford imprinted the festival early on: they were a big sponsor for the Country Music Hall of Fame, and the Ford Theater has its name because the company provided capital for the building. As the event grew, the CMA wanted more corporate commitment and Ford bowed out of the relationship. Chevrolet, which had been a sponsor for the annual CMA Awards show, filled the void.

These corporate relationships enter into the interactions and experiences at the festival. Armed with good relationships with sponsors in-

The Bic Soleil Bella Beach stage in a park, across from the symbolism-rich Country Music Hall of Fame and Museum façade, with the Music City Center construction to the right and hotel construction behind it.

vested in the country music market, the CMA was able to book activities and events into many downtown spaces. According to Wendy Pearl, CMA's vice president of corporate communications, there were fifty brands participating in the 2012 festival, and "we don't just ask them to be on a banner. They have to come up with things for the fan." There was a family zone with activities for kids (in 2004–2005 it was the "Bush's Baked Beans Family Zone," in 2007 it was the "Chevy Sports Zone," and in 2008–2009 it was called the "McDonald's and Dr Pepper Family Zone" with fishing and archery demos). In 2012, HGTV built a three-story lodge in a parking lot one block from Lower Broad that served as a hub for different activities from signings to performances. A temporary Bic Soleil Bella Beach stage—in a park nestled between Bridgestone Arena, the new symphony house, and the Country Music Hall of Fame and Museum—promoted a women's razor by hosting a lineup of mid-range artists. "We look at how every single partnership works for our customers," Pearl continued, and "our marketing and partnership team work very hard on our brand activation." *Activation* is marketing lingo for solidifying an emotional tie between a brand and its audience.

Sharpie set up a tent at CMA's street fair, where young kids passed out free markers to passersby. The trademark pen, so ubiquitous at Fan Fair, is a marker also of how CMA-sponsored commodities inflect the relationships between fans and the musicians, and between fans and the festival.[30] From the CMA's perspective, these brands need to be more than just visible. Brands must offer an activity. This, then, infuses explicit commercial interests into the place- and experience-making of the festival, branding both artist-fan interactions, and city spaces themselves.

((( )))

For the week of the festival, these corporate brands are tied into the banners, billboards, and spaces of the Lower Broad landscape. The festival's downtown move signified a change in the city's year-round image as well. Getting corporate buy-in benefits the festival's economic health, and provides an affordable experience for fans. For the city of Nashville, the festival is an opportunity to sell its image—along with its clear tie to the entertainment industry—to the world.

Successive mayors Bill Purcell and Karl Dean also envisioned the music industry as a strategic partner, and the CVB and chamber of commerce saw an opportunity to distinguish their city's brand. The city and the convention and visitors bureau began to fully adopt the logo of "Music City, USA," at the same time as the festival's downtown move. Though it is not a new term—the nickname comes from David Cobb, a 1950s DJ at WSM and early cohost of the Grand Ole Opry, who ad-libbed on air, "the sounds you are hearing on WSM radio were coming from Music City, USA"—the name was used only sporadically. Now, through a civic and industry alliance, this is the official slogan and brand of the convention and visitors bureau. Terry Clements, vice president of the CVB, explained:

> Delivering on a brand is some emotional tie that gives you what you want out of a product. Whether it's drinking a Coke every day, or using Gillette razors, whatever, that's a brand. The Music City one is just one that we

felt strong [about]. We've got this, but we don't own it totally, so let's make sure we own it totally.

As chamber of commerce president and CEO, Mike Neal echoed this interest in using the brand for strategic advantage. His organization saw an internationally known image, and "we as a community have got to do a better job of taking advantage of it... on a more frequent basis and use it in our marketing materials." The chamber and the CVB want to, in Clements's words, "deliver on that brand promise."

These conversations reveal how the festival serves as a marker of a different color: a prominent component for the CVB and the chamber of commerce's strategic configuring of Nashville as an entertainment machine. Just as all the corporate sponsors within the festival are "activated" through rituals and experiences, Clements's perspective makes it clear that the festival activates the city's brand as well. He asked, "Where do I really experience Music City?" As he walked through what he would want the perspective of the fans and visitors to be, he said, "Well, you can go to the Bluebird [Café] and you can hear some great songwriters, or you can go to the Ryman and hear a great concert, but how do you really touch it all?" He said that he aims to remind every visitor that they're in a creative place every chance they get. Mayor Dean reiterated this strategy to me when he talked about the new convention center, Music City Center, saying there would be "music references" throughout the project, even physically linking the new center with the Hall of Fame and Museum. The CVB wants to continue lending its marketing muscle to the CMA (they've provided logistical and financial assistance to the festival since 1977) through their promotional relationships with corporations, mass media, hotels, and airlines. "It's just a terrific little team," Dean concluded.

It's easy to see the connection between the CMA Music Festival and Music City, USA. The festival is the centerpiece for the brand's connection with the city. In interviews and on stages, it is repeatedly called Nashville's signature event—not only for providing a symbol for the city, but also because of its economic impact. However, in this triumphant mapping of commercial enterprise onto the civic sphere, I wondered what was left out.

The Scenes off Broadway

Cities are, of course, dynamic places. Not all locals are thrilled with the runaway success of contemporary country music, and this imprinting does, indeed, meet resistance in the other niches of music found around town. There are places where variants of country music with the same genealogical ancestry as the CMA festival still exist and thrive.[31] In an East Nashville dive called the 3 Crow Bar, bluegrass- and Americana-oriented musicians and industry professionals told me how their music contrasts with the CMA's careful packaging. Their opinions on the CMA's dominance expressed a pained sadness over their shared musical landscape.

In 2006, I conducted an interview with two executives at Sugar Hill Records, a small but well-respected bluegrass label: Kim Fowler, vice president of artist and media relations, and Molly Nagel, senior director of artist development. As we sat at the picnic tables behind the bar, a few people joined us, perhaps inevitable in a place where musicians and label insiders are regulars.[32] A fiddler who performs with more contemporary country acts was unwilling to be named for fear of losing gigs, but told me: "I don't go anywhere near downtown during the festival. I love this town, but during those days, it's not my town. It's not my music, and it's not my town." Avoiding Nashville's so-called signature event is not solely because of a strong aversion to contemporary country music. These industry professionals and musicians certainly still respect folks in the industry. "It's just, why would I go downtown *now*?" one asks. "I love some country music. But I've been a native Nashvillian for fourteen years, and I've never been to Fan Fair. Why would I go with the hordes of people to see bands I get to see 361 other days of the year?" Another echoed feelings of having better access to musicians they respect, like when they pay $10 and see Vince Gill or Marty Stuart stop in at the Bluebird Café. These professionals have the privilege of year-round admission to the Music City.

Not, they caution, to say there aren't tensions. They use the example of a young bluegrass band at their label, Nickel Creek, to explain what it is like to operate within the country Music City. Even though they had a hit single on Country Music Television and played a lot of country music festivals as children, Nickel Creek found that, according to Fowler, "they weren't a great fit with the other bands" as they grew older. She said she felt discomfort in promoting bluegrass at the CMA and Fan Fair because it was a harder sell. The fans were great, according to Nagel, although their interests, as she says, "were more Carrie Underwood than Nickel Creek." After peaking at #2 on the *Billboard* Country Music charts with their album *This Side* (which also received a Grammy for Best Contemporary Folk Album), they drifted away from contemporary country music. The conversation around the picnic table served as a testimony to the abundance and diversity of the city's music, and to the limited scope of the CMA festival itself. The band found a better fit at bluegrass festivals and at the Newport Folk Festival, where they reunited after a five-year hiatus in 2012.[33]

Asked about how she sees the relationship between the festival and the city, Fowler expressed that she "hates that people that aren't familiar with Tennessee immediately think of Nashville as country music, but it's a much richer place." I thought about our conversation at the 3 Crow Bar when I returned in 2012. I wanted to hear about that greater diversity, not something radically different but rather music that is more proximate, closely tied to the traditions of country while also stretching those boundaries. In order to see another variation on country music and festivalization writ small, I headed to a barn behind the famous Loveless Café, about fifteen miles from the site of the CMA.

((( )))

I pull up to a big barn behind the Loveless Café, just on the outskirts of town. The producers of tonight's performance told me I was on the "chicken-and-beer list," and when I arrive, folks point me directly to a backstage area where I'm greeted by piles of fried chicken, green beans, biscuits, mashed potatoes, gravy, and peach and blackberry jams. The banquet is for the crew and musicians of the weekly *Music City Roots* variety show. The person ahead of me—who turns out to be in one of the bands for tonight's show—expresses unreserved excitement: "This is a real treat. Being on the road for weeks, and to roll in to this.... I'm amazed." The bands swarm the food, eyes agog.

The two founders of the event, the middle-aged Todd Mayo and John Walker, tell me that they were inspired by nineteenth- and twentieth-century medicine shows, barn dances, and church events but also the more contemporary *Austin City Limits*, Garrison Keillor's *A Prairie Home Companion*, and, of course, the Opry itself. Every Wednesday they book four or five acts to perform twenty-minute sets, and the show is broadcast to over 170 stations nationwide.

Dressed in jeans and casual button-down shirts, Walker and Mayo both describe themselves as country music "commercial radio ex-pats" who got into advertising and then decided to develop live-music events in town. They relish the moments when new musicians arrive and are excited about the venue and the experience. "We get a kick out of it," Walker says, "when old-timers like Ricky Skaggs come in and say, 'This is how the Opry used to be.'" Quick to use metaphor, Mayo and Walker feel the Loveless Café barn itself is a perfect symbol for their show: rustic and far removed from the dominant corporate feel of the CMA Fest. Before the night's events get underway, and on the eve of the 2012 CMA Fest, Mayo speaks of the musical diversity of Nashville as he shows me around backstage, pointing out the recording equipment and cameras:

> We think the music from this municipality is like a good meal, and the organic stuff is on the outskirts. People's interest in this is a natural backlash to the more commercial music. It's like craft beer or organic food. People want to know what's in their food now, and some people want to listen to music without [sound-engineering software] Pro Tools.

He adds, "We're stewards of a tradition. We're preaching this." As with the Newport Festival, Mayo and Walker do some site sacralization too, albeit on a smaller scale.

They both tell me how the show started on WSM, earning praise in its first two years for providing an alternative to the Opry. In their opinion, the local media's insistence on casting their show in an oppositional light, calling it the Grand *Alt* Opry, created a narrative that prompted some pressure from the ownership of Gaylord Entertainment for them to either sell or give up control of the show when their contract came up. Walker felt *Music City Roots* was "a convergence of interests rather than a conflict," but, "you know, Gaylord Entertainment felt otherwise." They found a new on-air home, and the Loveless barn was their location on the outskirts of town.

Sitting at the edge of the room, I watch folks enter. I see scraggly old graybeards and young handlebar-mustachioed hipsters, some people with khakis and others with Western snap shirts. Lots of families. Above their heads are advertisements on old-fashioned-looking signs: Griffin Electronics, Vietti Chili, Ole Smoky Tennessee Moonshine, the Nature Conservancy, Nissan, and Ascend Credit Union.[34] Mayo and I talk a bit more while I finish up a biscuit, and I ask about the brands. "We are careful with our brands, even our bank sponsor," he tells me. "We are OK with them because they're a local credit union." When Walker comes back over, he adds that they're proud because "the sponsorships keep the lights on and everything else, which allows all the ticket sales to go directly to the artists." In the presentation of brands, authenticity is important to the organizers.

The lights dim, the on-air sign is illuminated, and former WSM announcer Keith Bilbrey starts the show. A veteran of WSM from 1974 to 2009 for both the Opry and the Ernest Tubb Midnite Jamboree, Bilbrey was recently let go to "cut costs." His deep, smooth voice announces the lineup for the evening, ending with an introduction of the master of ceremonies with a theatrical "Here's our host, Jiiiiiiiiiiiiiiiiiiiiim Lauderdale." Lauderdale, a Grammy Award–winning musician who has written songs for acts like George Strait and the Dixie Chicks, has been the host for the Americana Music Awards show nine years running. Through some banter, Bilbrey and Lauderdale inform us that the evening is divided into five sponsored segments, called branches, and that between sets music journalist Craig Havighurst will interview the bands.

Two North Carolina acts start the show. Between the second and third acts, the Vietti Chili Girl comes out with bright blond locks in a cowboy hat and short jean shorts to introduce the company's sponsored branch. After some banter with her guitarist, the two sing a jingle: "It's good for your heart, good for your soul, good in a can, better in a bowl. It's tastes so good I might lose control . . . Vietti Chili." Before the show, Walker had previewed the shtick as an ongoing bit: "It's definitely hokey, but it's also memorable and affective." The show and the chili company are running an "old-school, old-fashioned mail-in promotion": when you send in labels, you get a "real authentic" vinyl record of selections from the first season of *Music City Roots*.

The top-billed act for the night, Goose Creek Symphony, has been playing their brand of southern rock intermittently since 1968. Two dozen audience members crook their arms in the air—fingers and thumb pointed together, and elbows and wrists bent in the shape of a gooseneck—apparently flashing an established band symbol. The final set is called the Loveless Jam (named after the jam the restaurant is known for). All the acts return to the stage, with Lauderdale in front, and sing Woody Guthrie's "Going Down the Road Feeling Bad" (a song countrified by Buck Owens in 1968, and a Grateful Dead standard). Lauderdale nods to each musician to take a solo (trumpet, fiddle, then guitar), and cycles through all four acts, ensuring that everyone gets a verse. The older audience members sing along.

Conclusions: The Nashville Sound

With a full house and a sustaining business model, *Music City Roots* was hitting a stride. Mayo told me, "It's been great, Jon. Leaving WSM was for the best, really." One of the last things we spoke of that night was about how proud Mayo and Walker were about a Country Music Television broadcast that listed *Music City Roots* as "One of the top ten things to do while in Nashville during CMA Fest." They felt like acknowledged outsiders. They appreciate the nod from commercial country.

There have been arguments that country music has lost its sense of soul or tradition as compared with places like *Music City Roots*. In the 1970s, traditional country singers objected to Olivia Newton-John and John Denver winning awards, and in 2002 the Dixie Chicks song "Long Time Gone" made a similar lyrical lament: "they sound tired but they don't sound Haggard, they've got money but they don't have Cash." One can think about the smaller spaces in the festivalized city for sounds like Travis Mann's rockabilly or Nickel Creek's bluegrass. And as *Music City Roots* serves its time in exile out in a country barn while the festival is nestled between shiny office buildings, and as the country affectations of Skip Towne get overrun by Little Big Town's corporate pop- and rock-influenced style, one can't help but ponder.

But Nashville as a place and as a music scene has always been a mix of insiders and outsiders, town and country. Born in Music Row studios, what came to be called the Nashville Sound *wasn't* the rougher honky-tonk music of Hank Williams, but rather Chet Atkins's and "Honkytonk Angel" Patsy Cline's mixture of rural themes and polished, sophisticated string arrangements. The style then moved to the more "countrypolitan" feel of Tammy Wynette, Charlie Rich, Ray Pride, and Glen Campbell that contrasted even more with the rougher, more feral outlaw country music of Nelson and Haggard that Big and Rich try so hard to emulate. The old fusing of the urbane and the rural to create a distinctive brand of music presages many of the tensions at the festival today.

Vanderbilt sociologist Richard Peterson studied how country music professionals in this city shaped the content and style of what came to be the Nashville Sound, but this chapter turns that relationship on its head.[35] While there appears to be a truce between the country music industry and the Nashville elite, there is still the story of how the tensions of Nashville's sounds imprint themselves back onto the city through the festival and its experiences. The resultant discontinuities abound: the Music City, USA, branding and the Athens of the South imagery; the gritty honkytonks and glossy big-lights stages; the buskers and big stars, the street preachers and politicians, the locals and out-of-towners; the intimate interactions like the Photo Line at Fan Fair and the emotional impact of a big stadium show. While the Newport Folk Festival seemingly embraced its traditions as well as its new Americana sound, the CMA festival lacks an easy or clean relationship across these different experiences.

Perhaps the pieces should not fit perfectly anyway. Fan Fair's move from the Tennessee State Fairgrounds back to Lower Broad is the opposite move from Newport's relocation from the city's downtown to Fort Adams. Once somewhat isolated, the festival transitioned from a citadel to a core pattern, allowing for a wider use of downtown places: parks and the convention center, but also streets and parking lots. This transition allows for not just a mix of spaces, but also a mingling of different people and motivations. The more open pattern does create some uncomfortable interactions: Kerrigan Skelly's experiences indicate the challenges faced by organizers in controlling the public sphere in this arrangement, as well as the opportunities for other voices and perspectives. Skelly and buskers on the streets, as well as the experiences of the honkytonk musicians in local bars, offer up some important caveats to the festival's use of these downtown spaces. Contrary opinions, even unpopular ones, still have a place. "Because of the First Amendment," Skelly told me, "I've got every right to do what I do." His lawyers told him that the city could not limit the amplification he uses without having to limit the ambient noise rolling out of the honkytonks and bars as well. "It seems," he concluded, "that you cannot have the one without the other." Reverend Skelly's comment unlocks the struggle within the core pattern.

As the strong commercial imperative runs through contemporary country music, festivalization presses it onto the streets of the city. But when faced with the public sphere and the downtown set of businesses in the event's core pattern, limitations of that imprinting materialize. There are the honkytonks, which are private places hosting a variety of musicians who might not match the ethos of the CMA's events, and perhaps even bristle against it. What is a drawback for organizers is also an opportunity for others, and festivalization in the core of Nashville is available to unscripted events as well, from the honkytonk stage to the buskers and street preachers who are well within their rights to use these festivalized spaces too. The process brands city spaces, but it can open up street-level interactions and experiences as well.

4 Part-Time Indie Music Club
Austin's South by Southwest

Smells like nothing, back to beatnik.
And I want a partner, a big shot rock star.
She said "yoo hoo"
I'll sign something, when I'm ready.
I'll kill someone, blood confetti.
She said "yoo hoo"
—"YOO HOO," IMPERIAL TEEN

Weird City

We find the venue, the Tap Room at West Fourth and Colorado; Austin's street grid makes it easy enough. We pull up to the curb and weave through the sidewalk traffic to unload our gear. Once inside, I look around and take in the old converted warehouse space's high ceiling, old brick walls, and steel I-beam columns. In the back is a balcony and a bar, while the entrance is immediately stage left. I realize this is where I will set up my bass and be standing next to the bouncer and the volunteer checking badges and wristbands. I unpack my instrument and tune up as my stomach lurches in mixed excitement.

Tonight we're playing an official South by Southwest 2007 festival showcase. An indie label called spinART submitted a lineup of three bands; it was accepted along with thousands of other acts and dozens of showcases, placed on the schedule, and assigned this venue. As the Tap Room fills to capacity, I get off the stage so the first band can set up. The Trucks, a quartet of punk rock/rap women, have just released an album on spinART. From the first few notes they are raw and charming, poppy and smart, and like the band I am performing with, they bring a sharp feminist edge to their performance. As they launch into their set, they jump, swear, and coo at the audience. In sharp staccato, they spit out their lyrics:

> You. Are. In. Luck. We. Are. The. Lay. Dees. Of. The. Trucks.
> And. We. Don't. Give. A. Fuck. When. We're. Tripp. In'. On. Your. Butts.

Crowds at the festival act differently depending on the event—at some places the audience gravitates to the edges, and only when the audience swells is there the kind of crowding the stage I see here from the start. The packed room seems to bounce in unison.

Our band, Northern State, gets onstage at 11:30, and I take my place behind the three singers and in front of a banner of sponsors: Yaris, IFC, Verizon, the *Austin Chronicle*, Miller Lite, and *Blender* magazine. As I run through the descending bass line of the first song, "Mic Tester," I realize that there's no reason anyone would pay attention to me as I stand behind the band's three edgy, white female rappers. I relax a bit, spread my feet apart, lean over the bass, and bob my head to the beat. I feel the heat of the lights, and the ebb and flow of the verse-chorus-verse. There is a crowd of about 400 faces, and I watch their expressions as they learn the lyrics and sing along when a rhyme comes around a second time. Enthusiasm becomes general. Occasionally, I turn toward the door to my left to watch people look in, confirming that the venue is "on." Three women have their IDs checked by the bouncer and run down to gleefully meld into the miscellany of the crowd.

It is a quick forty-minute set. In my mind, it was over before it began and I was still ready for more. There are no encores at SXSW. The festival has a tight schedule, and in an air of cheers and applause, the three singers all head to the merchandise table to sell CDs and T-shirts.[1] As I pack up my gear so the third act can come on, I watch the audience quickly exit to the cool Texas air, off to the next showcase.

((( )))

Different from Newport and CMA Fest, "South By" (or "SXSW," as it is also abbreviated) is mainly an event for the music industry to conduct business and nurture new music, while also allowing limited access for everyday folk to treat it as just another music festival. Whereas organizers for Nashville's DJ convention and the local music industry developed Fan Fair to deflect public interest so they could continue their more business-oriented event, South By arose out of the city's alternative music scene and now walks the line between out-of-town commerce and local cool, as an industry event with some space for Austin's hip public, about four-to-one industry-to-nonindustry attendees.[2]

The audience at the Tap Room was typical for SXSW in many ways. Wendy Fonarow's book on British indie rock, *Empire of Dirt*, maps out the usual crowd arrangement as different "zones of participation": fans charge the stage as a few music industry folk stay to the back, asserting their position as industry insiders by being physically and socially distant, not clapping or interacting with fans.[3] As an official event, there were industry insiders. During the performance, I kept an eye on the door and saw many people with official badges hanging around their necks—these are mostly industry professionals who pay a lot (or have it paid by their label or media outlet) for admission to the SXSW business conference and receive priority treatment at music showcases. But I also saw a lot more people with wristbands, which are mostly for performing musicians and the general public to gain access to showcases like spinART's—after badge holders are admitted—but not to the business conference part of SXSW. In 2014, a badge could cost up to $795 whereas a wristband cost $225.

According to a record promoter and longtime attendee, Ronda Chollock, "SXSW *always* runs on time." Saying that the whole operation would fall apart otherwise, she said bands have to start on the dot and end in short order so industry people like her can come, see a show, and still have time to make it to the next gig. In that way, the badge, according to Ronda, is "pretty magic." She tells me South By's organizers are strict about no guest lists for the bands, which for her is "a ballsy move that means everyone has a pretty good shot to get into a show, and it keeps the badge worth the money: I can walk right up and get in." (In 2014, Chollock noted that SXSW badge holders could claim an "SXX-press pass" each day, allowing them to jump ahead of other badge holders for one specific venue: "although it understandably irritated the list of badge holders behind you, it worked like a charm." Platinum badge holders get two SXXpress passes a day.) This results in a different audience hierarchy and composition than at other festivals.

This is the reason that SXSW crowds often hover around the edges of a room, as music professionals check out an unsigned or lesser-known band in a rather uncommitted fashion. As Chris, a badge-wielding DJ from a college radio station, told me in an interview, "We're here to work, to see bands, not to crowd the stage like fanboys. You listen, you watch the crowd, you look to see if the band has some spark and if they do I might play it." Standing in the back allows industry professionals the chance to observe nonindustry attendees as a potential market, but it also allows for an easy exit. As Chris pointed out, "If I have to check out three or four bands in the same hour, I'm clearly not staying for a whole set." Audience members of our show were crowding the stage and buying merch, indicating that there were likely more fans than industry folk. Why did the audience leave during the third set? Even the South By fans move very quickly from one venue to another, often picking and choosing their way through a dense network of downtown venues, as Chris and Ronda indicated.

The festivalizing of downtown Austin requires a nearly herculean effort on the part of the festival's organizers. As I will show later, the event's success has also led to an eruption of overlapping activities unaffiliated with the official South By proceedings.

((( )))

When those attendees left, they spilled out into a downtown grid that is largely the same as its original 1839 plan. Austin was to sit north of the Colorado River (now dammed to create Lady Bird Lake), with Congress Avenue running north to the State Capitol, First to Fifteenth Streets fanning out eight blocks in either direction, and four public parks. The downtown framework is largely still in place. The Tap Room is one block west of Congress, and two blocks east is one of those parks, Republic Square. At the start of the twentieth century, rail lines ran along Third and Fourth Streets, servicing warehouses like the building I performed in between West Avenue and East Avenue.

In the light of day, the area on the west side of Congress is mostly composed of the shabby and windowless exteriors of old warehouses, giving the area its name of the Warehouse District. Since the Civil War, when General Custer's troops flooded downtown bars, entertainment drew folks here and it gained a reputation as a red-light district, called Guy Town, until 1913.[4] For decades, downtown venues on both sides of Congress have offered an odd mix of music. In the absence of a formal recording industry like Nashville's, places like Antone's (founded in 1975, settling a block and a half away on West Fifth in the 1990s) and the Vulcan Gas Company (in operation from 1967 to 1970, on the other side of the same block) and other nearby venues, such as Raul's, the Hole in the Wall, the Continental Club, Threadgill's, and the Armadillo World Headquarters, became centers for the city's cultural scene. They provided a loose but vibrant mix of blues, progressive "cosmic cowboy" country in the late 1960s, and punk rock in the 1970s and '80s.[5] Although music was and can still be found throughout the city, the Warehouse District, along with the Red River and Sixth Street areas on the east side of Congress, provides a walkable set of venues that holds a strong place character as downtown Austin has emerged as a residential and entertainment district, providing a mix of work, play, and living for an increasing number of condo owners, transplants, and out-of-town visitors.

Part of South by Southwest's draw is the offering of "all the music and Texas barbeque you can handle" for fans, and of a place for music industry professionals to conduct business outside their normal New York and Los Angeles routines in a relaxed environment. The focal point of the city's culture is set within these downtown blocks.

As a rather odd place—particularly when compared with the rest of Texas—Austin evokes contrasts seen in the last two chapters: Nashville's Athens of the South versus its Music City, USA, imagery, or the elite harbor-town residents of Newport wrestling with their folk and jazz festivals. Still, while the story of Austin and SXSW certainly has its conflicts, the city and its festival perhaps have a stronger bond than in the other two cases. The relationship of Austin and SXSW, however, adds new layers to our understanding of how festivals and urban culture can work. Offering a more decentralized experience than either of the two cases discussed so far, South By is dispersed across a wider urban landscape, attracting many more people and activities than either Newport's or Nashville's festivals. As a business-oriented event, SXSW is a more dynamic place, where musicians, industry professionals, and fans mingle, making for a more diverse range of expectations and motivations among participants.

These are not minor dissimilarities. The discussion of Newport and Nashville presented, among other things, the experiences on either side of the stage, emphasizing the musicians' and the fans' experiences, respectively. South by Southwest attendees, however, are often onstage, backstage, and in front of the stage at various times at the various official and unofficial events. Many attendees volunteer to work long shifts at the festival to earn a badge or wristband, but also perform as musicians looking to sign with a label, then stand in the audience as fans for other bands, and may even participate as performers or fans at other guerilla events. This third substantive chapter, then, continues to investigate how space and place are used for a festival but also adds new wrinkles on how participants operate on multiple levels in this curious corner of the music industry, negotiating an uncertain cultural and geographic terrain. Whereas Newport Folk tells the story of a rather elite event marginalized by the city, and Nashville's CMA is a tale of how a consortium of core institutions brought city and country music together, SXSW offers an image of how local countercultural chic and "indie cred" draws international corporate attention, and how its pattern blurs both together into a Music City cacophony.

There are several stories woven together in the following pages to underscore this fluidity of roles and cultural rituals. The first is how Austin's underground countercultural spirit became entwined with its city identity over the course of the past four decades, and how SXSW became a focal point of that synthesis. The following sections then look at how people participate in the festival in a variety of ways. There are two musicians (a headlining musician comparing the festival to others where he's performed, and a struggling singer-songwriter trying to network and gain what sociologists would call a *career foothold*), a label representative (trying to promote his bands through a variety of methods and settings), a festival organizer (working to maintain the festival's balance as both an industry and a fan event), a talent buyer (mixing fun and business), a mayor (seeking to marry economic growth and Austin's creative industries), and two promoters of unofficial events (struggling to make a name for themselves in the shadow of the official festival). The multiple roles and motivations of these participants mirror the hybrid part-industry-conference, part-music-festival nature of SXSW itself. It is a dynamic that has fueled the festival's growth; as thousands of participants serve as volunteers, they support the weight of its myriad activities.

Counterculture Crescendo

The CMA's chockablock advertising is somewhat unsurprising due to the genre's early embrace of commercialism. SXSW's eventual commercial success—the collective "buy-in" from major labels and independent ones, and all the auxiliary culture and technology that comes along with music—stems from Austin's countercultural mix and its ability to attract creative arts and technology folks.

One of the people attracted to the city's weird sensibility was Roland Swenson, who enrolled at the University of Texas at Austin in the late 1970s and ended up producing and managing a rock band (the Standing Waves) and running a small independent record label. His work organizing events placed him, in his words, "at the heart of Austin's music and arts scene." When the legal drinking age in Texas rose to twenty-one in 1986, it took a significant revenue stream away from music venues, stirring concerns over how to nurture the city's small but vibrant music scene. A group called the Austin Music Advisory Committee (AMAC)—a mix of influential local music critics, journalists, live-music industry workers, and David Lord, then head of the Austin Convention and Visitors Bureau—sought to protect and expand the city's unique blend of blues, alternative country, new wave, and punk.[6] The AMAC group, according to Swenson, got together because "the club owners, agents, and managers all saw the live scene as being in trouble." The result of those meetings was a 1985 white paper, "Austin Music: Into the Future," aimed at tying the local scene to the city's overall health. The report was presented at a symposium convened by the chamber of commerce at the Austin Opera House (co-owned by local music icon Willie Nelson) in 1977. Over the course of the following few years, many of the recommendations from that report were set in motion, including establishing music liaisons in the chamber of commerce, city hall, and state government, opening a medium-sized (1,000- to 2,000-seat) venue, and promoting music as the hook for the city's marketing for business and tourism.[7]

Hosting a music festival was a central recommendation of the report, and a few players from that AMAC group looked to New York City's New Music Seminar—a series of music showcases curated by industry executives—for inspiration. Through managing the Standing Waves, Swenson got to know the founders of the New Music Seminar, and began a conversation about organizing something similar in Austin.[8] His group "wanted to bring the music industry from LA and New York to Austin, while still giving Austinites a chance to see some great music," and he described how, in 1986, the chamber of commerce and CVB helped put together a serious pitch for a Southwestern Music Seminar. When New Music Seminar organizers backed out of the negotiations, Swenson joined booking agent Louis Jay Meyers, *Austin Chronicle* publisher and cofounder Nick Barbaro, and *Chronicle* cofounder and editor Louis Black and decided to go forward anyway.[9] With the tight connections between key figures in the local music industry, alternative media, and downtown venues in place, they felt they could pull off their own event. Scheduling it for Spring Break, when the venues were emptied of their usual college-student clientele, Black came up with the name South by Southwest as a riff off Hitchcock's film *North by Northwest*. In 1987 they planned for a small event, expecting only 150 registrants. Instead, they got 700 and interest from major labels in Los Angeles, New York, and Nashville. There were 150 acts (two-thirds of which were local). The chamber and the CVB contributed advertising money.[10] According to Swenson, now managing director of the entire festival, "it grew exponentially from there." (So much so that he complains that he spends too much of his time attending to various crises to enjoy any of the music.)

President and member of the chamber of commerce from 1983 to '87, and Austin mayor from 1988 to '91, Lee Cooke insisted on developing the local music industry as a "critical strategy," and Mayor Kirk Watson worked to merge economic growth with Austin's creative community during his term (1997–2001).[11] Watson, cited by Richard Florida as a prime example of the "creative class" argument, said:

> Austin has benefited from a convergence between technology and our laid-back, progressive, creative lifestyle and music scene.... The key is that we continue to preserve this lifestyle and diversity, which enables us to lure companies and people from places like Silicon Valley. We are building the habitat to do that.[12]

Another recommendation of that white paper, which connects with this approach, became a reality on August 29, 1991, when City Council Resolution 910829-46—adopting the suggestion of local musician Lillian Standfield with the backing of the city's music commission—made "Live Music Capital of the World" the city's official slogan.

Fortuitously, 1991 also happened to be the year when "indie" or "alternative" rock went mainstream. Less than a month after Austin's rebranding, Nirvana's single "Smells Like Teen Spirit" (sarcastically referenced in this chapter's epigraph) dominated the college radio charts and then its album *Nevermind* knocked Michael Jackson's *Dangerous* off *Billboard's* #1 album position. SXSW's heavy emphasis on college radio and indie rock bands rode that wave. When Nirvana's tortured lead singer, Kurt Cobain, was repeatedly photographed wearing Austinite Daniel Johnston's "Hi, How Are You?" T-shirt, the city's indie cred was second only to Nirvana's home, Seattle.

Austin was poised to be one of the genre's major nodes, and SXSW a significant engine for new music. According to one journalist's account of the rise of indie rock, the festival "started with hand-stapled schedules and a good deal of local music [and] had quickly swollen quickly and earned a near-mythical reputation as a place to catch an express train to rock fortune."[13] When the New Music Seminar folded in 1994, SXSW emerged as the primary indie rock industry event.

The 1990s saw an expansion of new venues in the central business district, providing a density of amenities to draw college crowds, other countercultural types, and tourists. Along Red River Street, the eastern

Austin indie musician Daniel Johnston's "Jeremiah the Innocent" graffiti has existed at the corner of Twenty-First and Guadalupe since 1993, and serves as an icon of the "Keep Austin Weird" ethos.

edge of the central business district (CBD), venues sprouted up, including Emo's (opened in May 1992), Stubb's BBQ (1996), and Club de Ville (1997). Stubb's is a grungy and dark indoor honkytonk stage and a couple-thousand-capacity outdoor space, and is co-owned by Charles Attal, who founded C3 Presents, a promotions and booking agency.[14] In 1992 the city built a convention center at the foot of Red River Street, and the festival moved in the following year. (The convention center doubled in size ten years later, and now includes two music venues.)

Balancing entertainment and economic growth was neither easy, nor uniformly successful. The city established a Downtown Venue Relocation Program in 1999, expressly for the purposes of offering one of those downtown venues, the Liberty Lunch, a $600,000 loan to relocate from city-owned property west of Congress to a new venue on Red River Street in order to make way for a lease to a tech company.[15] The loan arrangement was unsuccessful, and the city lost one of its iconic venues.

By 2000, Austin's overall economy was feeling the effects of the burst of its dotcom bubble. As a city councilor at the time, Will Wynn was appointed chair of the city's first Economic Development Committee a few years before his eventual role as the "Mayor of Rock 'n' Roll." "Up until that point," he told me, "we didn't really need a committee for a centralized city council study group on growth—whether because we were doing just fine or because it wasn't particularly politically correct to want to go out and attract business." A year later, he completed a set of white papers on managing the city's development in a way that resonated with the AMAC's earlier findings. Wynn believed the city should embrace its music and offbeat culture as a strategy, epitomized by its unofficial slogan: Keep Austin Weird. This phrase first appeared in 2000 when a man by the name of Red Wassenich called up a local radio station to donate money, saying it was to help keep Austin weird, and it ended up being a motto of sorts for Austin's countercultural and anticommodification spirit, even being printed on bumper stickers and T-shirts.[16] "Sure, you saw a few bumper stickers," Wynn acknowledged, "but it's not like there was a Keep Austin Weird store." It was, rather, "just a sentiment" that he felt the city could use as a city councilor and mayor. He found firm purchase for the argument within the city's live-music sector, despite some reservations:

> Of course, the chamber of commerce rolled their eyes. But I thought it
> could fly politically in town. Ultimately I believed it: this whole idea of
> jobs following people. So, we tried to pass ordinances to make it a little
> easier to open live venues, or have a small business. We started building
> more bike lanes. We tried to keep it hip, having festivals, more live-music
> venues, we essentially decriminalized marijuana. Pretty much focusing
> on strategies to keep Austin at the forefront of those young college kids'
> minds.

It was at this point that SXSW organizers began to see significant support. Swenson told me, "We were flying under the radar of the city government for those early years. . . . We were getting a lot of media, and then the fire department and the police cracked down, and noticed what we were doing."[17] And although there were tensions about music permits and the like, Swenson saw improvements in the "long, entangled history" between the city and the festival. As the chamber was invested in attracting tech companies from the 1970s through the '90s, they came around to music, too. Swenson told me his event was only "tolerated" until the chamber started searching for another way to market Austin as a tourist destination. The eventual allegiance made it easier to file for Change of Use permits, providing oxygen for the festival to grow further.[18]

This growth was seen on both sides of Congress. By 2007, a strip of Red River clubs—Stubb's, Club de Ville, and the Mohawk (opened in 2006)—were all seeking expansion permits in order to attract more successful musical acts and larger crowds.[19] On the western half of downtown, the venue I performed in, the Tap Room, was part of an upscale bar called the Six Lounge (named for bar-financier Lance Armstrong's now-rescinded six Tour de France wins), which opened in 2004. The building itself is like others around it: a two- or three-story brick building converted into a bar or restaurant.

To keep the momentum, in 2008 Mayor Wynn launched a fifteen-member Live Music Task Force (including Wynn, two city council members, a CVB representative, Mohawk owner James Moody, Stubb's owner Charles Attal, Gibson Guitars executive Don Pitts, and a few working musicians) to take on some of the perennial issues of balancing business and residential growth and the downtown live-entertainment industry.[20] One of the recommendations was having a music manager in City Hall's Economic Growth and Redevelopment Services Office. The task force also recommended designating the entire central business district as an entertainment district, which could lend considerable benefits to live-music venues, including less restrictive sound levels, better parking and loading zones, expanded hours of operation, increased publicity and marketing, more security, tax breaks, and an improvement of late-night public transportation.[21] The city's involvement continued. In 2012, the old Music Venue Relocation Program emerged in yet another form as a Music Venue Assistance Program, allowing the city manager to offer low-interest loans of up to $40,000 to implement noise-mitigation measures in hopes of balancing residential and entertainment interests.[22]

Wynn explained, "I won't go so far as to say that we're the victim of our own success, but we're still growing so dramatically that a lot of people are pushing back on growth," and he doesn't want it to happen at the expense of the city's diverse community, nor its music culture. The downtown scene, in fact, has had some setbacks as of late. In 2011, Emo's—the setting for hundreds of SXSW showcases over almost twenty years—closed and was eventually sold to Charles Attal and his live-music promotions company, C3 Presents. And at the end of 2013, the SXSW festival saw the shuttering of Antone's on the west side of Congress. As owner of Emo's and co-owner of Antone's, Frank Hendrix felt the pressures of these changes, evoking the gentrification of New York's East Village to claim his venues were priced out of the downtown core, telling *Billboard*, "We were going the way of CBGB's."[23] The fall of the two venues might be symbolic to some locals who express concern over the city's music district, but there are over 250 other music venues in Austin (and dozens still within a few minutes' walk from the convention center: thirteen on Sixth Street, eleven along Red River Street, and thirteen in the Warehouse District), offering thousands of live-music performances each year.[24]

Looking back on his time at city hall, Mayor Wynn talked about the business community's continued support for the "creative city" idea and ongoing relationship with the live-music industry and the festival. He says it is only possible because the city also managed to keep all the other components of city life moving as well:

> In very general terms, the chamber of commerce was won over, but you can't drop those other balls. You need to have a fiscally sound financial statement for your city. You can't raise taxes too much. You have to fight crime and be known for being a safe city. You better pick up garbage. All those are really important, in the trenches, public works stuff.... The chamber came around to the Richard Florida/creative class/Keep Austin Weird thing because they saw that we weren't dropping the ball.

Wynn easily tied the two slogans, Live Music Capital of the World and Keep Austin Weird, to the quality of life and pro-growth argument.

Austin's power brokers and place entrepreneurs were hard at work transforming these downtown blocks. By 2007—the year I first visited

Austin—new condo towers were being built around the CBD, and SXSW far eclipsed the New Music Seminar, with over 12,000 attendees registering and over 1,300 bands and ancillary film and technology festivals augmenting the event.[25] In 2014, there were almost 2,300 bands, 111 stages, and almost 28,000 conference participants (which includes artists with wristbands). South By is, according to the *Austin American-Statesman*, the city's trademark.[26]

Whereas the downtown area attempts to attract growth with a balance of both entertainment and residential life, the festival attempts to attract attendees with a mixture of work and entertainment, as industry personnel and fans all descend upon this downtown nexus every March for the part–business conference, part–music festival. The festival's multiple audiences and varied roles for participants within it are key to its organizational apparatus, its eventual expansion, and some of its greatest challenges.

"It's a Double Thing"

I arrive at the convention center early to get my volunteer assignment for the conference, and am handed a bright-red shirt with SXSW STAFF 2012 on the back. Eager to see the festival from the inside, I head to room 19AB at 9:30 a.m. and join a pack of forty sleepy-eyed twentysomethings sprawled out on chairs and tables. Most seemed to be recovering from attending late-night shows, save for the volunteer crew chief, Cindy, who cheerily announces that she doesn't go to shows anymore (the carrot for most volunteers) even though she works enough to get access to almost any event. "I just enjoy meeting people," she says. The volunteer staff has thinned out after a few days, precisely because the volunteers spend late nights going to shows and sleeping in.

Cindy warns me that she's going to "throw me in the deep end" and assigns me to the mentoring sessions. After a quick pep talk chiding volunteers for not making it to their assignments, and offering a few directions for the entire crew, I join a team of five who wend their way through the back halls of the convention center, past folded-up tables and stacks of clean tumblers for the day's sessions, to a big room with a few tables set up. A twentysomething woman gives us the drill:

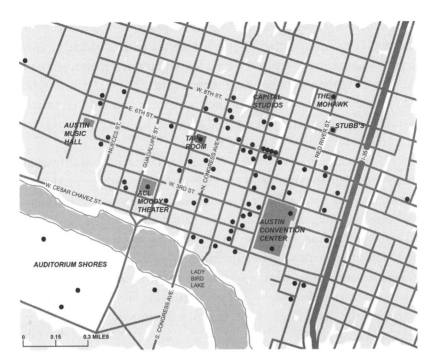

Map labels:
W. 8TH ST.
CAPITAL STUDIOS
THE MOHAWK
E. 6TH ST.
AUSTIN MUSIC HALL
STUBB'S
NUECES ST.
GUADALUPE ST.
TAP ROOM
RED RIVER ST.
I-35
N. CONGRESS AVE.
W. CESAR CHAVEZ ST.
ACL MOODY THEATER
W. 3RD ST.
AUSTIN CONVENTION CENTER
AUDITORIUM SHORES
LADY BIRD LAKE
S. CONGRESS AVE.
0   0.15   0.3 MILES

South by Southwest venues, 2012.

Musicians sign up for unvarnished advice from professionals. For ten minutes they can ask anything. It's your job to direct them to the people they signed up with, and if someone walks in and there's a space available, you have to match them up with someone. Coach them beforehand: tell 'em it's a waste of time to pitch their material and, instead, they should just ask any questions they want about the business side of things.

With that, our coordinator leaves and, since I am the eldest of the group by a decade, the other four look immediately to me. I divvy up responsibilities: one person flags people looking for the session, two escort the aspiring musicians to their intended mentor, one person keeps time, and I oversee it all. We put out placards for the mentors, and prepare the sign-up list. One of the volunteers is Drew, a music student from Wisconsin, who is logging hours for a badge and hopes to get into band management at a record label. Soon, the mentors arrive: a few musicians, as well as label executives, the owner of a PR firm, the music booker for NBC's *Late*

Night with Jimmy Fallon, and a college radio promotions director, Justin Gressley. For an hour of their time, each mentor earns a badge. As aspiring musicians arrive, we sign them up for ten-minute appointments and usher them to their mentor tables. After the first round, I'm astonished that people aren't showing up for their appointments, and I begin redirecting people who have just finished a session back to another mentor so as to not waste anyone's time.

Although there are many aspiring musicians who know exactly whom they want to speak with, there are others who want advice on the best person to speak with, or are nervous about being paired up with someone they do not know anything about. At the end of the session, when no one else is in line, my fellow volunteer Drew asks if it would be okay for him to speak with a mentor. Rather than grabbing someone from the hallway to see if they want a session, or spinning around yet another aspiring musician, I agree. "Why not?" I say. He pulls a notebook out of his pocket and sits at a table. Once the last pairs are matched up, my head continues to spin.

((( )))

The mentoring sessions are a window into the business-minded motivations and multiple roles that attendees embody at SXSW. Although musicians comprise the Newport Folk Festival's advisory board, and a few top musicians serve in the Country Music Association, for the most part, roles at festivals are circumscribed. There are producers, production crews, musicians, and audiences, and not a lot of overlap or movement between these categories. The hybrid nature of South by Southwest as both a conference and a music festival, however, means that roles are often more blurred.

First, there's the musician. Newport's musicians include both up-and-comers and old-timers, and Nashville's CMA lineups also feature both proven stars and new musicians with established hits. Central to the image of South By is that aspiring bands travel from across the country and, increasingly, from across the globe, for the chance to play in front of label Artist and Repertoire (A&R) people,[27] make contacts, and get signed. Landing a record deal is the explicit draw for most, but it is an increasingly rare occurrence. Many label executives told me this is "largely a myth," and the best that musicians can hope for these days is to "make a few contacts." When bands agree to play SXSW, they contractually agree to play only one event during the festival.

Established artists get invited as well—to perform headlining gigs, talk at panels at the conference, or serve in mentoring sessions.[28] For the rest of the hundreds of artists, there are two ways to book a show. The first is to apply to the festival directly. In the early days, bands would mail tapes and CDs, and organizers would sift through hundreds of boxes and select only a fraction of them. Musicians now submit a digital press kit, upload MP3s of their songs, and pay a $40 submission fee through the SXSW website. In 2012, over 10,000 bands applied. According to one SXSW official, if they "possess a combination of artistry and a sense that they're at a level where participation could help them further their career, they're invited." The other way for musicians to attend is by being invited to perform as part of a label's or media outlet's showcase, like the one at the Tap Room. These showcases feature primarily a label's own signed acts, but there are exceptions. Music showcases, which tend to have three to six acts, used to be only at night, but there are now shows nearly all day long. Now there are official day parties organized to promote music from other countries, cultural institutions, or media organizations. In 2013, a showcase was even put together by the Newport Folk Festival (sponsored by familiar underwriters *Paste* magazine and Sennheiser) as a way to highlight artists performing at Newport later in the year.[29] As these groups embrace the idea of the festival as a place to market themselves, and are willing to pay for hosting these showcases, the festival can accommodate a greater number of acts.

Whichever way they entered, the bands that performed in 2014 had the choice of being compensated with $250 ($100 if a solo musician), or all the members of the band get wristbands (which gives wearers access to the shows, mentoring sessions with industry professionals, and panels) and no compensation. About 20% take the cash, which can barely pay for a night in an Austin hotel room during SXSW. Like the rest, the band I performed with, Northern State, took the wristbands.

Two interviews illustrate the experiences of the musicians at opposing ends of the spectrum. The first was with Mike Watt, a legendary bass player who has played countless festivals around the world, who was performing at SXSW with Iggy Pop and the Stooges. As one of the quintessential punk bands of the 1970s, they were a headlining act at the festival. I spoke with him before his headlining performance at Stubb's.

Like many more established musicians, it took time for the fifty-year-old Watt to warm to the idea of discussing festivals and places rather than his own career or current projects. However, once the interview got on track, he talked enthusiastically about festivals as places where he both got to see "old buds" onstage and was excited to discover new bands too, saying he "trips out" over seeing "young cats" play. "I'm a lot less younger," he told me, "and really the gigs I go to are the ones I play, so at a festival I hear a lot of bands and I get out there and see as much as I can." After all these years, Watt remains a music fan. When asked about the differences between performing as part of an established act like the Stooges and the experiences of the aspiring musicians he sees onstage, he talked about the mistaken hopes of being signed at an industry event like this. He called it "the taunt":

> This is more like an insider clusterfuck. Although it's a double thing, because a lot of kids come here, too. And they really think they are gonna be signed. The reality is that the acts here are already signed, and it's a bunch of big wheels putting their bands out there to get some hype.... The real bands that come here and play, they bring a reality to it, though, and that is genuine.... That's the groovy thing about it, man.

So, while he is both a musician and a fan at the festival, the divide between musicians and insiders, and fans and industry professionals, isn't lost on him either. He lamented that only a few "cats" will be able to see his headlining show because people with badges will get first dibs and only a few wristbands will make it into the much-hyped performance. Laughing, he told me he is still happy to perform for anyone because "people are getting to see us doing it in our fifties and sixties and that's pretty cool." Even if it is all "industry stiffs," he said, they're still "going to get a face full of Iggy!"

It is this awareness of multiple audiences and multiple motivations for participating that makes the event, in Watt's terms, a "double thing." Watt knows the industry from the ground up, having struggled as a member in the now-iconic punk band the Minutemen and then participated in other projects for decades before he arrived at SXSW in 2007 as a proven musician and part of a headlining act.

The second interview was with Dani Linnetz, who is a good example of those musicians who come to SXSW trying to make it, and therefore lend the festival its indie cred and populate the vast majority of its showcases. A thirty-three-year-old singer-songwriter, Linnetz put out six self-produced albums over the span of seven years, and attended SXSW six times in the same period. Participating at this level means having to negotiate the "double thing" quality of the festival—accepting the challenge of what Watt called "the taunt" while at the same time representing what Watt saw as the more "genuine" aspect of the festival.

The first time Linnetz applied, she didn't get in. Although organizers disagree, she believes that good connections make all the difference: "If you're not a cool band on a cool label, it's hard to get in." She described her first application as a "really sassy package," all tongue in cheek with a letter pretending she was someone else reviewing her music. She admitted she did not really expect to get in, saying, "They have so many people applying, it's crazy." She availed herself of conference sessions that focused on the nitty-gritty of industry work, both to learn and to network:

> In the beginning, I used all kinds of tactics. I was eager to meet every person I could. . . . I schmoozed with everyone. I was very much a one-woman show, marketing myself like crazy and trying to make it. I had a ton of business cards. I certainly tried to exchange business cards with every single person I would meet. I met people in every area of the industry, from all over the country.

With panel topics like "Marketing Your Music in an Overloaded World," "Music Deals and Artist Compensation of the Future," and "Touring Nuts and Bolts," and mentoring and demo-listening sessions, the conference aspect of the festival is oriented toward artists precisely at Linnetz's level.[30] "Oh, the showcases and the late nights are a lot of fun," she explained, "but if you're actually a musician trying to network, you should be at the convention center, sitting at panels, meeting other musicians, trying to meet managers, and producers and the speakers." Aspiring musicians often spend the weeks leading up to the festival contacting people in the industry in hopes of generating some buzz, getting people to their showcase, or scheduling a meeting. Artists and volunteers aren't compensated much in terms of cash. They are paid with access.

In addition to the musicians, there are those industry professionals that the aspiring musicians want to meet: managers, booking agents, A&R, media reporters, talent buyers, and other people around the music business. They are engaged in a variety of business activities, from participating in the convention to promoting their own artists to trying to find new artists to book at their hometown venues.

Label executives and A&R reps promote their bands, seek out new bands to sign, and network. Erik Courson, the thirty-one-year-old label representative from spinART who put together the showcase at the Tap Room, has been coming to the festival for years. In the 1990s he attended as a fan, but when he opened a record store in Dallas in 2000 he shifted his involvement to checking out new music and promoting his store. And then, in 2004, he had moved to New York City and worked for the small indie label, shifting his work again to promoting his acts and setting up the 2006 showcase featuring Northern State and the Trucks. He explained how they put that showcase together:

> We had to submit bands to play a sanctioned showcase. The problem
> with that is, if you're a label and you do a showcase: you are not going to
> farm your bands out to any other indies for their own radio promotion
> or digital marketing whatever. You want them to play *your* showcase, it's
> *your* evening. And SXSW only allows bands one showcase. So, it is really
> difficult to get a band you feel confident to be a draw—because you are
> competing with everyone else.

Drawing on his days as a record-shop owner, Courson told me how he works the event by going to his band's gigs, but he tries to promote his acts at other events too:

> When I'm out and about, my role while I am talking to people I know or
> meeting new people is to tell them when our bands are playing. Hope-
> fully they'll come. If someone manages a store in some town and comes
> to see one of my bands, maybe they've never really listened to the CD, or

never heard about them, well, if I get them to the show and they enjoy it, they go back to their store, put the CD in the listening station, tell friends about it, and play it more in the store. Any time you can get a fan in a store, that's a good thing.

For Courson, the festival is fun, but there are what he called "layers of obligations" that necessitate a different set of expectations. He has to pitch his acts to friends in the industry, but he also has to be at their shows, pretending to be an enthusiastic fan to keep up the image. "The free booze," he told me, "helps a lot."

The talent buyers travel from all over the country to check out bands they think might be good to bring to their hometown music club. Brendan Leith books music venues in a small college town; he loves the surprise of seeing bands just by walking down the street—what he called "letting the wind take me"—or going to a show a friend tells him about, but there is a less glamorous business side to it as well. One of his highlights for the festival is getting the chance to meet with other talent buyers and comparing notes, hearing what works, what doesn't, and even "all the pretty dry stuff" like discussing changes in tax withholding from foreign bands. And while free booze may be a help to some, he admitted, laughing, that "there's only so much you can take before you want to say 'Enough!'" As the number of parties during the day increases, he has become disappointed that people choose to go to shows rather than have productive business meetings. "I mean, I want to see bands I like, too, but I also have work to do."

Justin Gressley is an executive in his early thirties who heads up radio promotion for college radio stations and participated in the 2012 mentoring sessions. He was eager to describe the informality of the work at SXSW in comparison with the CMJ Music Marathon—the annual event in New York City run by the College Music Journal, a music promotions company. "There are more meetings at CMJ," he said, "where you meet here at this time and go see this band right away." SXSW, however, has a more relaxed pace: "You're like, 'Yeah, let's get some barbeque, and ah, I'll see ya there.' There are more parties and it's more loose."

Ronda Chollock, an independent record promoter, spent her time at SXSW talking up bands; she described her job at the festival as "schmoozing and seeing bands." She watched her bands perform for crowds, gauged people's reactions, and then was able to talk about their stage presence to talent bookers like Leith.

Each had a different agenda, and yet all of them emphasized the business they conducted at the festival, while also appreciating SXSW's relaxed format. In contrast, the band managers seemed highly focused, seeking every opportunity to promote their bands and to follow up on any contacts they've made over the years. Zach, after encouraging me to go see one of his bands at a showcase, told me that after eight straight years of coming to the festival, he felt it is increasingly difficult to get one of his unsigned bands signed. "A&R people already know what they are looking for, having done their homework, read blogs, and watched a lot of YouTube. They arrive with a wish list." In the technological era, vetting is done earlier, and a live show is less about discovering a band than it is about verifying a live performance. "I still stumble upon a band that's quite good," Zach continued, but he encouraged his bands to "generate buzz well before the festival itself." He continued:

> No one goes under the radar anymore. There are few chances to get signed. Take, for example, the band Illinois. Everybody is talking about them this year, and everyone will be at their show. But they were [already] signed to an indie label.

Zach was disappointed about these kinds of acts being at the festival because they "absorb a lot of buzz."

One indie label rep described the ideal experience for a band coming to SXSW: they should be focused on filling their room with "anyone from the major labels to music blog writers and anyone else off the street." "Coming into South By, you want attention," he told me, "and coming out of it you want to be one of the two or three bands being *the* buzz band." A twenty-four-year-old band manager, looking for a deal for one of the bands he was managing at South By, said that the "attention-grabbing techniques" he sees on the sidewalks (e.g., giving out stickers, etc.) are "nowhere near as important as getting some cool blog to write about them" so people hear about them before they even arrive in Austin.

Many professionals I spoke with wondered if SXSW's size inhibited such attention-grabbing tactics. A twenty-seven-year-old A&R rep for a

Convention center rock: Cameras rolling in a near-empty room.

major label described SXSW as "just so chaotic" that it's not really serving its purpose. He felt that most attendees would agree that it is "impossible to see all I want to in the short period of time I'm there, but I guess that's a good thing, right?" This "chaotic-but-relaxed" theme arose as industry insiders talked about the SXSW balance between business and fun.

After the musicians and the industry professionals, there are the volunteers: a few hundred red-shirted, mostly college-aged folk assigning badges at check-in, helping at a panel, or working backstage at a show, all logging hours for access to the festival itself. In 2014, volunteering fifty hours earned a wristband and sixty hours earned a badge.

Although there is a great deal of monotony working panels at the conference, being a volunteer has benefits. Not being invited to perform at an official showcase did not dissuade Dani Linnetz from participating. Like many aspiring musicians (or aspiring music industry professionals, like Drew), volunteering is another way to get in the door. Linnetz arrived in Austin a week before the music festival to log enough volunteer hours at the SXSW Film Festival to earn a platinum badge (allowing her access to all three festivals—music, film, and interactive), and she took every opportunity to meet managers, producers, and other musicians at panels and shows during her second week in town.[31] In her years at SXSW she never played an official show, yet she always booked performances at other unaffiliated shows around the city. She worked with people she knew at local venues, and she was able to use her access from volunteering to convince industry people to come to these unofficial gigs (she learned that 6 p.m. was a good time to book an unofficial show because it was between official showcases). She was able to find some success, and by her third volunteering stint, she had developed enough contacts to piece together a tour to Austin, culminating with an unofficial show at her favored 6 p.m. slot, and then playing a second set of gigs on the way home. At a panel at that year's SXSW, she met a man from the William Morris Agency, the largest talent agency in the world:

> He was really just flirting with me, but I didn't care. I knew enough to have my guard up about that, but also how to use it to my advantage. He came to one of my shows. He was into it. He bought me drinks, and invited me up to his hotel room to play him some songs, but because everyone schmoozes in the lobby of the hotel, he ran into some of his friends who were actually promoters and he invited them up to the room, too. After I sang a few songs one of them said, "Hey, well, I have some opening slots for John Hiatt. I'd love for you to do them." And I followed up as soon as I got home.

Although she was not able to get signed, Linnetz was a rare example of an unsigned, independent artist opening for an established artist at the level of John Hiatt. Most attendees would call that a major success.

((( )))

The last few pages show the multiple roles that people play, and how SXSW brings out a different set of roles and interactions than most festivals. A classic study like Howard Becker's "The Professional Dance Musician and His Audience," which examines the tensions that arise when a musician's sense of self is deeply connected to the viewer's enjoyment, relies on a clear distinction between the performer and the audience. SXSW garbles up categories, and while some tensions emerge, other antagonisms are pacified. There are certainly individual figures and generic types familiar from the other two festivals—the musicians both young and established who come to perform; the fans who come to see a favorite band or discover a new one—but taken collectively, the stories of Mike Watt and Dani Linnetz; of Erik Courson, Brendan Leith, Justin Gressley, and Ronda Chollock; and of Zach and Drew make the picture a more complex one. It is not even that SXSW can be divided into three, rather than simply two, groups: the badge-holding "industry stiffs" of Watt's description; the more enthusiastic wristband-wearing musicians and fans; and Watt's authentic "cats" looking to build a career. Rather, SXSW stands out for the way it does not structure clear and distinct roles for its participants. Established artists and industry personnel enjoy becoming fans of (or mentors for) new musicians; beginning artists work as their own managers and booking agents; and volunteers aspire to be musicians. Label people like Courson and promoters like Chollock have to pitch their bands throughout the conference, but also have to stand in the audience at every gig, looking as enthusiastic as the fans. Some volunteers use their wristband access simply to enjoy late nights partying; others, like Linnetz and Drew, use their wristbands as a way to achieve other goals.

SXSW is, then, a double thing both in its structure as a conference and festival and in its ability to offer participants the chance to occupy multiple positions in and around its activities. Yet another way SXSW is a double thing is in the interplay between the officially scheduled program and the unofficial performances that take place around it. This quality makes for an urban festival quite different from the other two.

Buzz Overload: A Walk through Official and Unofficial SXSW

As befits an industry conference, South By also features a range of panel discussions devoted to topics relevant to music industry professionals. Participants receive a badge, but also a hefty swag bag that includes a variety of CDs, magazines, promotional stickers and flyers, a thick conference program, and a weird mix of aspirin, earplugs, and even a voodoo doll. I start my day at the "Covering Music in New Media" panel, where representatives from AOL.com, Pitchfork, and eMusic discuss the revolutionary changes that digital music and media have brought to the industry. Michael Azarrad (author of a book highlighting Mike Watt's

Minutemen, *Our Band Could Be Your Life*) makes the case for online media while also lamenting the death of music magazines. Things get lively with a question-and-answer session, and conclude with audience members drowning the speakers in a wave of business cards.

After attending two other panels, I tour the convention center, passing by a Verizon Phone Charging Station, a Dell Computers Lounge, and another lounge sponsored and furnished by IKEA. Thousands of flyers and ads are strewn everywhere. The convention center has two state-of-the-art music venues running performances all day. At these shows, however, as at a great many of the official showcases where the bands are neither signed nor "buzzed about" on social-networking sites, the rooms are mostly empty, with only a few viewers hovering around the edges—not unlike a few music showcases.

Outside these venues, sponsors, imagery, and sounds bombard me. Music rumbles across the street as a band plays on a makeshift stage in an empty dirt lot that is definitely not in the official program. Farther down, women in black shorts and white button-down shirts on roller skates are passing out flyers to an unofficial party. An old school bus in a parking spot on Red River Street has a makeshift stage inside it. Young men and women roam the streets with refrigerator carts of free Fuze beverages.

Austin's Sixth Street is closed off to automobile traffic for pedestrians, as it is for many celebratory holidays. There are buskers and bands, people handing out flyers for gigs and ads for Microsoft. There is a hazy aural aura. The music from open windows pulls in pedestrians. Like Nashville's Lower Broad, Sixth Street has a party atmosphere, but SXSW does not dominate the public space as heavily. It has a much looser feeling. One twenty-one-year-old local told me that his primary impression is that "music is coming out of every other doorway down here," and that it is unlike anything else he has experienced because he can "just pop in, check out a band for a while, drink some free beer, and go find something new." Another attendee described it as "definitely more of a Mardi-Gras-for-hipsters atmosphere."

A very large percentage of the passersby have interesting, asymmetrical haircuts, tight jeans, and ironic T-shirts, which makes the whole procession look like one big, hip band. The official music venues often take

An empty lot becomes an unofficial SXSW venue.

Two drummers, one playing an official showcase.

advantage of the mild March weather to use outdoor parking lots and patios for stage areas, with green plastic sheeting threaded through the gaps of the fences to obscure sight lines, but the music washes over the temporary fences and people peek between the slats or stand on each other's shoulders to catch a glimpse of the performance. A walk down just a few blocks of Red River Street offers music by ten or twelve different bands.

At Seventh and Red River, another parking lot has been converted into a music venue. There's a stage with a performance by She and Him, a band comprising M. Ward and indie-film actress Zooey Deschanel. The music is being broadcast live by a Minnesota public radio station, but the concert is a production of Free Yr Radio, a promotional strategy by a marketing company specializing in hip consumer engagement; the sponsor for this event is Yaris, a lower-priced Toyota model.

((( )))

With about 200 staff, South By books thousands of bands, and tries to keep control over the quality of bands and the walkability of the events.[32] Though SXSW will sometimes build a temporary venue, for the most part they use the existing downtown clubs and the convention center. The venues cede control over their spaces and booking, and in turn receive production costs (or additional tech staff from SXSW) and keep their beer and liquor sales, earning what one local reporter approximated as six weeks of revenue in four days. SXSW claims that venue revenues for March average 45% more than the next-highest-grossing month.[33] The digital age has diminished production costs, making it easier for advertisers, blogs, cultural magazines, promotions companies, and smaller music labels to participate in the industry. College radio promotions director Justin Gressley pointed out that it also makes it harder to get attention for your organization's events. He continued:

> You need to have visibility in regards to the industry, and that means putting on a showcase. We need our brand on the tent, we need to be associated with cool acts. We need to serve free beer so people will identify that whole experience with our company. But when we did our party, there were a lot of college kids and that worked for our college radio crowd.

With all these events, it is surprising there are any available locations, and yet there are spaces left over that have been increasingly rented out for unofficial shows during the past few years: dirt lots, vintage clothing stores, garages, art galleries, hotel lounges and swimming pools, and even parking spots for tour buses that double as traveling stages. There are some events that are official (like those at the convention center), others that are not (for example, the empty lot for rent), and still others that are semi-official (like the Free Yr Radio stage, which qualifies as a "sanctioned but not officially listed" show). There is so much signage downtown during the festival—dozens of official and unofficial day parties—and the experience of walking in and out of events is so fluid that it is easy to miss when there is no official banner hanging behind the stage.

The semi-official She and Him event, for example, took place only hours before their official performance at a SXSW showcase sponsored by Toyota, a headlining sponsor of the official SXSW. Even the event at the Mohawk described at the beginning of chapter 1—which featured a welcome speech by Austin Mayor Will Wynn—was not an official SXSW event at all. Austinist's "Gonna Gonna Get Down" day party characterizes the blurring of official and unofficial SXSW perfectly: though not an official event, it was held at a venue that did feature official SXSW events later in the evening, and thirteen out of the sixteen acts there also performed at other, official SXSW showcases. The appearance of the mayor, which lent credibility to the event, resulted from Austinist's editor-in-chief contacting Wynn's chief of staff and convincing him that an appearance at their event would be a good way to reach "the hip, urban, twenty-one- to thirty-five-year-old set." It was, assuredly, quite an ironic moment.

Far surpassing Newport's BridgeFest and Nightcap and the smattering of unofficial events around the CMA Fest, there are dozens of unofficial events (alternately called advertiser, side, shadow, or satellite events) occurring alongside the official SXSW. As one participant told me: "With the unofficial parties, you are probably assured to see a band, as opposed to the official showcases [where wristband holders may not be admitted]; people aren't buying badges as much anymore." People who want to see She and Him, for example, had the choice of getting a badge or wristband and hoping for a chance to see them in a crowded bar at the official show, or just strolling into the Free Yr Radio event in the middle of the day for free.

Although Austin during SXSW might appear similar to Nashville during the CMA Fest, it's quite a different scale. During the CMA Fest, most honkytonks kept their usual lineups of local, unsigned musicians while the official festival events occurred in the convention center, on temporary stages in the surrounding downtown parks, in empty lots, and in the football stadium. In contrast, Austin's unofficial venues field calls from outside companies looking to rent space and from bands wanting to book a show concurrent with SXSW. Whereas Newport had one such event (BridgeFest), SXSW has dozens of them vying for attention. These shadow events are beyond a mere nuisance: they threaten the economic health and brand dominance of the festival in ways that are very different from the other activities outside the CMA and Newport Folk festivals. Because SXSW is scattered across the entire downtown area, guerilla promoters can embed their events literally across the street from the convention center and sap attention and revenue from the official festival. In the marketing business, the brands that sponsor these alternative events are conducting *predatory* or *ambush marketing*.

These guerilla events are a byproduct of SXSW's use of the downtown area (as opposed to the fairgrounds outside Nashville or the bounded space of Newport's Fort Adams). They spring out of the social ecology of venues and physical spaces around the growth of Austin's downtown: new businesses (perhaps not even music venues) that are eager for the publicity and attention that come with a shadow event, or landowners who are awaiting a bid on an empty lot and rent out the space during SXSW for extra revenue. Just as there is a surplus of spaces for use, there is also a surplus of musicians who were not invited but still come to capitalize on the networking and industry attention; even musicians who are invited often still book an additional gig at one of these events to defray some of the travel and accommodation costs and garner even more attention by playing to multiple audiences. SXSW disallows artists from booking additional nighttime shows, but many artists ignore the warning.

Then there are the promoters of these guerilla events. Preferring to use a pseudonym for fear of negative attention from the festival, Sofia told me, "South By has always been my favorite music festival" because of the opportunities to create side events to extend the visibility of her promotions company. "Power drinks, beer, radio stations, local promotional companies, smaller magazines all want to be affiliated with cool events outside the festival," she explained, adding: "Look: our free beer isn't free for us and hanging up a sponsor's banner helps us to pay our bills and put on a good show, official or not." She recognized SXSW's concerns over the use of their name, saying, "Hell, I get it because we wouldn't want them to use *our* name either." However, she argued, "they don't run the town, either. It's not fair to have a monopoly on 'all events in Austin at such-and-such a time,' and I know that we're not taking something out of their pockets or their mouths." Sofia guessed that 80% of the people who have been to her unofficial showcases have badges. "Some of these bar and local shop owners," she said, drawing on the experience of setting up unofficial shows during the festival, "would rather chuck the whole [SXSW] system and cash in with an unofficial party rather than toe the party line. They could make a mint for those couple of days rather than follow the formula. It's their Christmas." Sofia never mentioned the term *ambush marketing*.

Another producer of shadow parties told me that some record labels and commercial entities are shy of explicitly tying themselves to unofficial events through sponsorships because they do not want to upset SXSW organizers. Also preferring to remain nameless, he told me how he is willing to partner with any number of eager sponsors for their unofficial day parties, letting them advertise their sport drinks, headphones, messenger bags, and so on. He explained: "We will tell them, 'Give us X amount of dollars and we will highlight your company,' or 'We will give out information virally, through the mail, or at the event.'" He said there is plenty of interest because "a lot of these companies don't get the chance to get involved in such a cool event and reach these kinds of people." The official event only has so many spaces for sponsors, and others want to get involved, too.

And, last, there are the people who attend these side events. Tina, a twenty-seven-year-old Austin local, sometimes buys a wristband and other years just attends the free shows, based on her economic situation and what her friends are doing. Another local said that he has attended enough to skip the official event: "It's too expensive and I'm too old and just don't want to deal with the crowds much anymore." Instead, he planned to go to several unofficial parties, which he called "free booze events."

((( )))

It is easy to see why an unofficial festival running concurrent to their own frustrates SXSW organizers. There is some question over how much they can really do about it. A 2006 law required some of these venues to get a Change of Use permit—meaning that a clothing store, for example, would need a permit to host a musical performance—and this set the stage for a bit of a brouhaha. In 2007, city officials shut down a number of these shadow events for improper permitting, being over capacity, and excessive noise. There was a debate over how much of a role SXSW officials played, with some locals claiming that SXSW organizers provided the local fire department with a list of unofficial parties.[34] Austin's Public Assembly Code Enforcement (PACE) officers—a mix of police, fire, and Texas Alcoholic Beverage Commission agents—started to patrol events from that point forward, checking permits and making sure that bands did not exceed 85 decibels or sell merchandise without the necessary sales tax ID. When PACE officers shut down a shadow event at a local clothing store called Factory People, the owners railed against festival organizers for being "imperial" but also admitted they "didn't obtain the permits" and "accept full responsibility."[35] Festival organizers Roland Swenson and Louis Black, in turn, make the case that SXSW expends hundreds of hours filing permits correctly for all their events, and that it is only fair if everyone else has to play by the same rules as well. In a less generous 2008 interview, Swenson described these events as "parasites," admitting that SXSW did, indeed, provide the police with a list of unofficial events.[36] While they do not want the SXSW brand to be exploited, they also know that if something goes wrong, South By will be mentioned whether it was an official event or not.[37]

In addition, SXSW organizers want to make sure that no unofficial events use their brand. When a promotions company called JellyNYC pitched a "concert series at SXSW" in the heart of the downtown area that coincided with the festival, SXSW lawyers took them, and another outfit called LIVEstyle, to court. Sofia, who sympathizes with JellyNYC, said that there were intense pressures placed by South By on people like her. "They built something," she acknowledged, "and we're doing something with what they built. It's not my fault that the younger bands, cooler bands want to align their identity with our company." According to one report, the court action not only claimed trademark infringement, but also requested that JellyNYC and LIVEstyle be blocked from producing any event in the entire county during SXSW.[38]

Among music professionals, many do feel that the glut of unofficial events drains their attentions and, writ large, their festival experience. As Brendan Leith described it, "It's almost like there are all these mini-festivals around the festival itself," but this makes him want to focus more, not less, on the official events. Interestingly, at least in this way, these shadow events can potentially reinforce the official festival as a "weird" event, enhancing its overall image.

Don't Move Here: The Struggle over an Indie Austin

At an official event, a Merge Records Showcase at Antone's, the lineup includes the "queer alt-rock band" Imperial Teen, which is returning to the stage after a five-year hiatus, and a "surprise special guest" people correctly assume is local indie rock heroes Spoon. The behavior of industry folk toward performers changes when there are cooler, more recognizable headlining acts. Antone's is packed to capacity. No one is getting in, and the "zones of participation" are blurred with a big act like Spoon promising to play in a smaller venue. It's still early in the night, and folks are chattering between songs, mixing business and pleasure. Imperial Teen snarls out lines from their most recognizable hit, "Yoo Hoo."

Even here, though, where the crowd is unified in its excitement about the show, the tensions between Austinites and industry insiders surface in interactions. As Ben, a local who works at a tech company, complains about the high price of his wristband, a woman wearing a SXSW badge interrupts our conversation as she squeezes between us to order a Lone Star beer: "Hey, guys, they're not running a nonprofit. It's not supposed to be just for Austin hipsters to get to see their favorite band-of-the-moment. I'm here for my fucking job, and no one's forcing you to come."

With a smile, she declares that "locals like us" are in the way of her and her business, just like we are standing between her and her beer. We laugh and move aside, but Ben continues by reinforcing that he is an Austinite, although he admits that the animosity felt by his local friends toward SXSW is likely "rooted in their collective imagination of some 'golden indie age' of South By, when everything was perfect and free and wasn't so fucking popular." He adds that they probably didn't even live here then, but just heard stories.

Lone Star in hand, our interloper continued, yelling loudly over the band: "Look, people with wristbands will not be able to get into everything, it's true. And I do feel bad breezing by people who are in the wristband line who waited for a long time and I see that they're upset, but it's an industry event." Besides, she notes, locals can see the headlining band, Spoon, "all year long... *because they live here!*"

Eventually introducing herself as Isabella, an A&R rep from the Los Angeles office of a large label, she finishes by noting that "it's as easy to get a free beer as it is to complain, but what's extremely motherfucking difficult is putting on an event of this magnitude." The talk moves to how Austinites use the festival's presence to pull out their SXSUX (South By Sucks) and Austin Sucks: Don't Move Here T-shirts. Like many interviews with locals who understand both sides of the event, the conversation cannot easily be summed up with catchphrases.

((( )))

Austin's local music community organized in the 1980s and '90s in hopes of blocking outside influences while preserving and supporting the local music scene.[39] SXSW, with its attention to the music industry from New York and Los Angeles, tests those aspirations. After out-of-town festivalgoers swing through, they leave behind a somewhat tense relationship between the festival and Austinites, and local concerns over temporary inconveniences echo what many Newport and Nashville residents describe. I found, however, Austinites participating in their festivalized downtown. Unlike Nashville, where organizers had to expend resources to attract locals, South By has had to find ways to ensure that locals have a chance to participate as well.

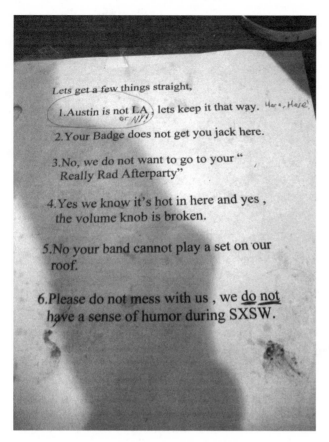

A notice posted at the counter of a pizza parlor near the convention center.

Roland Swenson told me that maintaining a positive relationship with locals is a chief concern for the festival that they have tackled in a number of ways:

A lot of people's expectations who have recently moved here is that "it's supposed to only be for Austin bands," "all these visitors displace the locals," "all the Austin bands that apply get turned down." Because of these perceptions, there are people who really resent what we do. That's a problem, but what they don't realize is that it was always about bringing people from out of town, to bring talent from out of town, and our belief was that it would benefit everyone here, locals, local businesses, and locals in the music industry.

Trying to keep everyone—visitors and locals alike—satisfied with the ever-growing event is neither an easy nor an enviable charter.

One tactic SXSW uses is a complicated admission system that aims to limit online scalping by selling a significant number of wristbands though a local record chain, only available in person and two at a time for $130 each. These are a hot commodity: for weeks prior to the festival, dozens of Craigslist ads sell them for up to $400. As noted, however, while badges get near-guaranteed entry, wristbands do not. Although most Austinites acknowledge SXSW as primarily an industry event, even locals who fully support the festival still harbor feelings of resentment as they watch out-of-town music industry representatives with badges breeze into venues while they have to stand in line.

On the other side of it, many music industry professionals grumble about the difficulty of doing business when surrounded by partying locals. Record promoter Ronda Chollock had her wallet stolen at the festival and said that, for the first time, SXSW was beginning to feel "like St. Patrick's Day in Boston:" "Look," she said, "I paid $700 [and] I have to fight my way around hundreds and hundreds of drunk children to see a show for a client." While she said it was irritating to have to deal with what she referred to, tongue in cheek, as "civilians," she also acknowledged that it was a "minor quibble," and one that came from the festival's ability to offer so many things to so many different people.

A second tactic has been used by SXSW to both assuage local dissatisfaction and keep the industry professionals happy. Much like the CMA's refashioning of Lower Broad into a public street fair, SXSW has recently organized three nights of huge free concerts at the nearby Auditorium Shores Park on the southern side of Lady Bird Lake with major artists like M. Ward (of She and Him). This is a way of giving something back to locals while at the same time pulling "civilians" away from official showcases; it also helps drown out the competing free guerilla events. These free shows include a marketplace for local artists and food trucks, similar to Newport Folk. Even here, though, there are privileges: there is a special hospitality area for badge holders.

M. Ward performing a SXSW free show at Auditorium Shores.

Another of Swenson's concerns is the overcommercialization of SXSW. Similar to folk music (though unlike contemporary country music), indie and punk rock have a long and deeply held anticommercial ethos, and this has lent a certain sense of hipness and countercultural credibility to SXSW. At the same time, the festival, with its history of being a tastemaker of indie rock music, has achieved a level of success that has attracted corporate sponsorships eager to affix their brand to the event.

For Mike Watt, whose band the Minutemen was deeply immersed in the anticommercialism of punk,[40] performing under the logos of corporate sponsors was less about compromise or selling out than it was about having to "deal with the realities." Watt speculated that when a festival like this one is "more of a genuine deal," the music industry people will "always see something happening and try to hustle it." Watt then returned to the duality of the experience—there are corporations "hustling" these events, but at the same time there are musicians hustling, too, and "there's something genuine in that." Watt focused on the goals of young aspirants over the more established music executives.

The hustle, then, comes from inside and outside the festival, from musicians and organizers and sponsors, too. Unlike the CMA's history of reaching out to corporate sponsors, SXSW sees it as a more careful and recent endeavor. Swenson told me that garnering major sponsors was "new but necessary territory" as the recorded-music industry comes under economic pressure as the money from labels diminishes and outside corporate interest rises. "Nine times out of ten," he tells me, "the sponsors come to us because, right now, we're an attractive property." This allows him to pick sponsors, but there are also corporate influences that the festival has less control over. Swenson noted that the more successful and established bands already come with their own brand relationships. "To survive on the road, these bands get sponsorships and, when they come to our event, we're having to grapple with that, too." However, the bands are themselves careful about what sponsors they choose. As Swenson laughingly noted, "Typically, they're not being sponsored by Tide but rather something endemic to music." He understands that bands need to do what's in their best interest as well.

The second concern for SXSW is the sponsorships *outside* the festival. The guerilla events bring another layer of branding that imprints itself onto the city. A good example is the Fort, hosted by the music magazine the *Fader*. Founded in 2002 by marketing and branding guru Rob Stone, the Fort pairs bigger-named, signed bands with non-SXSW sponsors like Levi's, Microsoft, and Southern Comfort. It is the epitome of the corporate-sponsored day party: located within a few blocks of the convention center, it offers free booze and gifts to everyone who RSVPs, and has a packed house with a line down the street. The event switches affiliation year to year, sometimes functioning as an official day party and sometimes not. In 2011, Fiat became a Fort sponsor, but this conflicted with one of that year's official SXSW corporate sponsors, Chevrolet; as a result, the Fort returned to unofficial status yet again. For Fiat, however, this presented its own advantage: a Fiat representative told the *New York Times*: "The Fort is more about the up-and-coming bands, not the mainstream... and we're not a mainstream brand."[41] The claim of an international corporation like Fiat to *not* be a mainstream brand is a good example of how sponsors spin their corporate image to take advantage of the alternative credibility offered by an association with SXSW—and even more so by an association with a non-SXSW event—but also of how brands clash in the festivalized city.

For Swenson, these guerilla events give the undesirable impression that "even though we try to control our sponsorships, we *seem* overly corporate and overly branded." In other words, the indie festival ends up being perceived as too mainstream because of the corporate sponsorship of events that it does not manage. SXSW loses its control over the symbolic landscape. As Swenson himself noted with a sigh: "Really, but I'm not sure what we can do." While guerilla promoters and musicians exploit the festival's looser organization (compared to the festivals at Newport or Nashville) to promote their own bands and brands, organizers fear that the unofficial events with their unofficial sponsors dilute the distinctiveness of their festival.

Once again, a sense of doubleness—and at times possibly even duplicity—ends up haunting South By, and this leads to some understandable confusion: the festival struggles to be diverse but also in control of its product; to be both a "genuine deal," in Watt's wording, and a viable commercial entity for the music industry; to celebrate the unique culture of Austin and also draw in out-of-town professionals; to offer an alternative to the mainstream music business and also cater directly to it. Advancing these misperceptions are the idealized (and perhaps imagined) past experiences that contrast with attendees' present-day frustrations, and the blurring of what exactly is an official and an unofficial event, particularly when the same musicians play official showcases, nonofficial guerilla events, and the official-yet-free Auditorium Shores show, all with differing sponsors. In this, the festival mirrors the city that hosts it, which also is engaged in an ongoing struggle: to stay weird and also be growth oriented. Austin's unofficial and official mottoes—Keep Austin Weird and the Live Music Capital of the World—may not have settled into an easy truce, any more so than have Nashville's competing slogans of Athens of the South and Music City, USA.

By 2014, tensions had escalated further. A SXSW-commissioned report by Populous—an event-planning and design company with experience working for and with twenty-fix Super Bowls, twelve Olympic Games, and five World Cups—concluded that the main problems with SXSW are actually the unaffiliated events, and that the festival cannot function for the best of itself and the city of Austin without stronger municipal assistance. The report recommends creating a "Legal Injunctive Zone" or "Clean Zone" around the festival with a "controlled, soft perimeter" of security checkpoints to search people walking on the public sidewalks of Sixth Street—a recommendation that could defy the First Amendment rights of buskers or people like Reverend Skelly in Nashville and would make the event more a citadel like the Newport Festival than its current incarnation.[42] Perhaps the report's biggest bombshells were that the city should start limiting what they call *splinter events* (and their *ambush marketing*) by giving priority in assistance, permissions, and permitting to specially designated "signature events" like SXSW, and that, if it doesn't get that support, the festival may have "no choice but to entertain notions of bidding their event to other cities to sustain their business model."[43] Cofounder and managing director Roland Swenson posted a response on the SXSW website reiterating the festival's commitment to and shared identity with Austin, admitting that managing other events has been a logistical nightmare but adamantly denying wanting to ban unofficial events like the Fader Fort.[44]

Conclusions: Inside and Outside the Club

I didn't get into the Fader Fort's unofficial event. Instead, I crossed the street to take a picture of the Fort's long queue. On the opposite corner was a man holding a sign for a nonprofit organization called Climate Counts. He was one of a handful of protesters, countering the counterevent. The sign named a main sponsor of the Fort, Levi's, as a "choice to avoid for the climate-conscious consumer." Asked about his organization, he admitted that, "Oh, um. I dunno... This guy just said he would give me twenty bucks to stand here." The man approached him outside the Austin Resource Center for the Homeless (built in 2004, near the Red River venues a few blocks away). When he showed me the other side of the sign, where Climate Counts gave Levi's a "one out of one hundred" score, he rotated his arm to reveal infected track marks along bright inflamed veins.

Later that night, while walking down Sixth Street, I ran into an entourage of street preachers. Marching with banners and bullhorns at 11 p.m., the group offered up fire and brimstone to the amusement of the crowds. One sign had a picture of a man and a woman drunkenly walking down a street. This group was followed by six men dressed in orange astronaut suits handing out flyers, promoting an altogether different otherworldly offering: a Jefferson Airplane/Starship show with "intergalactic give-aways" for Microsoft. The makeshift parade is a free-for-all, unlike Nashville's more careful coordination of zoned activities on Lower Broad.

Aspiring musician Dani Linnetz described South By as a "big networking party." She told me, that, "having worked at a label, toured around, having lived in New York and LA, I get to go to Austin and see everyone. It's a big party for everyone who is in this weird club called the Music Club." Like any club, there are those who are invited and others who are not, and yet, in contrast to the citadel pattern at Newport, South By's confetti-like looseness makes exclusion difficult. By using some—but not all—of downtown Austin's public spaces, the SXSW Music Club is open to all kinds of incursions. The spatial arrangement creates challenges for organizers as well as opportunities for other groups to compete for festivalgoers' attentions.[45] Within this loose fabric, a wide range of people are able to weave their way through it all, from aspiring musicians working the system for access, to savvy locals unwilling to pay for a wristband and filching off the free events, to corporations willing to pay for an unaffiliated party.

Although its logic is corporate, its experiential tone can appear shambolic. More so than in Newport or Nashville, then, SXSW is the site for a contradictory range of interactions—official, semi-official, and unofficial; corporately sponsored, nonsponsored, and even anticorporate. When indie comes to town, it carries along with it a bevy of other activities that challenge the ownership of its experience in a way distinct from the other two festivals discussed in this book. Both the experience outside the Fader Fort and the one on Sixth Street speak to South By's open, confetti-like plan and Linnetz's evocation of the festival as a big networking party to underscore the importance of thinking about access, and how the events inside the festival are used, too.

Will this dynamic change? With guerilla events and protesters, the idea of restricting the borders of the festival must be a tempting strategy for organizers. Limiting these kinds of activities would allow for greater control over downtown's economic, spatial, social and symbolic terrain. Without erecting walls, a "Clean Zone" would transform South By's confetti pattern into a citadel. In its present form, the fluidity between inside and outside gives SXSW a discordant energy, and it is a dynamic not without its benefits: there is a buzz over access that makes the experience hip, customers flock to a nexus of downtown music venues and businesses, and a rowdy mix of images and sounds helps the festival's weirdness reflect the ethos of Austin itself while still attracting corporations and developers. SXSW and its outsider events institutionalize that weirdness in a marketable package. While the SXSW organization attempts to control the unofficial events—not to downplay the weird and chaotic scene they create, but to control its commercialization, possibly with greater municipal involvement—the organization struggles to keep its cool in more ways than one.

5 The Long-Term Effects of Fleeting Moments Part One

I had my dream I held your hand on that broad avenue,
We crossed the road and never spoke to another as we flew
We left your man alone in drag, laughing there at us,
A romantic bust, a blunder turned explosive blunderbuss.
—"BLUNDERBUSS," JACK WHITE

After the Party

Lower Broad is already swept clean. The tents are gone. Nashville's Riverfront Park is silent, save for the trucks loading fresh supplies to the Second Avenue bars via the First Avenue delivery entrances. A lone jogger passes silently, headphones on. Now that food and T-shirt tents no longer blockade the park's edge, it is possible to see the rows of trees lining the river. On Lower Broad, men and women in business clothes stride at a determined pace, sunglasses on and Bluetooth headsets in their ears, chatting to seemingly no one. Everything is quieter. The bars and restaurants open their doors and let the breeze of air-conditioning flow out like a cool exhalation. In this post-party atmosphere, it is clear that understanding how festivals fit into a city's overall cultural landscape means knowing what happens not only during the festival, but after it as well. Once the 2012 CMA's big finale ended in fireworks, the city slowly returned to its normal rhythms, to what happens in the days, weeks, and months after the party.

When those bright lights fade and the out-of-towners return home, residents often open up their local newspapers and see articles touting estimates of success in economic terms: how many hotel rooms were booked, how many out-of-town dollars were spent, and so on. This sort of data can look fairly impressive. But impact reports mostly highlight monetary gains, and fail to encompass each longer-term change to cities at the ground level, as everyday folks experience them. This is where Henri Lefebvre's vision of urban life provides for a more nuanced view, one that contributes to a more holistic understanding of the components of festivalization.[1] Numbers of visitors, and especially numbers of visitor dollars, are persuasive measures, and yet miss the lived processes, interactions, experiences, and perspectives detailed in the past three chapters.

A larger analytical view of these events must include, in addition to the established *economic* data, a consideration of the *spatial resources* (i.e., the actual physical places, and the experiences generated within them), the *social + cultural resources* (i.e., the kinds of people involved, and the particular skills they hold), and the *symbolic resources* (i.e., the images, icons, and place branding). These four resources interlink and influence one another, and the following discussion raises particular questions about the festivalization process in real time and place. To tell that story requires two chapters (this chapter and the following one).

The first half of this chapter addresses the economic facet: What institutions and individuals are bound together for art- and culture-based urban development? What are some of the evident successes and failures? To answer these questions, the next section will discuss the economic and business growth associated with these three festivals.

The second half focuses on the spatial resources of a city, asking: With this kind of development in mind, how do neighborhoods change within and around festivalized areas? How are they experienced? For these questions, this section weaves together a sequence of facilities and venues through a series of walks in Newport and Providence, Nashville, and Austin.

The first half of chapter 6 examines the social and human resources, asking: How do the city government and music industry personnel—tied briefly together through a festival—directly or indirectly cultivate creative communities? What needs are targeted and which groups benefit? For these concerns, this section draws from interviews with musicians, festival organizers, and community members.

The second half of chapter 6 highlights the symbolic resources of a city, asking: With the official and unofficial festival events, how do corporate images shape the overall impression of the city via its symbolic landscape? What images are included? What role do alternative or unofficial events play? To address these concerns, I draw from interviews with festival organizers who are keenly aware of the issues and opportunities raised by branding, but I also look at what festival participants themselves think about these landscapes.

Although split into two chapters, the discussion and analysis of these four resources interlink, making comparisons and connections across different locations as resources are developed, reinforced, promoted, and exploited. This chapter and the next map the mobilization of resources surrounding the festival itself, to focus on the urban-culture placemakers, community stakeholders, and participants through the lens of the music cultures that these events and places have so strongly identified with.

The Business of the Arts and Urban Growth

Most festivals justify their effect on the community via their positive economic impact. City agencies, local universities, and sometimes the festivals themselves will conduct what is called an impact study. Data on these events are typically broken down into Direct Impact (i.e., the income from expenditures by the festival organization, sponsors, and attendees) and Indirect Impact (i.e., the income from sales, increased employment related to the festival, and the expenditures of those individuals who earned income at the event, sometimes called Induced Impact).[2]

A 1997 study by the Office of Travel, Tourism, and Recreation at the University of Rhode Island found that both Newport festivals had a combined direct impact of over $3.7 million, and a 2012 economic-impact report found the festivals to have close to a $5.1 million overall impact.[3] The CMA reports that the festival generated a $10 million impact in 1999, $24 million in 2010, and $31.5 million in 2013.[4] SXSW's year-round operations boast an overall impact of over $73.7 million,[5] while an economic-impact report showed that the three SXSW festivals combined (music, film, and interactive) pumped $168 million into the economy in 2011, over $190 million in 2012, $218.2 million in 2013, and $315 million ($208.6 million in direct impact, $55.6 million in indirect impact, and $51.1 million in induced impact) in 2014.[6]

There are also studies mapping the broader economic impact of the creative sectors of urban centers (a term used to encompass film, gaming, visual arts, and music industries as well as tourism and, at times, the not-for-profit sector).[7] An arts-advocacy group called Americans for the Arts found that in 2010, Providence nonprofit and cultural organizations generated $190 million in economic activity.[8] A 2006 study by Belmont University faculty found that Nashville's music industry—its eighty record labels, 130 music publishers, 180 recording studios, and 5,000 working union musicians—created a total economic impact of almost $6.4 billion a year, with over 19,000 jobs and an additional 14,000 jobs in "music-related" tourism that brings the city $2.42 billion.[9] A 2012 study by the Nashville Chamber of Commerce found the total economic impact to have increased to nearly $10 billion a year, with 56,000 created and sustained jobs within the Nashville Metropolitan Statistical Area.[10] In 2012, an Austin-based policy consulting firm, TXP, Inc., found that the city's overall creative sector generated $4.35 billion of economic activity, $71 million in city tax revenue ($9.6 million via music alone), and almost 49,000 jobs (almost 8,000 jobs via the music sector), claiming that their creative sector, as measured by employment, has "risen by about twenty-five percent over the past five years, a pace more rapid than the ten percent growth for the local economy as a whole."[11] They also found that live music and music tourism represent $1.7 billion of revenue, over 38% of the creative sector's contribution to the city's economy.

Festivals are not without costs. For the 2012 CMA, for example, the Metropolitan Nashville Police Department paid overtime to forty officers and ten sergeants for extra four-hour shifts to patrol the city streets at key times and locations.[12] From 2010 to 2012, Austin used a "special enforcement team" spanning six city departments to check that "all vendors, merchants, event holders and property owners are in compliance with municipal safety codes." In 2012, the Austin Police Department announced that, to streamline communication, it would have all of its 1,700 officers on duty, split among seven shifts, rather than having the festival hire off-duty officers as in the past.[13] (SXSW organizers contributed by making sure the police knew where the popular bands would be performing, and where any surprise shows would pop up.)

Then there is the labor, which is not such a clear economic gain. As temporary entities, festivals offer short-term employment (as compared with, for example, the more stable year-round attractions of a museum or an amusement park), and thus their benefits are more limited. The festivals generate extra jobs, along with seasonal employment for hotels, catering crews, and the like, as well as hundreds of temporary jobs for sound engineers, stage managers, and security. And even if it seems that festivals offer minimum-skill work, events often use volunteers who are eager to be a part of the festival and perhaps gain access to some of the events. In recent years the CMA used stadium tickets to entice hundreds to volunteer, and SXSW used wristbands to compensate over 3,000 volunteers. On a much smaller scale, Newport also has volunteer cleanup crews. Overall, these cost-saving measures—through either police or volunteers—reduce the potential employment impact.

It is now necessary to look at these three locales in terms of recent developments in relation to these numbers, to see how festivals and music culture shape urban growth at the ground level. First I will look at Newport and the greater Providence area, and then I will move to Nashville and Austin.

Uneven Cultural Providence

Rhode Island is experiencing tough economic times: an aging population, one of the worst unemployment rates in the country, the lowest college-graduation rate in New England, and a political establishment with long-standing corruption issues. The economic vitality of Newport, as the state's second-largest chamber of commerce, rests on the hospitality, boating, and defense industries. In describing the zeitgeist of

Newport for most of the past century, Didi Lorillard told me, "You have to remember this is where people retired to, not to earn a living, unless you are in the navy." Indeed, when the North Atlantic destroyer fleet pulled out of Newport's harbor in 1973, it removed one of the largest employers in the state. Now, the smaller navy presence—the Naval War College and the Naval Undersea Warfare Center provide education and training rather than fleet support—is still the single largest employer in the county, with roughly 7,400 civilian employees, military staff, and students, and an economic impact of over a billion dollars.[14] The defense industry keeps the area insulated, offering well-paying, year-round jobs. The seasonal tourism and leisure industries bolster Newport further. Boating, bars, mansions, and recreational events are all part of a wider effort to maintain Newport's place character as a destination: landscape, water, scenic buildings, and cool breezes.

Ed Lavallee, Newport's city manager, told me that, when it comes to cultural events, "success breeds success"; in other words, "it seems that, if you have enough of them under your belt, your town is a place-holder to create traction for other events." When asked how events are considered from the municipality's perspective, he continued, "From a government management standpoint, and the need for economic sustainability: it's important for the business population. Collectively, all those cornerstones—the other music festivals, the boat festival, the tennis—are what draw other events." Jody Sullivan, executive director of the Newport County Chamber of Commerce, said that her members look for any "quality thing that can bring quality people here"; when the festivals are in town, she says, "the bed-and-breakfasts are full, the restaurants are full.... All boats rise with that tide." It is what you would expect the executive director of the chamber to say, but business owners say similar things, both on and off the record: in a fragile tourism economy, sensitive to weather and fickle consumer spending habits, any stable, repeatable infusion of out-of-town spending is welcome. A Newport business owner explained to me that the summer resort season provides 60 to 70% of her overall business profits, and she is "super thankful" for the city's summer programming.

Whereas the resort town of Newport relies on its defense and tourism economy, Providence, twenty-three miles to the north and at the other end of the Metropolitan Statistical Area, is attempting to rally around its creative industries. Mayor David Cicilline places his hopes in arts- and culture-fueled economic growth. Cicilline worked with community members to issue a Creative Providence plan in 2009, hiring a Nashville- based consulting firm specializing in crafting brands for cities. The plan aims to boost programs like Buy Art; to improve arts education in the city (feedback generated from the plan indicated a dissatisfaction with the city's arts education); to raise the influence of the city's Art, Culture, and Tourism Office so that it is more officially engaged in business re- cruitment and public relations; and to rebrand Providence as the Crea- tive Capital. As sources of both cultural wares and social resources, the city's two major institutions of higher learning—Brown University and the Rhode Island School for Design (RISD)—both have programs de- signed to nurture creative-industry businesses too. The city's nonprofit arts and cultural organizations accounted for 4,669 jobs in 2010, up from under 3,000 in 2007.[15]

Prior to Mayor Cicilline's plan, Providence's arts-and-cultural- development-as-growth strategy had mixed success. Investors and pol- iticians made efforts to develop the city's surplus of empty paper and textile mills and old warehouses, built during a massive 1800s building boom in the western part of the city and vacated due to the now-familiar post–World War II deindustrialization. Some of these buildings were al- ready being used by musicians and artists looking for cheap rent and big spaces. Attempting to repeat the success of developing Baltimore's Harbor Point and Inner Harbor redevelopment, the Maryland-based company Struever Brothers, Eccles, and Rouse announced in 2006 an investment of over $333 million to redevelop twenty-six Providence fac- tory buildings, taking advantage of state and federal historic-renovation tax credits, and asking for a further $41 million in other public subsi- dies. They targeted former factory sites with a plan to build over 380,000 square feet of new construction; their announced goal was to make Prov- idence "the coolest city in the world."

In 2008, a Tax Increment Financing (TIF) plan—a public investment via a grant or an interest-free loan for projects in a designated geographic zone holding a kind of "civic value," usually awarded to a development company with the assumption that the project will generate future tax revenues—was approved by the city council, which seems to have been charmed by the developers' promises for improvements to the Woonasquatucket riverfront, along with the promise of rent subsidies and affordable housing. Condo growth statewide was on the rise, up 140% from 2005 to 2007, and there was reason for optimism that there would be continued demand for warehouse loft living.[16] The government loans (via a general obligation bond), however, were never issued, due to two factors: the existing working-class community in the area organized over the plan's displacement of thirty small businesses, and this slowed the process enough for Struever Brothers, Eccles, and Rouse to be hit by the 2008 recession. Financial troubles led the company to halt all work, leaving subcontractors unpaid and promises unfulfilled, and to relinquish ownership of the properties.[17]

The "creative-class dream" has had its bumps in Providence. The city made unwanted national headlines in 2012 when the semi-public Rhode Island Economic Development Corporation offered former Red Sox pitcher Curt Schilling $75 million in taxpayer-backed bonds to move his video-gaming company, 38 Studios, to Providence in 2010. The company's implosion two years later left taxpayers holding a $100 million debt, almost 300 people without jobs, Citizens Bank suing Schilling, and investigations into cronyism. The story symbolized Providence's continuing struggles and reinforced preexisting stereotypes of political dysfunction.[18]

In the shadow of these mishaps, Providence's Creative Economy plan includes no mention of Newport and its festivals, despite their geographic proximity, national and international reputation, and connection with local musicians. But this is not the end of the story. I will show that musicians themselves have brought the festival's assets back home, to provide a glimmer of hope for the state's music economy.

Lower Broad's Waves of Development

There might not be a clearer example of the meshing of music culture and economic development than Nashville over the past fifteen years. Although music has played a part in the city's economy for the past century, Nashville has turned to the local music community in an explicit way since the early 2000s to generate growth and attract business. Through mid-century suburbanization and disinvestment, Nashville underwent the kinds of change common enough to many downtowns: historic buildings were replaced by parking lots, and urban renewal (a euphemism for slum clearance) resulted in Nashville's core purging "nearly every resident, becoming a bland central business district," while Broadway became "a repository for sex shops, strip clubs, and the homeless."[19] Despite this, some commercial interests that could have moved out of the city's core stayed downtown, including office buildings for IBM and the Tennessee Education Foundation, First American National Bank, and the Opry's benefactor, National Life and Accident Insurance. The 1990s brought a wave of themed restaurants to the Lower Broad area that, however, coughed to a standstill at the turn of the century.[20]

The business climate improved in the early 2000s with a load of accolades directed to the business community and, for its efforts, the Nashville chamber was named Top Chamber of the Year by the American Chamber of Commerce Executives in 2009.[21] This economic upswing coincided with Mayor Bill Purcell injecting himself into the decision-making process to move the festival downtown, and the chamber of commerce making music a central part of their mission. Chamber CEO Mike Neal described how the CMA festival and awards show directly worked as part of the city's economic development strategy. He described how the city would host red-carpet tours for economic development prospects highlighting their cultural distinctiveness:

> It only made sense to us to bring them in the middle of this event and give them an opportunity to meet these stars, and we take them backstage, on the stage, underneath the stage, in the green rooms. The CMA has given us access to take these prospects, and it has helped us recruit some pretty major businesses, helped us land a couple of new corporate headquarters, and the music industry is a huge factor.

This approach to business recruitment differentiates Nashville and, according to current mayor Karl Dean, is "a big deal here." Upon his arrival, Dean assembled a blue-ribbon commission that included representatives from the Department of Economic and Community Development, the chamber of commerce, and professional associations within the music scene to plan how to better match the music industry and the city's growth. This advisory committee resulted in the forty-person Music City Music Council (or MC²), cochaired by the mayor himself.[22] Early initiatives included housing development for musicians, called the Ryman Lofts; a public-private partnership called Launch Tennessee; and the first southern culture and technology conference, called Southland. Staged between Middle Tennessee's two major festivals, CMA Fest and Bonnaroo, Southland aims to bring venture capitalists together with early stage technology startups (with musical entertainment provided by a Bonnaroo artist).

The communities around the CMA aim to use its prestige to attract new business and support the existing corporate fabric. When the city was hit with a "thousand-year flood" a few weeks before the 2010 CMA Fest, much of downtown was underwater, including the strip of businesses, lofts, and venues along Second Avenue, the Country Music Hall of Fame and Museum, the Schermerhorn Symphony Center, and the Bridgestone Arena. The epicenter of the festival, in the words of a CMA executive, "was a bathtub." The CMA donated almost half of the proceeds of the 2010 festival—over $3 million—to the Community Foundation of Middle Tennessee, which had been tasked with flood relief. City stakeholders said that continuing the festival was critical in projecting an image that Nashville was still "open for business."

Austin's Quality of Life

Austin's economic development followed a different path. In the 1960s and '70s, Austin's technology industry blossomed alongside its existing government and education sector. In the early 1980s, Austin was selected as the site for the Microelectronics and Computer Technology Corporation (a research consortium designed to compete with Japanese advancement in the high-tech industry, which survived until the consortium was dissolved in 2000), and the city government played a role in wooing IBM, Samsung, Dell, Intel, Apple, and Motorola to open branches throughout the 1990s.[23] Although their offices were mostly in the higher elevations in the north and west of downtown—dubbed "Silicon Hills" in a comparison with the Bay Area's Silicon Valley—these businesses attracted employees with good jobs to a liberal town with a warm climate and an offbeat culture. Relocations and expansions continued into the new century: Dell has over 16,000 employees in Austin, IBM has 6,000, and Apple increased the size of its Austin branch to 2,500 employees.[24] The abundance of parks and recreation by day and live entertainment at night provided a lifestyle that enticed businesses and talented employees.[25] As Xerox, Cisco, Hewlett-Packard, Samsung, and Intel all join the city's business ranks, the city is now working on plans to develop into clean energy and digital technology.[26] This managed balance of growth and the creative and high-tech economies set the stage for a bigger SXSW: in 1994, the festival extended to a ten-day event to include a Film and Interactive Festival, which split into two separate festivals the following year: SXSW Film, and SXSW Interactive. All three festivals drew strong crowds and further international and industry buzz. Twitter, for example, was unveiled at SXSW Interactive in 2007.

Key to this growth strategy is maintaining a distinct sense of place that has increasingly focused around the idea of music. The Live Music Task Force insisted on a "music department" similar to Nashville's Music City Music Council. In 2008, a senior advisor to Mayor Will Wynn told the alternative weekly that "the music office in Nashville is the mayor's office," and that they were working on developing an advisory committee within the city government facilitating growth in a similar way.[27] As Mayor Wynn explained, this was part of the overall quality-of-life campaign:

> These twenty-five- and thirty-year-old kids who have PhDs in electrical engineering from Michigan moved to Austin in part because of the music scene and outdoor recreation. So, it's far more organic, far less targeted. Our economic development model is that the jobs will follow the people. You want to be attractive to the people, and the people you want to attract are young, educated, creative, dynamic kids who have a passion for the outdoors, love live music, want to ride their mountain bikes to work.

Overall, the latest Census data show that Austin is becoming the youngest and most educated of the top cities in the United States, and is the fastest-growing city for postcollegiate transplants. Twenty-five- to thirty-four-year-olds have disproportionately moved to Austin rather than Los Angeles, New York, or anywhere else. Mayor Will Wynn calls it "remarkable" and says the age group is a "sweet spot" for residential growth.[28]

Wynn's development strategy targeted the downtown central business district rather than the Silicon Hills. The Austin Downtown Alliance Business Improvement District cites their positive growth figures: in 1993, the downtown area had about 4,000 residents and 67,000 jobs, while in 2012, it had close to 10,000 residents and over 116,000 workers. Facebook's short-lived investment in Austin's downtown sat near the location-based social media company Gowalla's headquarters, which Facebook bought and then closed down.[29] Still, good tech news followed thereafter: Apple announced on March 9, 2012, that it would double its workforce in Austin by building a $300 million, 3,600-job campus, in return for $8.6 million in tax rebates over ten years from the city of Austin, up to $6.4 million in tax rebates over fifteen years from Travis County, and a $21 million investment by the state.[30] Apple's announcement during SXSW was not the only link between economic development and the festival. SXSW Interactive generated a number of interactions: local, national, and international tech companies participated in a career expo, and visiting international delegations of tech companies were hosted by the chamber of commerce.[31] By 2012, condo occupancy in Austin's CBD matched that of the city as a whole (around 97%) and, according to the communications director at the convention and visitors bureau, the success of the SXSW and Austin City Limits festivals and conventions means the city needs all its 6,000 hotel rooms, as well as the additional 2,000 under construction.[32]

((( )))

After the 2008 economic crisis, these three second-tier cities outperformed first-tier, alpha cities: according to a 2010 report by the Brookings Institution and the London School of Economics, Austin ranked as the twenty-sixth best-performing metro *in the world* postrecession, Nashville ranked forty-eighth, and Providence ranked seventy-third (New York City ranked seventy-seventh, Chicago eighty-second, and Los Angeles one-hundred-sixteenth).[33] Whereas Providence's Metropolitan Statistical Area saw only 1.1% population growth, representing one of the slowest growth rates between 2000 and 2010 of any of the top forty MSAs, Nashville's was 21.2% and Austin's 37.3% in the same time period—making them two of the fastest-growing cities in the United States. With regard to music, Newport's festivals are downplayed as just a part of a wider palette of tourist offerings and Providence struggles with developing its creative economy. Nashville and Austin, meanwhile, established music departments in their mayors' offices, tied their creative industries to economic development, saw similar rates of growth after 2000, and targeted their downtowns for cultural placemaking.

However, economic-impact reports are largely tools of the chamber and the festivals themselves, produced to mollify critics, justify public investments in targeted industries, and have the unintended consequence of monetizing the arts. It is necessary to bore down into these places further to get to the other ways music influences the city.

On the Streets Again: Walking through Neighborhoods

So, how do these kinds of developments "hit the ground"? If Music City is to be seen as a set of spatial resources, built up, used, altered, and possibly destroyed, a series of purposeful walks around these city neighborhoods could provide a good complementary perspective to the first half of this chapter. Changes in the arts and urban life can be grounded through a "shoe-leather" view of these neighborhoods, to see how music and culture are tied to, or disconnected from, some of their communities.

The notion of a "walk with a purpose" comes from a group called the Situationists. Led by Guy Debord, a onetime compatriot of Henri Lefebvre, these experimental social and spatial investigators would take what they called *dérives* (from the French verb meaning "to drift"). Debord described such a practice as a "rapid passage through varied ambiances," in order to understand how capitalist endeavors mesh with the practices of everyday life by letting the mind and body wander through city geographies.[34] Over the course of 2012, I walked through the neighborhoods of these cities to note some changes and similarities—a two-part trip of Newport and Providence's West Side, Nashville's Gulch and Rolling Mill Hills area, and Austin's central business district.

These *dérives* give a necessary, though only partial, view and connect some of the economic development data from the previous section with what I have shown of festivals so far. Instead of the tourist sets that are carefully constructed by chambers of commerce and convention and visitors bureaus, these tours offer a package for understanding how festivals and the urban culture that hosts them interrelate.

Down and Up the Narragansett Bay

The Newport Historic District, designated as a National Historic Landmark in 1968, is a 250-acre envelope that includes the famous mansions to the south, the Redwood Library (where Lois Vaughan played Bridge-Fest) to the north, and the shopping center along Thames to the west. I start at the corner of Memorial Boulevard and Bellevue Avenue in the middle of the district. On the east side of Bellevue is a two-story Victorian shingle-style façade that now hosts a Talbots and a few other shops, but which once was the Charles McKim and Stanford White–designed Newport Casino. The casino was the cultural center for Newport's elite residents, housing a 500-seat theater and ballroom space. Didi Lorillard, daughter of Newport socialite and Newport Jazz Festival founder Elaine, reminded me that music in the Gilded Age was primarily a private affair. There was no "public space" for culture. "The mansions had their music rooms for performances," she told me, and "then there was the casino." Unlike the patchworks of honkytonks and bars in Nashville and Austin, Newport's music was for the privileged.

Long after the Gilded Age had passed, this onetime social club for the upper crust was the location of the first Newport Jazz Festival in 1954. Now, in addition to the few shops, the complex houses the International Tennis Hall of Fame, and its onetime glorious performance hall has been vacant since the 1980s. A $4.5 million renovation is proceeding, and will provide another entertainment space for the city. Still, there's hope of getting a bigger events venue. "We don't have a very large indoor space," chamber CEO Jody Sullivan acknowledged. "People talk about building a convention center," but that requires several thousand more hotel rooms, and there is no space for a new hotel.

I head down to the Narragansett Bay waterfront and walk along the cobblestoned Thames. This stretch has remained lively as a perennially popular tourist destination. The expansion of Newport Folk Festival's prestige, media attention, and ticket sales has had only a muted effect. The business community is stable. As the city's main tourist and shopping artery, rents are high. These places capitalize on the cool breezes, and foot traffic strolling along the waterfront.

With a small local population, big temporary tents on the piers are used as larger venues, hosting summertime comedy nights and other special events. On the east side of Thames is the only year-round home to music in Newport, Jim Quinn's ivy-covered Newport Blues Café. Using his status as a Newport native and the limited options for music downtown as leverage, Quinn successfully lobbied the city's zoning board and the city council to allow construction of an outdoor patio for the café. He told me, "We can now shift the dining we're missing during the festival and do twenty tables out there while our music goes on inside."

A short ride up to the top of Narragansett Bay sits the city of Providence, an entirely different part of the MSA. On the city's West Side sit the factories and mills of Olneyville that once utilized the river for waterpower and more recently served as spaces for the area's informal and underground music scene. Musicians and artists took up residence in the old factories and mills, establishing artist collectives with names like Dirt Palace, Hive Archive, and Fort Thunder. The latter has become the stuff of local legend: operating as an underground music and art space, the building was torn down and replaced by a grocery store in 2001. And then, in 2003, a deadly, preventable fire at a nearby hard rock club called the Station changed the city's music landscape further.[35] Officials clamped down on music spaces that were not up to code and on other illegal occupancies. Inspectors evicted squatters in one building in early January 2004, and many feared a full collapse of the underground music scene. The result, however, was an unexpected formalization and institutionalization of the area's cultural revitalization.[36]

A few years earlier, RISD graduate Nick Bauta, Clay Rockefeller (Brown graduate and great-great-grandson of John D. Rockefeller), and two others took advantage of historic-renovation tax credits and new zoning that allowed for live-work spaces to purchase an Olneyville mill building, converting it into thirty-six artist lofts and studios, with six of them designated as affordable housing. Attracted to the edgy scene and cheap real estate, these college graduates started cultivating amenities on the West Side. On the same block, Bauta and Rockefeller purchased a manufacturing complex across the street from one of the ill-fated Struever Brothers development sites—half a block from the site of Fort Thunder, and half a block from a windowless strip club called Club Fantasies—to develop a nonprofit called the Steel Yard. This complex was repurposed around the ideas of urban revitalization, arts promotion, workforce development, and community growth.

Frank Shea, executive director of the Olneyville Housing Corporation (OHC), says that the Steel Yard is one of his favorite pieces of the neighborhood's puzzle. Taking me on a tour of the area, he points to various aspects of the site, including how grass was used as part of the remediation of the brownfield. The Steel Yard uses its facilities for metallurgy education, teaching locals skills to produce goods for the neighborhood and the city, thanks to a Weld to Work program (funded with $62,000 from Bank of America). Shea told the story of how the OHC convinced the Steel Yard to have one of their job-training programs work on a fence for the nearby elementary school and that, when they did a celebration event, he saw a student's father proudly bring his child over to the piece he had worked on. "That," he tells me, "is the 'full circle' of what we want to do. And it works. No big grant. Just, kinda, 'Here's the resources we have, here's the resources you have. Let's do something.'" By offering job-training and skills-building workshops for local residents, he sees it as "less of an arts-fartsy endeavor and more of a real connection with the community." As the head of an organization designated to develop the community through partnerships with local groups, he should know.

Midway through our tour, we see a woman standing alone on a blind corner, on the sidewalk in front of a large fence. She sees us coming and signals a compatriot around the way, bowing her head. As we turn the corner ourselves, I see a man take a white plastic bag out from under the open hood of his car. The dealer and his lookout are two of the only people to be seen in this desolate elbow of Olneyville. Shea and I pass them, and make a right to see another of Bauta's music-based projects on a barren street a mile away. Fête, a collaboration with another Brown graduate, is a 900-plus-capacity venue built out of a onetime auto garage. Bauta invested $2 million; two banks contributed $850,000;

and the Providence Economic Development Partnership added a loan of $365,000 from a federal community development block grant.[37] Fête has a more refined look and feel than the illegal venues that were a part of the area's underground music scene, and it advertises itself as "New England's boutique live music venue." These music and cultural projects connect to the community in various ways. On the one hand, there is the hope that projects like the Steel Yard's education program can bring together different groups, while at the same time, these activities bring concerns of creative-class gentrification and concerns over the neighborhood becoming a party destination. Fête and the converted mills draw new residents but also attract college students from Boston who come to Providence (sometimes in buses) to listen to music, party, and barhop to take advantage of the city's lower drinking age.

Leaving Olneyville, I walk down Broadway, across Route 6-10, and toward Federal Hill. In ten minutes I reach the Columbus Theatre. The building is the latest manifestation of the Low Anthem's rise. The Brown University alum, hometown-hero band formed the Columbus Cooperative to purchase this building—a onetime vaudeville hall, then a triple-X movie theater—to record their fifth album and turn the building into a live performance space. They also established the Columbus Recording Company, to record not just their own new album, but also other bands in the community.

On November 17 and 18, 2012, the Low Anthem marked the building's grand reopening with a two-night celebration titled Revival! 1 and 2. The first night sold out and featured Providence Mayor Angel Taveras providing the welcoming address. The second night opened with the lead-in band addressing the crowd by saying, "It's nice to be a part of something *official* here," a wink to the fact that the theater had previously been part of the area's underground scene. The food came from a restaurant two blocks away, the beer was provided by a local brewing company, and sponsors included the Rhode Island Music Hall of Fame. The night ended with the Low Anthem's performance, which brought everyone onstage, including Newport alum Dave Lamb from Brown Bird.

Tom Weyman, the theater's booking agent and also manager of Brown Bird, has lived in Providence since high school, and though he acknowledges that there are many genres of music played in the city, he believes

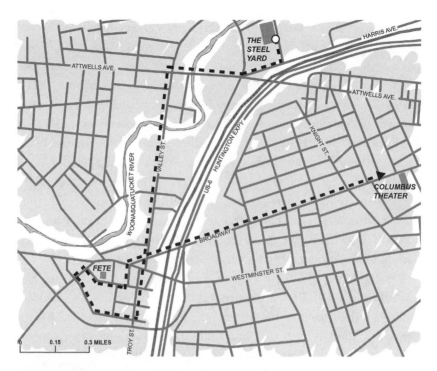

Map of Olneyville and Federal Hill neighborhood tour.

Johnny Cash graffiti, near "The Opry Has Sinned: Reinstate Hank" graffiti, and the new Music City Convention Center construction in the background.

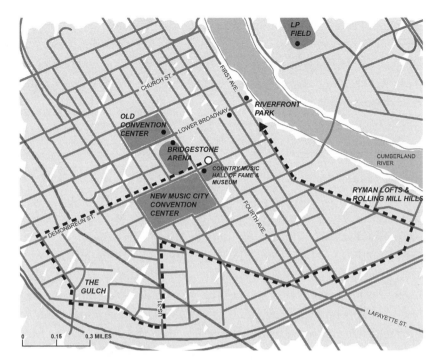

Map of downtown Nashville tour.

the theater fully connects Newport with the Americana and folk scene in Providence:

It's no secret that in the first six months of operation the majority of acts had played the folk festival in the last five years, although that's not necessarily a conscious thing, but it's been on my mind. Whether it's intentional or not, with the Newport connection there's been a bit of curation that's going on. We only do a few shows a month, so we are very deliberate. On one hand that's purely for financial reasons: we're trying to have shows that sell out, and we price tickets to sell. But then we also present the music that we want to know and support the music scene.

The ties between Newport and Providence continue. The Revival! series featured a third event, "Revival! at Newport," which was an opening showcase for the 2013 Newport Folk Festival held at the Blues Café—the lineup included Joe Fletcher and the Low Anthem and served as the first official kickoff to the festival. At the Folk Festival, there was a Newport Homegrown showcase at which the Low Anthem curated a series of Providence musicians, tying the festival to its earlier traditions. Deer Tick's after-parties at the Blues Café feature Providence bands. All these events show the growing feedback loop between Newport and Providence's music scene.

From the Gulch to the Hills

American Idol alum Casey James sings a few songs on the steps of the Country Music Hall of Fame and Museum while, just behind him, construction on the new million-square-foot Nashville Music City Center continues. Backed by city-assured revenue bonds funded by a hotel room tax and TIFs (Tax Increment Financing), the center's undulating roof and open maw of an entrance give it the look of a giant sandworm, gasping to eat the smaller Hall of Fame. The new facility is ten times the size of the still-operational convention center a block to the north (built in 1987 and housing some festival activities since the downtown move), dwarfs the city's other convention center at Opryland, and even humbles the hockey arena across the street. The structure will eventually physically connect the Country Music Hall of Fame and Museum to a new 800-room Omni Hotel (incentivized with tax breaks and funded through sales tax revenues and tourism funds).[38]

I start my walk by the Music City Center and head southwest to "the Gulch," an area nestled between train tracks and a bend of interstate highway. These barriers kept the Gulch isolated despite its centrality—it is only a few blocks from Lower Broad, or, heading northwest, a short distance to Music Row. The area was once a massive railroad roundhouse for train maintenance, including a warehouse and distribution center. Now the hulking building is gone, and new condos and apartments have taken its place.

Two major movements shaped these recent changes. First, the Tennessee Department of Environment and Conservation, along with assistance from EPA brownfield cleanup grants, helped Gulch development. Second, zoning changes in the early 2000s led to residential development in the central business district: the second and third stories of buildings along Second Avenue were converted into lofts, and some projects just outside the central business district were created within walking distance of the downtown area, including the Farmers' Market and Hope Gardens to the north and the Gulch to the south. The 2007 Downtown Development Plan's stated aim was for a "thoughtful mixture of uses including residential, retail and office, to ensure that Downtown doesn't close at 5 p.m. or even after the concert ends or the restaurants close, but is instead a welcoming home for a more diverse residential population."[39] A realty company called MarketStreet was centrally positioned in those efforts: it owned almost half of the Gulch's acreage by 2001 and entered into a public-private partnership with the Metropolitan Development and Housing Authority and city hall, which contributed $7 million in infrastructure improvements (e.g., traffic calming, street improvements, and underground utilities) and $15 million in TIF funds.[40] With these funds, the Gulch became the thirteenth LEED-certified (Leadership in Energy and Environmental Design) neighborhood in the country, and the first in the South.

When I first visited the 2006 CMA festival, I ducked away to see hip-hop icons Blackalicious and the Roots at a Gulch venue called City Hall. At that time, the master-planned, mixed-use, revitalized area had a Business Improvement District, and shiny new condos were sprouting up that incorporated music venues as part of the same complex. In accordance with receiving TIF funds and infrastructure development, these MarketStreet developments also offered affordable housing. The owner of ICON—a former brownfield, now profitable condo development—described to sociologist Richard Lloyd his target demographic as "younger music professionals, twenty-five to thirty-five, with a pretty significant amount of disposable income, that wanna have a big city lifestyle, go to a big city place."[41] To receive municipal aid, however, ICON needs 10% of its housing stock to be occupied by people making under 80% of the area's median income.

In the intervening years since my visit in 2006, the City Hall venue closed, and MarketStreet Realty did not renew their lease; the hipster clothing chain store Urban Outfitters took their place.[42] One of the last remnants of the predevelopment Gulch is the legendary bluegrass oasis the Station Inn: open since 1974, its simple one-story stone building stands in sharp contrast to the new developments rising around it.

The Station Inn and new condo complex, ICON, "Nashville's Hippest Urban Condo," in the background. Note the official "Nashville: Live Music Venue" sign shaped like a guitar pick in the center of the picture (photo courtesy of Alexandre Frenette).

Five minutes by foot from the Station Inn, east across Eighth Avenue and the train tracks that border the Gulch, are the offices of Third Man Records, run by Jack White, recently of the successful alternative rock band the White Stripes. White relocated to Nashville from Detroit in 2008 in a move that many locals—including the mayor—saw as emblematic of the city's new, more diverse, and hipper public image.[43] Mayor Dean dubbed White a Music City Ambassador in 2011. The low building complex, painted all black, combines under one roof the label's office, a recording and production studio, a performance space, and a record store offering an eclectic mix of old-timey roots and country music along with more contemporary rock recorded in the adjacent studio. Inside, glass cases display guitar picks, vinyl iPhone cases, and a portable record player, all in Third Man's brand colors of bright yellow and black. Another glass case features the Third Man Monkey Band—seven pint-sized animatronic monkeys who for a quarter will play "Blunderbuss," a song from White's latest album.

Another ten-minute walk to the west passes through mute warehouses with long brick façades and leads to the Ryman Lofts development, located only a short walk away from Lower Broad. Like the Providence Steel Yard and the Gulch, it is another brownfield, the site of old trolley barns and a long-since-shuttered public hospital.[44] A single smokestack remains as a token from the past. It is now an affordable urban housing complex, initiated by the Music City Music Council. Part of the development is occupied, but there are other buildings still under construction, and a few flat parcels ready for further development, too. The $5.2 million, sixty-apartment Ryman Lofts portion of the area takes its name from the iconic Ryman Auditorium. Mayor Dean proudly highlighted this site during an interview two days earlier, calling it "perhaps the most innovative thing they've done [which] should be a strong pull for people to continue to come to the city. And the music industry has been real cooperative in wanting us to continue moving in this direction." The floor plan for the complex, he said, provides spaces for creative collaboration, and the units themselves are targeted to artists and musicians who earn 60% or less of the area's median income.

A young white couple passing by and walking their dog tell me: "There's probably less than 300 people who live up here now," adding, "and there's not enough retail nearby." Still, they moved here from a nearby suburb called Murfreesboro because they "could finally afford to live downtown" and hope that shops will come in time, especially when Ryman Lofts is fully operational.

I complete my loop back at Lower Broad in under an hour. Unlike my walk through Olneyville and Federal Hill, this area has seen significant transformations. The Struever Brothers' failures in Providence's West Side resulted in smaller-scale repurposing of their brownfields. In Nashville, however, with little housing stock immediately south of Lower Broad, new neighborhoods—along with the new convention center—have been made out of whole cloth.

Rock 'n' Roll Condos

Calling it "pretty exciting," one of the industry professionals at South by Southwest tells me that, after ten years, he sees the growth happening through his own experiences. "I can see the changes to the neighborhood culture," he tells me.

To see what he was talking about, I strike out on a walk from the convention center (about two-thirds the size of Nashville's Music City Center). I first walk north through the Red River district of bars and venues that partially comprise the tax base for a massive nearby TIF-funded $100 million flood-management public works project.[45] I pass Emo's and the Mohawk, avoiding the Sixth Street entertainment strip, and turn west on East Eighth to a development on Trinity called Capital Studios. In collaboration with a nonprofit called Foundation Communities, which operates seventeen affordable-housing properties in the area, the development is downtown Austin's first affordable-housing project in forty-five years and will provide 135 efficiency apartments, with ten earmarked for low-income musicians. It is a similar, though smaller-scale, project to the Ryman Lofts in Nashville.

Turning south on Congress, I head to Las Manitas' unassuming diner in hopes of having the delicious *molé* I remembered from my first two SXSWs, only to arrive at a dirt lot with a sign for a massive new Marriott Hotel.

There seem to be transformations on the other side of Congress, too,

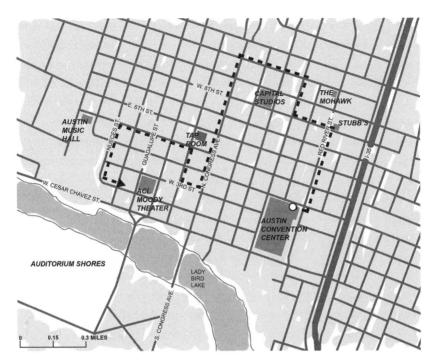

Map of downtown Austin tour.

similar to what is taking place in Nashville's Gulch. The Warehouse District has been pockmarked by vacant lots since the middle of the last century, and preservationists are fighting to maintain some of the area's history by encouraging owners to see the benefits of landmarking their buildings, through educating them on programs to help them receive partial property-tax abatements. In August 2009, the city council eased the requirements for designating a historical district—it now requires the approval of only 51% of property owners rather than the earlier 60%—and developers are seeking to use Transfer of Development Rights to exploit zoning entitlements to continue developing other spaces in the downtown area while conserving the scale of the warehouse spaces.[46] The council has yet to approve the designation.

Up Colorado Street near the Tap Room, there is a continued expansion of this commercial Warehouse District: art galleries, condos, new restaurants, and boutique stores. Heading west on West Fifth, passing through the shade of a massive parking garage, I come to Antone's. Like

Nashville's Station Inn and Newport's Blues Café, this place has brought music to a onetime rough neighborhood since 1975, hosting Texas blues musicians like Stevie Ray Vaughn and Charlie Sexton. Continuing on, my stroll further connects the downtown business district with music and a growth spurt of residential complexes. Three blocks farther west are the now-shuttered Austin branch of Facebook and the location-based social media company Gowalla. I turn south on Nueces Street to see an example of Mayor Wynn's vision of increasing the downtown population from today's 10,000 people to over 25,000, and of the close relationship between downtown real estate and the music district: the recently renovated Austin Music Hall. Even more formalized than the music venue–condo relationship in Nashville's Gulch area, this is a $5 million joint venture between the Music Hall and two real estate companies, the Novare Group and the Austin-based Andrews Urban LLC, which saw rebuilding the venue as a way to improve the value of their nearby forty-four-story condo complex that opened in 2008. A block away I see another condo building, where I attended JellyNYC's unofficial party (with a music lineup including Providence's Deer Tick) after their 2007 legal battle with SXSW. And farther still I see the towering Austonian—the tallest residential building west of the Mississippi. In an area once known as Guy Town, a center for prostitution, gambling, and crime, the condo stock along West Third sold at a healthy clip until the same recession that knocked growth in Providence arrived here, although with less impact.

I walk past Third and turn back toward the convention center. Directly to the north of the nine-year-old, sustainably built city hall is Moody Theater, the brand-new location for the *Austin City Limits* live-music television program. Talent booker Brendan Leith told me he was "shocked" that it took so long for Austin to build this kind of space. "For being the Live Music Capital of the World," Leith said, "the live clubs aren't all that stellar.... There are a lot of 'black boxes' and bars that just become venues for South By"; and then, bigger shows had to be held at the nearby Austin Music Hall, which is, according to Leith, "like a glorified gymnasium." Moody Theater's seating capacity of 2,700 solves that problem. The new space for *Austin City Limits* is housed in a chic $300 million, thirty-seven-story W Hotel and condo tower, and served as the location for "A Celebration of American Startups" during SXSW, sponsored by the chamber of commerce. The event highlighted local music and sought to recruit startup companies to the city.

After thirty minutes of walking, I end up back on West Second Street, which, in an institutionalized tribute to Austin's most iconoclastic musician, has recently been renamed Willie Nelson Boulevard.

A Downtown Set to Music

As meditations on the economic and spatial resources of these Music Cities, these paths compared experiences in festivalized places, showing similarities and differences in how music culture and economic development "hit the ground" and the ways neighborhoods have absorbed these changes. They identified key markers in Newport/Providence (Newport Casino, the Blues Café, Steel Yard, and Columbus Opera House), Nashville (Music City Music Center, ICON and City Hall/Urban Outfitters, Third Man Records, Ryman Lofts), and Austin (Capital Studios, Las Manitas, Tap Room, Austin Music Hall, W Hotel, *Austin City Limits*) and tied together many of the stories about Music City.

These *dérives*, or walks with a purpose, aren't only routes to understand the shape and feel of these Music Cities. If I made a right at one intersection, or a left around another, I would have found different things in Nashville's Hope Gardens, Austin's East César Chávez neighborhood, or Providence's College Hill.

Still, by considering both economic development and spatial resources at a walkable scale, one sees how short-term events and longer-term festivalization link up with place: for example, how musicians contributed to crafting Providence's Olneyville underground scene only to have it transform into a more formalized music culture in places like the Steel Yard and Fête; how Nashville's and Austin's municipal governments and nonprofits worked to develop spaces for musicians proximate to their entertainment community, as was the case with Ryman Lofts and Capital Studios; how the drive to occupy downtown Nashville and Austin with both entertainment venues and residences fashioned condo/music multiplexes like ICON and the Austin Music Hall. One also sees the festivals flow through these multilayered points of connection: JellyNYC's use of a condo complex for an unofficial SXSW event, the Columbus

Cooperative as a vehicle for Providence musicians to infiltrate Newport and its festival. Furthermore, each walk illustrates how developers and urban planners capitalize on music culture. On Providence's West Side there was a nascent scene that attracted a major international developer and a smaller group of enterprising university alumni. In Nashville's Gulch and Rolling Mill Hill areas, as well as Austin's Warehouse District, developers reused brownfield spaces and attracted a variety of redevelopment strategies to facilitate their missions (e.g., EPA grants, local economic development grants, TIFs, landmarking, or historical tax credits), often promising a few affordable-housing units to do so.

These routes also touched upon how development in the Music City encounters local community concerns in different ways. The troubling aspects of gentrification, when more wealthy residents move into and displace existing working-class communities, come into play primarily in the case in Providence's West Side. It is, perhaps, the clearest and most familiar example of what scholars see as the negative consequences of this form of urban revitalization. Olneyville offers a tale of artists building a scene, developing an underground culture by taking advantage of cheap rents, and then finding themselves out in the cold, along with existing working-class residents. Although the neighborhood has not felt the same effects as more famously gentrified places like New York's Soho, Providence musicians—like Joe Fletcher, David Lamb, and MorganEve Swain, who moved to Warren, Rhode Island—did cite rising rents as one reason for leaving. As those with certain kinds of leverage can craft more formalized urban culture, via either economic resources (in the case of RISD graduates Bauta and Rockefeller) or cultural status (as when the Low Anthem used their national success at the Newport Folk Festival to institutionalize the area's Americana and folk scene through the Columbus Theatre), others are left out.

Frank Shea talked about the dislocation of the local working-class community but still explained it as an opportunity for new Olneyville artists and the existing community. Indeed, some Olneyville neighbors were upset over the displacement of thirty local businesses by Struever Brothers' development of mill properties, just as Austin environmentalists once mobilized against development that threatened the very quality of life so many were attracted to in the first place. The rowdy college kids who come to the neighborhood, and the hipsters who crowd into Fête, are mixed portents for locals, just as the folks coming in for SXSW are seen as potential competitors for rent and the enjoyment of Austin's natural amenities. Will the increased attention of these locales bring collaborations with community groups, or higher taxes and further displacement? The visitors leave with less money in their pockets, but will they return with a willingness to pay higher rents in a hip neighborhood?

Although neighborhood processes like these often attract criticism for favoring developers and tourist dollars over local residents and stoking fears of gentrification, these three cases do offer some variation.[47] Austin's Warehouse District and Nashville's Gulch and Ryman Lofts are crafted out of formerly industrial areas, though even in these locations there is resistance from some long-established businesses and neighborhood groups. In Nashville, for example, some downtown dwellers have bristled as growth radiates from these inner-ring districts and developers seek to buy up houses to further stoke a growing unaffordability in a bursting metropolis. In the face of a process of destroying old housing stock for bigger, newer buildings—something the local weekly called "teardown fever"—Nashville groups are attempting to implement neighborhood preservation through the Metro Historical Commission as others point to the development in the Gulch as a model for using TIF funds to secure affordable housing.[48]

And in Austin I can revisit my missing *molé*. The two proprietors of Las Manitas restaurant, sisters Lidia and Cynthia Perez, refused their landlord's request for them to leave. Property owner Tim Finley was eager to sell his land to the Marriott hotel chain, which also chipped in an initial offer of $72,000 for the sisters to leave. A kind of public shaming came after their second refusal. A 2006 letter penned by J. Willard Marriott and published in the *Austin American-Statesman* posed the question to the sisters and local readers: "Why should you hold up a several-hundred-million-dollar investment because of a small little restaurant?"[49] In 2007, the city offered the sisters a $750,000 forgivable loan if they agreed to terms with the developers and relocated, but they turned that offer down too, and the offer generated resentment from other business owners, who complained about special treatment. Eventually, the developers, the building owner, and the Perez sisters reached an undisclosed settlement, and a twenty-seven-year-old Austin standby was bulldozed. The following year, the sisters founded La Peña, a Latino art and community center, down the block, and in 2011 the city approved a plan to waive $4.3 million in fees to the hotel chain.

It is difficult to score gains and losses. Even in the clearest case of adverse consequences, in Providence there is evidence that muddies the waters. Nashville and Austin, with little to no downtown housing stock—due either to mid-century urban renewal, or to the existence of light-manufacturing areas—are different cases altogether, while the Steel Yard shows how gentrifiers can work with their community and contribute to the local fabric. And then there are the realizations of those gentrifiers themselves. While Austin's environmental groups struggled with developers in the 1980s and '90s to eventually settle into a kind of mutual appreciation, there are still plenty of signs of strife. Once charmed by the idea of living in a Music City, some of those who moved into downtown Austin soured at the actual experience of living in an entertainment district, citing a 2009 city council resolution that waived fees for permits, expedited the application process, and allowed restaurants in the CBD to have music outside at an 85 dB level.[50] In response, the city established a 311 system in which noise complaints are sent to the city's Music Division.

Collectively, these walks show different levels of success and concern in building around and within music scenes that are related to these music festivals. From Providence neighborhoods several miles away from Newport, to the "first ring" neighborhoods surrounding Nashville's downtown, to Austin condos embedding venues into their buildings, the Music City is crafted and nurtured in new high-rises and old brownfields. The effects of music culture radiate and connect on both neighborhood and regional scales.

((( )))

As these stories link economic and spatial resources in these cities, they also point to other concerns: How are the particular musicians, artists, and local organizations that fill these spaces affected by these changes? What are their experiences? What do festivals do to shape and brand the image of the cities themselves?

6 The Long-Term Effects of Fleeting Moments Part Two

I know of a city to steal from,
And I know of a city to cheat on,
And I know of a City of Sin,
and that's the place I wanna meet you in.
—"ART ISN'T REAL," DEER TICK

Music in the Back Alley

After playing our official SXSW gig at the Tap Room, the band I am with also performs the next day at the Yard Dog Art Gallery on South Congress, a mile and a half from the convention center and on the other side of the Colorado River. The neighborhood seems to be the very incarnation of "Austin Weird" with its boutiques, thrift stores, bars, hip restaurants, and cafés crammed end to end. The gallery itself is filled with beautiful—but pricey—folk art collected from the Deep South. Before our set, I mill around the busy gallery and search in vain for a painting under $100 as people stream in from the street to the event space in the back alley.

Gallery owner Randy Franklin hosts local bands in the alley twice a month, and the week of SXSW is no exception. This year he is partnering with a North Carolina independent music distribution company called Redeye for an 11 a.m. to 7 p.m. lineup. "Business," the woman behind the counter tells me, "is rarely more brisk than during South By." This time of year the Yard Dog takes advantage of the hundreds of bands at SXSW eager to perform multiple shows, official and unofficial.

In the gravel alleyway behind the gallery, there is a little orange and white striped tent, a temporary bar, a taco truck, and roughly five dozen people in the audience. Fourteen bands are scheduled back to back. When it is our turn to hit the stage, we do a quick sound check in front of the audience, and proceed to tear through the set we did the night before at our official showcase. As soon as we hit our last notes, we pack our gear to make way for the next act; there is only time to grab a few tacos and beers and chat for a few minutes with the audience before we have to load up the van and head off to our third gig in two days.

((( )))

At places like the Yard Dog, where the official music festival intersects with the local cultural scene through an infusion of imported talent that makes use of the place-based "neighborhood cool" within the larger cultural occasion, the relationships between the seemingly intangible resources of urban culture become a little more evident. To illustrate this further, the following two sections tease out the less obvious relationships regarding the nurturing and use of social + cultural and symbolic resources. Such an emphasis does not leave behind economic and spatial matters but in fact expands upon them.

Again, a given community's cultural knowledge and social capital is referred to here as *social + cultural resources*,[1] and the term *symbolic resources* refers to the image- and idea-based goods that can be linked to, or promoted within, a festival or its surrounding communities. Whereas the previous chapter ended with a series of "walks with a purpose" to show how music and urban culture work—and don't work—in these locales, this chapter will end with data illustrating the mixed results of the marriage between the idea of Music City and its local and visiting communities.

Growing Muses: Nurturing the Social + Cultural beyond the Creative Class

Just as in Olneyville and Providence, and in Nashville's hipper enclave East Nashville, many Austinites fear that their city is becoming *too* crowded and *too* hip—this is perhaps nowhere more evident than in the area around the Yard Dog known as South Congress.[2] Local musicians and artists lament the rising cost of living in their community. Some feel SXSW is partially to blame, and believe that growth squeezes out the very creative community responsible for the music and weirdness that Austin tries to capitalize on. This is not a particularly new concern. One longtime SXSW volunteer told me about how a local band, the Wannabes, wore T-shirts for their 1997 SXSW gig with their name on the front and "Don't Move Here" on the back, spawning a variety of T-shirts on this theme: "Welcome to Austin. Don't Move Here" and "I Hear Dallas Is Quite Nice."

The ubiquity of these shirts isn't the only way to measure locals' anxiety about newcomers. The fancy condos and higher-priced boutiques in Austin's downtown alter the physical and cultural landscape and represent a familiar story for those who studied New York's Soho in the 1980s, Chicago's Wicker Park in the 1990s, and Williamsburg Brooklyn in the early 2000s. Rapid growth causes apprehension among members of creative communities, who fear a rise in rent and a drop in hip credibility.[3]

Richard Florida's thesis—that creative communities can have positive effects for cities in the new technology- and culture-based economy—has taken root among municipal power brokers, and over the course of my research I saw several moves to develop and support local artistic and creative communities, through efforts to either attract artistically inclined residents or support those groups already present. Though Florida's argument has been fairly criticized by many members of these cities' creative communities—and the many concerns over gentrification are well founded and documented[4]—I also found other musicians and culture-industry groups happy to find allies in city hall and government agencies, and eager to develop strategies for bolstering and exploiting a wider swath of a city's social + cultural resources, beyond "the creative class." These connections neither discount nor offset more troubling concerns over arts development. They do, however, trace a few of the benefits of festivals for these communities.

((( )))

As chapter 2 indicated, there is a contentious history between the people of Newport and the festival, from the old memories of the riots to more perennial complaints over traffic. According to Didi Lorillard, daughter of founders Elaine and Louis, the Newport festivals were supposed to be not-for-profits to benefit the cultural fabric of the community. "The original document that allowed them to have a public event in the city of Newport," she told me, intended that the profits would go to the only high school in Newport (equidistant between Fort Adams and down-town), with the idea that the music education program would be funded. And yet, according to locals, the decades-long relationship between the festivals and their locale has offered few of these kinds of gains.

After years of weaving through corporate sponsorships, the takeover of Festival Productions, Inc., and the eventual transformation into the Newport Festivals Foundation, it seems both Newport festivals are re-turning to the Lorillards' original intent, trying to keep music traditions alive in the region. There are three ways Newport Folk works to nurture social + cultural resources: through strengthening social ties among re-gional musicians, using those ties for benefit concerts for local agencies and groups, and broadening access to the event in a very limited capacity.

First, although Newport itself has not generated a vibrant music scene, there are broader regional ties between artists.[5] Festival producer Jay Sweet has stated that one of the key goals of his new leadership is to create a strong bond with Rhode Island bands because they lend "real authenticity" via their pride in being from the Ocean State: "John [McCauley of Deer Tick] is very proud of his Rhode Island connection. The Low Anthem is very, very proud of their Rhode Island connection. Brown Bird is very, very proud of where they are from." Sweet explained that he started small, but the development of the place-based network of musicians was further deepened when he allowed an advisory board of musicians to be a part of the conversation to pick performers for the folk festival. With repeat visits by the Low Anthem, Brown Bird, Joe Fletcher,

Deer Tick, and nearby Massachusetts-based David Wax, now, Sweet explained, "it's all their festival too."[6]

While the after-parties augment the festival's program and bind these artists together, they also raise money for the Newport Festivals Foundation. As mentioned before, Sweet had the Low Anthem curate a revue called Newport Homegrown. As Columbus Theatre booker and Brown Bird manager Tom Weyman told me: "We see the Columbus Cooperative as a hub for Rhode Island music." He said they feel immense support from the festival and Sweet, who has let them have the Homegrown event, in his words, "as a way to raise money, promote the endeavor, and be a presence there." And because of the relationship between the bands, the festival organizers, and Newport Blues Café owner Jim Quinn, the 2012 and 2013 events were also benefits, as Quinn detailed in a very personal anecdote:

> I'm very fortunate to be friendly with a lot of the members of the bands that played here, Deer Tick especially, and they know that my wife suffers from a very bad type of cancer, multiple myeloma, which is a terminal cancer. They decided that the proceeds from the third night of the 2011 after-parties would go to multiple myeloma research, which was very nice on their part. This year they wanted to split the proceeds with multiple myeloma research and festival foundations and the ticket was a twenty-dollar ticket and, again, all the bands were playing for nothing.

Half the proceeds went to the NFF and half to the Multiple Myeloma Research Foundation, headquartered nearby in Connecticut.

A third effort to strengthen local social + cultural resources was the festival's early efforts to reach out to Newport nonprofits. Historically, there has always been a presence of political and nonprofit groups in the tents, like Betsy Siggins's New England Folk Music Archives. Now, however, part of the money raised for the Newport Festivals Foundation is also directed toward nurturing a Newport community not necessarily to grow a generation of new musicians per se, but to infuse music education into a variety of different settings. In 2011, this money funded instruments and computer software, hired a year-round professional music teacher, and established a music component to a summer camp, all for the Newport Boys and Girls Club. The following year, the Boys and Girls

Club was on site and musicians were encouraged to set up workshops with the group. Spirit Family Reunion, for example, ran a washboard workshop. Though these activities form an important symbolic project for the festival, the interactions between less advantaged children and folk musicians are not always, in Joe Fletcher's words, "as magical as you would picture." The former schoolteacher said he really enjoyed the experience, and it reinforced his commitments to the festival, folk traditions, and music education, but at the same time, the participating children sometimes had the "hostage vibe" of being begrudging participants at the event:

> These kids weren't necessarily interested in the music that was going on that day, they... didn't want to hear about folk music. But I gave them a little talk and used my teaching skills to engage them with what they were interested in, tried to do a couple sing-alongs. It ended up being okay.

Debbie Bailey, the countywide after-school program director for the Boys and Girls Club, told me the children thought the music was good but a little too "old-timey" for them; she remembers one child who "really enjoyed all the ethnic vendors that were there, in particular one that was selling African art, and she liked how it was homemade and that a portion of the profits would go back to the community that was making them."

((( )))

In the early days of the Opry, WSM radio set up an Artist Service Bureau, modeled after a similar office for NBC's booking agency, to bring in better talent and improve musicians' lives; it allowed artists to make money on the road yet always return to Nashville by Saturday night's Opry show. Frances Williams Preston (a WSM receptionist who eventually rose to become president and CEO of BMI) described the bureau's activities as getting involved in almost every aspect of an artist's life:

> When an artist signed on to the Grand Ole Opry, they just took his career over, and they were a part of his family. I mean, they got him out of jail, they put him in hospitals, they put him in rehabilitation places. They helped pay for the new baby coming along. You know, everything they

could do to keep that artist's life, trying to make it a normal life, they would try and do it.[7]

The days of such personal attention to artists might be long gone, but the city is still a significant draw for artists and organizations attempting to keep their music culture alive.

Because of the strong connection between Nashville and the country music industry, it is unsurprising to know that a large group of country musicians call Nashville home. And yet, country music maven Hazel Smith made an important stipulation by pointing out that many of the most prominent people in the business aren't from here: "The people working the music business are not from Nashville. The people that sing the music are not from Nashville. [People] come from all over the world to sing our music, to write our songs, it's just not a local gig." With such a tradition, it is easy to forget that the Music City nickname originated with the Jubilee Singers, the more-than-a-century-old a cappella group from Fisk University.

And over the past decade, even more new talent has been pouring into Nashville, diversifying that palette further. In addition to the home-grown, non-country talent, like Kings of Leon, Ke$ha, and Paramore, recent migrants include Jack White, members of bands like the Americana act Old Crow Medicine Show, and indie rockers Black Keys and My Morning Jacket; the city is now a center for contemporary Christian pop as well. Even Newport Folk musician Joe Fletcher relocated his honkytonk sound to the city at the end of 2013, a move he telegraphed by hosting a collection of Tennessee artists at his Newport-to-Nashville set at the folk festival that year.

A variety of organizations and actors worked to ensure that Nashville lived up to its Music City name for future generations, and those efforts were often channeled through the festival. Country musicians had a long-standing tradition of using their time at Fan Fair to organize charity events on the side. When the CMA's Artist Relations Committee realized that acts donated to over a hundred charities in and around the festival, they decided to consolidate their giving for a more focused impact. To the disappointment of other local groups, they settled on the Nashville Alliance for Public Education, a nonprofit for music education for the city's 87,000 public school students. The CMA launched Cause for Celebration in 2001, corresponding with their move to downtown, which began the era of more organized philanthropic work, collaborating with community organizations each year to benefit charities designated by participating artists. CMA Executive Director Ed Benson told me the organization "felt it was a good fit," and expanded the program:

> Even the [schools with] music teachers, those kids live in households where they can't afford to buy an instrument to play in the band. Some of schools have old, beat-up instruments, and not enough to go around. You look at that and say, "Well this is Music City, of all places in America where music education in the school system should be a primary component…" Hopefully as the festival grows, more and more money will be poured into this endeavor and it will really help to build Music City as Music City.

Renamed Keep the Music Playing, and partnered with Chevrolet, the program then targeted purchasing student instruments—eventually over 4,000 of them, or about 90% of the instruments in the city's schools. Chevrolet and the CMA touted their efforts in promotional materials.[8] The CMA donated $368,500 and $655,600 from the 2006 and 2007 festivals, respectively, and the CMA Foundation, a nonprofit established in 2011 to better connect the industry to the community, donated $1.4 million to the music education programs, totaling $6.1 million since my research began in 2006.

Compared with Newport's support for its arts community, the much larger CMA Fest has a greater capacity to support Nashville's social + cultural resources. For one, the CMA's Keep the Music Playing program joined with Mayor Karl Dean's Music City Music Council to focus on Nashville's public schools through another program called Music Makes Us. Dean described it as a "major initiative" and "the next step." The project, as he sees it, "refreshes" music curricula to include more contemporary music courses, beyond orchestra-, choir-, and marching band–based music, and not just country.[9] Dean explained that many visitors see Nashville as the kind of place where all the public school music teachers "are banjo players or are songwriters, but that's not the case."

An organization on the other side of these efforts is the nonprofit

W. O. Smith School of Music. A CMA executive described the school's mission as "want[ing] to bring music education 365 days out of the year" by providing intensive music education to kids from low-income families, who enroll in after-school classes for fifty cents per lesson and are lent instruments. The school's $5.2 million building (unrecognizably repurposed from a tire-repair station) was partially financed with a million-dollar grant from Bank of America's Charitable Foundation, with other support from the Predators (Nashville's professional hockey team) and Great American Country television. It features brand-new lesson rooms, a library, and a 200-seat concert hall. The school benefits as well from a good number of famous and working musicians who volunteer their time in workshops and seminars, and both the organization and the building have been recognized for several arts and community awards.

In his office, the executive director of the music school, Jonah Rabinowitz, describes Nashville as "real fertile ground" for collaboration and partnerships. By his count, he's worked with dozens of CMA board members, and credits years of good interactions for the CMA's recent commitment to their summer program. Their $50,000 gift provided an intensive, weeklong "traditional camp experience" for over a hundred staff members and children. The kids get swimming, and three meals a day (which they don't often get at home, he noted), but they focus mainly on music all day long: choir, lessons, and ensembles. At the end of the week, every child participates in a performance for family and friends. Rabinowitz added that the greater Nashville community "really doesn't grasp the scope of what the CMA has done for the public school system in general." Specifically, he sees the festivals and the experience of running a nonprofit in Nashville as deeply connected. When I asked about changes in his relationship to the music community, Rabinowitz told me that, over his seventeen years of leading this nonprofit, he has observed the industry move from what he called "the golden age of Garth Brooks" to today, as the recorded-music industry struggles, and he noted that the industry's economic difficulties are a paradoxical gain for Nashville's community organizations:

> Back then, the country music industry wasn't as attached to the general
> business and the workings of the city. They had companies headquartered

out of LA, Germany, and Japan. Big conglomerates. There's *much* more attention being paid to what takes place in Nashville now. I think that's good. I'm sure they'd like to have the glory days of CD sales and money, but I think when it comes to somebody who lives here, there's much more of a feeling to me of their participation in the everyday life of the city.

He says that the industry used to be very selective with their contributions. Now they "almost always choose to be community oriented," having moved from a "feeling of obligation to a feeling of participation and community building."[10] Rabinowitz knows that a healthy relationship with the private sector makes sense for any nonprofit, and notes that it is an easier relationship when the "connective tissue" is music: he believes that a place like W. O. Smith couldn't exist in its present form without that support.

There are other moves that benefit local music folk. Housing is one example, but another is event planning on a regional scale. City hall and the festival organizations have tried to ensure that people who work in the live-production part of the industry do well, too. In 2012, people complained that the two major music festivals—CMA and Bonnaroo, which collectively brought over 150,000 visitors and over $40 million in economic impact—were both the same weekend, straining resources, overflowing taxi stands at the airport, and overbooking hotels, while also denying local production crews the chance to exploit both events. And indeed, one of the first orders of business for the Music City Music Council was to encourage the festivals to stagger the two events on different weekends, which they did in 2013 and 2014.

((( )))

Down in Austin, there are other ways of supporting creative communities afoot. Austin's chamber of commerce has taken to giving the city another motto—the Human Capital—corresponding with strategies to attract and nurture talent. Whereas public institutions in other states train students and then lose them to places like Austin—as Will Wynn reminded me in our interview—the state wants to retain their brightest University of Texas graduates; they've spent money on them, and they want to keep that capital while adding new blood. The city's overall job growth is the envy of many metro areas.

As Nashville's strategies indicate, enticing new talent is one thing, while nurturing and supporting local folk is another. Just as the CMA worked to siphon economic resources through their festival to local groups, there have been efforts in Austin's city hall and community organizations to use SXSW for their own ends. The 8,000 musicians and thousands of others who make their living in and around Austin's music scene are always, according to Mayor Wynn's chief of staff Rick Bailey, in need of support.[11] In an effort to provide that assistance, local musicians mobilized with the help of city hall to advocate for themselves. Wynn's Live Music Task Force was composed of fifteen people hoping to address the needs of the local creative community while at the same time further developing the downtown entertainment district. The group surveyed over 500 local musicians and found some of their chief concerns to be the increasing cost of living and a lack of affordable healthcare. Because the task force found that only 40% of their respondents had healthcare,[12] there was newfound support for two not-for-profits, the Health Alliance for Austin Musicians (HAAM) and the SIMS Foundation.

Since 1995, HAAM has provided primary medical care, mental health counseling, and basic dental care to area musicians. In 2008, they were at their cap of 1,000 enrollees—65% of whom were under forty and 67% making under $15,000 a year—and in 2012, they were able to expand services to 2,000 local working musicians.[13] The SIMS Foundation started in 2005 and offers mental health services and support for substance addiction treatment to Austin musicians. Lila Johnson, a native Austinite who is director of outreach for SIMS, told me, "we all know tons of musicians, and we all know that they struggle with finances, medical care, and mental health care." SIMS and HAAM hold monthly communications meetings, but across all the nonprofit and professional agencies, Johnson says they've reached "a new level of collaboration by doing outreach together, meeting regularly to stay informed about each other, sharing resources, and even occasionally sharing board members." There's a strong sense of mutual support among the city's creative community because of such connections.

In addition to these groups, there's the Austin Music Foundation, a nonprofit partially funded by contributions from the city of Austin, the NEA, and Fender Guitars, operating since 2002. They offer local musicians free training, private consulting, and workshops on a variety of facets of the business, from audio and video recording techniques to legal issues. In 2011, several prominent members of Austin's professional organizations, nonprofit communities, and government agencies—including Roland Swenson, music-venue owner James Moody, Will Wynn, and others from SXSW and *Austin City Limits*—came together to form Austin Music People (AMP) as an advocacy group for the music scene.[14]

AMP held a fund-raising concert at SXSW 2013. The festival, in fact, serves as a rallying point for these organizations. Healthcare corporation Aetna, and booking and events corporation C3 Presents, served as underwriters for the seventh annual HAAM Benefit Day at SXSW, which collected $235,000. Lila Johnson told me she conducts constant outreach at South By, educating and raising awareness of what she sees as the tenuous conditions for local musicians.

((( )))

As the existence of these nonprofits makes clear, the long-term effects of participating in the music industry are not always affirmative. While touring through Texas in May 2013 in support of their new album, *Fits of Reason*, tragedy struck Newport folk musicians Brown Bird. Dave Lamb grew weak with flu-like symptoms and ended up in an emergency room after being unable to finish a show. Tests brought terrible news: leukemia. Their burgeoning success could not shield the thirty-five-year-old Lamb and MorganEve Swain from the economic consequences of the diagnosis. With few financial resources, no healthcare, and no social support system in Texas, they had to take to social media to ask for donations from fans to get them back to Rhode Island and help with establishing insurance. Without touring, the band couldn't make ends meet and, without the support of their fans, they were uncertain how they could pay for Lamb's chemotherapy. In place of a canceled Brown Bird show in Boston, Joe Fletcher and other Newport and Providence bands held a benefit, tapping the local social network of musicians, and held another fund-raiser at Olneyville's Fête. At Cambridge's Club Passim, the newest incarnation of Betsy Siggins's 1960s folk hotspot Club 47, a series of artists (including the Low Anthem) performed Brown Bird songs as a benefit in late 2013. Through an online donation site, 1,600 of the band's fans donated almost $68,000, and hundreds more donated an additional $22,000 a few months later.

Tragically, Lamb died after an aggressive relapse in April 2014. Family, friends, and fans filled the Columbus Theatre in Providence for a service three days later. The memorial concert included a series of performances of local musicians, culminating in a tearful sing-along of Brown Bird's song "Mabel Grey," led by Joe Fletcher. The night was a bittersweet showcase of all the lives Lamb touched and yet a heartbreaking reminder of the precarious state of being an uninsured musician. For me, it was also a reminder of the vulnerabilities of the creative subset of uninsured Americans in general.

David Lamb provides a distressing story of life as a musician, but across the three cities there are differences in how the festivalized economic and spatial resources of these places support the social + cultural resources. Along with the general worries over gentrification and displacement, there are also stories within, like how these social ties within Rhode Island's community of folk and Americana musicians can benefit the members of its smaller network. Of the three cases, Austin's organizations show best how musicians and nonprofits can organize for supporting their creative class, and use the festivals to do so. If Providence had a similar program to Austin's HAAM, or if the Affordable Care Act had gone into effect months earlier, one could imagine a better outcome.

In Nashville, the municipal government and the music industry's promotion of music education as an initiative to cultivate social + cultural resources more generally is not without its critics. As an East Nashville musician (who preferred to remain anonymous because of his dependence on work as a backing musician at large CMA events and occasional music sessions) put it, "Look, I'm all for music education for kids but, I mean, who isn't? Everyone can get on board with that." Another musician describes the money she makes at the local honkytonks—"playing the stuff everyone already knows but wants to hear, but *definitely not originals*"—as barely enough to get by. She agrees that supporting children's musical education is worthwhile, but asks, "What are we going to do with the musicians who are fucking already musicians, man?" Calling moves by city hall for supporting local musicians "largely symbolic," she continued by saying that "a handful of apartments named after the Ryman isn't enough. It isn't easy these days, even here." Across town, John Walker from *Music City Roots* talked about what he offers to the music community. On show night, at the back of the Loveless Café, he told me that in the digital age he wants to "keep a space for our emerging middle class of musicians and industry folks in Nashville." Walker sees a strong reason to keep developing different kinds of outlets like his, and using them to support musicians: "we put the content online for free—it's out there anyway—and move to a sponsorship model. We need to subsidize housing and healthcare as a community and we're doing our part here." He cites the need for corporate sponsorship in order to provide as much revenue for musicians as possible. "Look," he said, "being able to provide these bands with a good meal is great, but we have to help music people pay their bills, too." By coordinating sponsors and paying musicians fair wages, *Music City Roots* offers a different way of thinking about music, as a kind of patronage system based around the live-music venues where the musicians perform.

Urban Signatures: City Sights and Miller Lites

Urban sociologists, in general, are rather critical of the commercialization of contemporary cities, and when seeing these festivalized spaces festooned with corporate logos it is easy to see why. When John Walker justifies corporate sponsorships for *Music City Roots*, he is referring to the opportunity to pay his musicians by hanging a sign on the wall, or by having a jingle sung between sets. Festivals, on a larger scale, need to pay bills, too. During my first visit to Newport, the orange, brown, and pink of Dunkin' Donuts was visible on nearly every sign. The CMA Fest had ads for Chevy, Crisco, and Wrangler, as well as Chevrolet's sponsorship of the Keep the Music Playing program. At SXSW, official sponsors like Verizon, Miller Lite, IFC, Doritos, IKEA, and Toyota Yaris were on the banners, and unofficial events added even more logos.

My field notes are filled with brands, which were, in turn, tied to my own identifications of those places. When thinking through this mixture of corporate and place-based symbolic resources, though, I first had to find out how these logos made their way onto the visual field in the first place, and then how festivalgoers responded to them. Thomas, the festivalgoer in chapter 2 who complained about Dunkin' Donuts wedging itself into every sight line, would certainly share urbanist Sharon Zukin's lament for older, less commercialized landscapes, yet surprisingly few festivalgoers shared this perspective. Most of the participants I spoke with retained very positive images of festivals and were undisturbed by what I saw as the high level of corporate imagery.

Cultural scholar Hans Mommaas writes that when a location is branded, it allows for a continual and collective recognition and identification of place—called alternately *territorial trademarking* or *place branding*.[15] Such trademarking comes about in various ways. Just as festivalization as a process allows for various for-profit and nonprofit groups to collaborate in shaping the social fabric of the city, these three cases provide an intersection of different kinds of visual imprinting. Many place identifiers or nicknames originate in an organic fashion: both Austin's Keep Austin Weird and Nashville's Music City, USA, nicknames came from unplanned statements made on the radio, and Austin's Live Music Capital of the World came from a local blues musician. Then there are city stakeholders, eager to proffer their own brands, whether it is Providence's marketing-firm-generated the Creative Capital, or Austin's the Human Capital, born from the chamber of commerce's office of business retention and expansion. Corporations represent a third major force in shaping these visual landscapes, and corporate marketing reaches its peak during festivals, which, as a city's signature event, provide a symbolic panorama for the imprinting of logos. I wanted to know how festival participants, coming from a variety of different backgrounds and with a variety of different agendas, shape, recognize, and identify brands—and, in particular, how corporate brands enter the mix.

Each setting tells its own story of how these different groups exploit or shape place brands and nicknames, and how they slip their way into the landscape. Newport's small resort town, for example, grapples with the attention it receives as the home for the historically significant festivals that occupy only two weekends in the summer. There is little consensus among residents on whether Newport is a Music City; most stakeholders are eager to lessen or at least relativize the festivals' importance as "two events in a long list of leisure activities." City Manager Ed Lavallee, furthermore, was troubled about the amount of corporate branding brought in by the festivals. Without prompting, he gave special emphasis to this issue:

> We regulate the event, but we regulate the signage as well. The festivals tell us what they want, to put banners and flags up here and there, and from this date to this date, and we tell them what our rules are. We don't care if it's Dunkin' Donuts or Campbell's Soup. We define how many of those flags can go up, and where, and for how long. That's for a couple of reasons. First of all, marketing is an important part of business, but it can get overloaded with exposure to these things. There's a sense of balance as to what appears to be attractive to a community... so that somebody can come and see our signs and see that they are reflective of the character of the community. And for us that means it's colonial, it's balanced, it's tasteful, it's historic.

The symbolic relationship between city, festival, and brands plays out on Thames Street.

Festival producer Jay Sweet expressed trepidation over the symbolic relationship between city and festival as well. After years of corporate underwriting, the new nonprofit sought cultural relevance and economic solvency in an era when headlining corporate brands grew harder to come by; this resulted in a strategy that highlighted Newport as a brand, rather than corporate sponsors like Dunkin' Donuts, and a symbolic tethering to the music scene in Providence in its lineup. As Sweet explained, "the signature brand is really Newport itself, and we're proud of that." Economic necessity may have prompted the reorientation, but the result is, for Sweet, a more "authentic" event. Corporate brands remain at Newport, of course, but they play a more subservient role to the festival and to local brands, and are mostly tied to particular activities (e.g., the Sennheiser Ruins, Gibson Guitars open mic), just as they are at Nashville's CMA.

In 2006, Nashville Chamber of Commerce President and CEO Mike Neal spoke about his organization's relationship with the CMA and their branding strategies. He noted that the city "now knows we need to take advantage of this great Music City brand we have." In his mind, keeping the city's signature event, its brand as Music City, and his constituents in harmony requires a coordinated effort of four entities: the city government, the chamber, the convention and visitors bureau, and the Country Music Association. The closer partnerships between the CMA and their brands, coinciding with the festival's return from the more isolated location of the Tennessee State Fairgrounds to its present downtown epicenter, offered the chance to better coordinate corporate sponsorships with territorial trademarking, and to include a variety of country- and family-oriented brands. Those brands are filtered through the festival since the Country Music Association, in the words of CEO Ed Benson, has always had the "good fortune" of being attractive to "corporate America." He continued by describing the CMA as an early adopter, making direct pitches to corporations for advertising since the early 1980s.

In my experience of the three festivals, the official branding seemed the most pervasive at the CMA, and the most complex in Austin. There was a clear connection between the city's more organic Live Music Capital of the World and Keep Austin Weird brands and its music festival, in part because of the ubiquity of music venues in downtown. Yet, with all of the guerilla marketing, from unofficial events to bands trying to promote their gigs, the resulting symbolic imprinting in Austin far surpassed the festival organizers' intentions and hopes, and was, perhaps, just as evident as in Nashville. For the marketing they can control, SXSW Managing Director Roland Swenson expressed concern over corporate advertising in spaces both inside venues and on city streets. South By cofounder Louis Black, in an interview with an Austin zine, talked about the expansion and policing of the festival's own brand:

> I have mixed feelings—I love the fact that it's everywhere. On the other hand, once SXSW [is] trademarked, if we let people imitate it than we lose ownership. That's the way it works. The reason why Disney are such fascists over Mickey Mouse is because if they know there is a kindergarten with Mickey Mouse on the wall and [if] they don't do anything they are passing it on to the public domain. Look at Sundance—they didn't do it and so there is Slamdance and One-Dance and up-dance and down-dance . . . so we protect ours because we don't want to confuse people.[16]

An official SXSW stage, designed to look like a Doritos vending machine, with the conference hotel in the background.

From the perspective of the organizers to the festivalgoers, the end result is that SXSW gets branded both inside and outside the music events themselves.

((( )))

All these efforts—from the corporate sponsor (e.g., Miller Lite) to the festival (e.g., SXSW) to the municipal (e.g., Live Music Capital of the World) branding—however, cannot make festivalgoers take notice. For all the strategy and expense, sociologist Michael Schudson notes that "advertising is much less powerful than advertisers and critics of advertising claim" and, indeed, I wondered just how much these activities impact festivalgoers' experiences.[17] Does it really matter to participants, for example, that Gibson sponsored the open-mic tent one year and C. F. Martin and Company the next? From the folks I spoke with around them, it seemed unlikely that any more people signed up because of one or the other, nor did it seem any songs were sung much differently, and both seemed to lend positive feelings toward the particular guitar manufacturers. Correspondingly, would a Ford CMA Block Party be any different from a Chevy CMA Block Party? It is, rather, the case that participants' experiences were quite similar. As much as I noticed these differences, and as much as organizers and promoters talked about it, fans I spoke with seemed less troubled. This is due to the extensive negotiating and careful matching of brands, events, and audiences: there might be little difference between a Ford CMA Block Party and a Chevy one, but there would be a difference between those and a Yaris CMA Block Party. Bands, then, aren't the only carefully crafted pieces of a festival.

To find out more of the audience's feelings on the matter, I administered a small number of surveys at all three sites, asking festivalgoers about both their participation in local culture and music as well as their perceptions of place and branding. Although I was only able to survey a limited sample of 200 participants, these results were balanced against my findings from ethnographic interviews about how participants reported "seeing" these events. The survey allowed respondents to identify as locals or out-of-towners but also queried other factors, such as levels of involvement in the music world and number of times attending the festival.[18] I did my best to tease out these variables to then compare perceptions of branding and place across the three locales. Separating out the locals (a quarter of the respondents) meant that I could zero in on the perceptions of visitors rather than of residents, who were more likely to notice the dramatic changes to their city. I also wanted to see if these repeat visitors were more aware of corporate branding, and if they had a positive, negative, or neutral impression of the symbolic landscape.

Much to my surprise, there was an overwhelmingly *positive* impression of branding in all three places. Festivalgoers visiting Newport, Nashville, and Austin were unconcerned with the corporate imagery. There was some important nuance, however. For example, first-time attendees to the Newport Folk Festival in 2007—questioned at the height of the Dunkin' Donuts branding—had a better impression of brands and sponsors than those who attended the festival previously; this latter group was more likely to talk about how the festival "used to be," and to express regret that festivals in general were becoming increasingly corporatized. At the same time, they seemed savvy enough to know that while corporate branding of a folk festival was somewhat paradoxical, it was also unavoidable.

Conversely, the more often festivalgoers went to SXSW, the more likely they were to have a *positive* impression of the corporate branding. Ironically, despite the "hipness" of such an "indie" event, South By attendees are likely to be working in the music industry itself or, as is more often the case, hoping to find a career there. This connection in the minds of participants was more nuanced when prompted for further thought. For example, when Erik Courson from the spinART record label spoke about how the festival had changed, his description immediately turned to the rise of corporate sponsorship—he noticed a little bit of marketing in the 1990s, but the "big corporations spending a lot of money" marked his more recent experiences; even his taxi receipt and hotel keycard had advertisements for new albums on them. Record promoter Ronda Chollock expressed a similar qualified unease. Despite recognizing the need for corporate "buy-in," and her own participation in the industry at large, she told me she thinks "Austin and South By need to be careful [of] the increasingly obnoxious level of branding." Even though attendees griped in interviews, when it came to participants answering survey questions, respondents showed clear acceptance of the imagery.

The country music festivalgoers in Nashville were altogether different than those in either Newport or Austin. More than 70% of those surveyed reported having *no* impressions of sponsors or brand awareness, regardless of how many times they had attended the festival. I followed up on this finding in 2012 by asking CMA festivalgoers about their impressions in informal interviews; the interviewees seemed uniformly nonplussed by corporate sponsors. Similar to hip-hop, country songs like Toby Keith's hit "Red Solo Cup" (which led to people strolling down Lower Broad wearing necklaces made of Solo cups), Blake Shelton's "Kiss My Country Ass" (which includes lyrics like "Well, I love turkey calls, overalls, Wrangler jeans/smoke nothin' but Marlboro Reds"), and Jason Aldean's "Big Green Tractor" make the comfort with commercialism understandable. In songs like these, product placement is almost as common as shout-outs to Hank Williams and evocations of simple, small-town living. Representative of many of those I spoke with on these matters, one interviewee explained, "Well, that's just the air I breathe, I guess. I don't pay no notice." On Lower Broad, when asked about what they noticed at the festival, most folks would eagerly talk about the musicians and their fellow audience members, whom they described as "earthy" and "down home" people. When asked to discuss corporate imagery, few responded directly, preferring to talk more vaguely about "country living." Millionaire musicians deploy corporate logos in lyrics in order to reassure their middle- and working-class listeners that they are just like them. By adopting such brand imagery, the festival serves as an opportunity for those corporations to coordinate their efforts and market to their shared audiences.

Because of the higher levels of commitment and participation in the music industry by SXSW participants, I was eager to compare results across all three locations by respondents who reported having "high participation" in the music (i.e., respondents who not only bought music, but also played an instrument, or wrote about or performed music) with those who had little participation (i.e., respondents who went to the festival, but had bought only a few albums or songs over the course of the previous year). Sure enough, a greater percentage of people surveyed at SXSW participated in a wider range of music activities than those at the other two locations. Their overwhelmingly positive impressions of corporate imagery were, therefore, unsurprising: South By attendees with a high level of music participation reported positive brand awareness and sponsor impressions more than two and a half times those who had lower levels of music participation. In fact, *no* SXSW respondents reported negative brand awareness or sponsor impressions, despite the festival's seemingly anti-establishment and hip reputation and Austin's overarching Weird City spirit. Teasing out this dynamic led to some solid differences between SXSW participants and the festivalgoers at the other two locations. In Nashville, three-fourths of those who reported no or limited music participation said they had no brand awareness or sponsor impressions, compared to almost 15 and 10%, respectively, of participants who reported having positive and negative brand awareness or sponsor impressions. In sum: whereas CMA attendees didn't notice, SXSW attendees noticed but didn't mind, and repeat Newport attendees noticed and *did* mind.

How closely do festivalgoers perceive the tie between festivals and their locations or, as referred to here, their *place character*? This certainly was a major concern among city stakeholders and festival organizers. For example, South By cofounder Louis Black emphasized the link between the festival and the city's territorial branding:

> If we tried to do this anywhere else it wouldn't work. You go to Park City, Utah, the week before or after Sundance and you would never know that this was a town that had a film festival because there is nothing there about it. You go to Austin any day of the year and it is exactly the same as SXSW—it's just not as intense.... There is more programming of films in this town and better music in this town than almost anywhere else on a regular basis. And it's accessible and affordable.[19]

Black's point about Sundance could be equally well applied to Newport, although he would have a harder time making these claims when comparing Austin to Nashville rather than to Park City, Utah (home of the Sundance Film Festival). And more recently, in response to the Populous report that suggested SXSW could move to another city, Roland Swenson underscored the importance of Austin and its music scene.

One could approach the issue of the connection between these festivals and their locations in the minds of the attendees with a similar skepticism as to the topic of corporate branding. If most festivalgoers either did not notice or did not mind how corporations imprinted themselves onto the visual field, would they actually have strong feelings about the relationship between festivals and their locations? For mayors, city managers, and organizers, these festivals are their city's "signature event," and survey respondents at all three locales certainly echoed Black's feelings of a strong connection between place and event. All three festivals were positively linked with the hosting cities in the minds of those surveyed, all three contributed to the identity of the place, and repeated participation strengthened the attachment between festivals and their cities.

The survey determined this through an initial question as to whether the respondent liked the festival where it was, and then followed up on this later in the survey by asking whether the respondent would like the festival better if it were in New York or Los Angeles. The first question elicited a predominately positive response, whereas the second received an overwhelmingly negative response.[20] People like the festivals, and they like their placedness (which doesn't bode well for any argument for moving SXSW).

Perhaps the most notable takeaway from this exercise was the overwhelming lack of concern about the high level of corporate sponsorship among these respondents. In particular, the loose, confetti-like structure of SXSW—neither as well coordinated as the core pattern of Nashville nor as confined and controllable as the citadel pattern in Newport—led to an excess of corporate sponsorship. This destabilized the distinctiveness and the monopoly of festival brands, and blurred the experience of being at the festival, as South By festivalgoers (including the mayor himself) seemed to care little about moving from official to unofficial events. In contrast, the CMA festival's corporate branding seemed to harmonize with the festival's contemporary country music content and with Nashville's place as the home of the genre. And despite its countercultural roots, festivalgoers at Newport during the height of its Dunkin' Donuts branding were similarly nonplussed. So, although I had my own difficulty accepting the pervasive branding I witnessed, for most participants, the corporate brands were either a necessary part of the festival business or an integral part of the festival landscape. I was, in this sense, wrong.

Conclusions: The Shape of Things

With the conclusion of the discussion of these four resources, some summarization is necessary. To do so, I return to our three patterns of festivalized spaces—the citadel in Newport, the core in Nashville, and the confetti in Austin—to better compare how festivals reinforce and exploit city resources, how different kinds of actors and groups engage with their events, and how one can think through the varied relationships, opportunities, and obstacles in the management and fortification of these economic, spatial, social + cultural, and symbolic resources.

These patterns serve as good guides for understanding these activities, yet they should not draw the reader into the *fallacy of physical determinism*: festival shapes do not stipulate specific outcomes; they only lend themselves toward certain kinds of events, activities, and interactions.[21] A keen awareness of change—from the founding of these festivals, throughout my research, and to the present—and an eye to variation within cases guards against such an error. These patterns are, again, good to "think through."

Although Newport's two festivals started in spaces more central to downtown (i.e., the Newport Casino, Freebody Park, and Festival Field), altercations with police and locals led city stakeholders to confine and even marginalize the events. Newport's Fort Adams State Park is a citadel that does just that. For the festival organizers, performers, and attendees, the citadel is separate from Newport in some ways and still connected in others. The limited space, both of Fort Adams itself and also of the resort town of Newport, means that the symbolic resources of the traditions at the folk festival are directed in limited yet curious ways. Over time, as the festival's organizational structure changed from for-profit to nonprofit, its symbolic character shifted as well. This meant not only a decrease in corporate logos from my first visit to my last (although that was certainly the case), but also the rebranding of the festival for a closer tie to its closest metropolis, Providence. In this case, the economic and noneconomic benefits are partially used by and for a Providence-based network of musicians more so than affecting any local music scene. The symbiotic relationship of Providence's nascent Americana and folk scene and the newly nonprofit and re-sacralized festival makes for a tightly bound, controlled, and curated event. Newport Folk's citadel pattern limits the possibility of significant redirecting of resources to unofficial events like BridgeFest and the Newport Nightcap, but even minor efforts in this direction (e.g., new attempts to link the festival with local venues like the Blues Café) are more strongly felt in a smaller community.

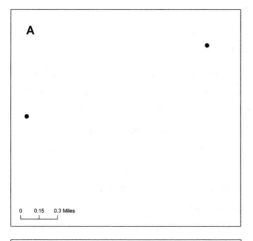

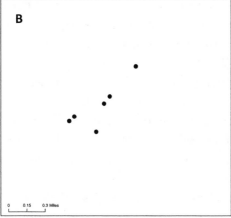

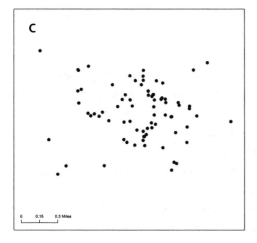

The spatial distribution of festival activities: (a) Newport Folk's citadel pattern, (b) CMA Fest's core pattern, and (c) South by Southwest's confetti pattern.

Unlike Newport, SXSW's confetti pattern allows for a variety of venues and businesses to join in the festivalization of their Music City. With its far more open organizational logic, this pattern presents a challenge for organizers, who struggle to maintain control of their resource use, both in claiming exclusive purview over downtown Austin for their corporate sponsors and in managing their own SXSW brand. Swenson and Black expressed anxiety over Austin becoming overly branded in the eyes of participants and locals. It has been, in their mind, potentially *too* open, *too* informal. Furthermore, people in and around Austin have perceived the growth of events in the city as too unwieldy, although attendees do not seem to mind and some of the local not-for-profits see mixed support directed through and around SXSW. When thinking about the economic benefits of the festival, local business owners have been less troubled. "I love it when tourists come in. Everybody wants the money," said one. Nonetheless, the same business owner, speaking from the point of view of also being a resident, said, "We just want to minimize the impact on our daily lives and avoid downtown when South By is on. . . . I just want to hide from all the people." The openness of the confetti pattern, in other words, has led to a bit of a struggle over the economic and symbolic landscape in Austin, more so than in the cases of Nashville and Newport. Over time, the festival has grown exponentially, drawn more attention from guerilla events, and heightened concern among locals.

The core pattern of the CMA Fest illustrates how festivalization reinforces and uses existing infrastructure, parks, hotels, and convention centers, attracting institutional support from the local community and, in the process, strengthening the local talent base in a targeted fashion. As with Newport, examining Nashville's change in organizational pattern offers a perspective on how the festival itself has developed over time. Many factors worked in coordination—both intended (e.g., municipal government investment, the convention and visitors bureau branding) and unintended (e.g., the reorganization of the larger music industry and its effects on the country music business in the city)—that corresponded with the move from Fan Fair's citadel pattern at the Tennessee State Fairgrounds to the more open core pattern using the Lower Broad area and its multiple downtown facilities. The citadel of the fairgrounds partially isolated Fan Fair in its 1982 to 2000 incarnations, similar to

Newport today. Yet, while Newport has remained exiled from the city's core, Nashville's CMA has been embraced.

((( )))

In comparison with the looser confetti pattern and the more confined citadel pattern, the core arrangement emerges as a kind of "Goldilocks" arrangement, where the weather is neither too hot nor too cold, and the music is neither too hard nor too soft; the CMA Music Fest, indeed, does seem to offer a lot of this "in between" quality. It uses big stadium venues and small venues, offers shows in a public park on scorching June days and events in the icebox AC of the convention center, and is structured around carefully choreographed showcases but features some off-script interactions in Nashville's public streets and honkytonks. In addition, the core pattern keeps the festival bounded within the resources it has while also allowing for expansion. Though it seems to strike a balance between the corporate branding and the more unaffiliated activities, the events of the festival do not reflect the cultural diversity of Nashville's wider cultural offerings, nor is it under an obligation to do so. The CMA provides resources for Nashville's other cultural organizations; tertiary benefits spill over and social + cultural resources are reinforced, but the festival still reinforces the city's dominant contemporary country music brand.

Thinking of the core pattern as the perfect middle-ground strategy for urban cultural policy also ignores some of the specific attributes exhibited by the confetti and citadel patterns. Both SXSW and Newport have, for example, diversified their content, while the CMA has only narrowed theirs. SXSW, for its part, started with local alternative rock and expanded to include a wide range of music: over my seven years of research, South By grew from listing twenty genres of music to forty, adding hip-hop, classical, bluegrass, Tejano, funk, metal, and reggae (although rock remains the major category). Though Newport's citadel pattern would seem to incline toward a very limited range, since it needs to attract only 10,000 festivalgoers, it actually offers a broad range of content—so much so that discussions and debates among the fans and musicians over what qualifies as folk music are reminiscent of when the Kingston Trio were invited to the Newport Folk Festival or when Led

Zeppelin and Sly and the Family Stone performed at the 1969 Newport Jazz Festival.

Festivals can, of course, hold more fidelity to a particular genre or style regardless of pattern. However, there is something to be said for the patterns themselves, as indicated in these discussions. The confetti pattern allows for alternative or unofficial events in and between a festival's scheduled activities. Assuredly not an advantage for organizers, this openness manages to be a greater gain to a wider network of organizations and participants. SXSW, in this way, is more democratic compared with the spatially bound Newport Folk Festival or the rather narrow CMA Fest. Although the slow growth of BridgeFest indicates some opportunity for other cultural events to sneak in around the edges of the Newport fortress, for the most part the citadel allows for the Newport Festival to stamp its brand more clearly through its official lineup than in the other two patterns. Pushing this line of thought even further, an argument could and perhaps should be made that a rather robust confetti pattern works as an incredibly vibrant and vital urban social space: as guerilla events cause headaches for festival organizers and further glut the visual landscape, participants seldom mind the symbolic discord and relish the access to a wider range of music and other cultural resources.

((( )))

These two chapters illuminate some of the struggles around the idea of the Music City through the lens of three music festivals, identifying how resources are reinforced and extracted, exploited and appropriated. There are those who benefit from such activities, and those who are left outside. The confetti pattern seems to benefit a wider array of unaffiliated individuals and groups, while it is less the case in the core pattern and even less so in the citadel. And yet, the dynamic is quite the inverse for festival organizers: perhaps it is because Newport is so enclosed that festival producers are finding ways to reach out to the city and to introduce a little controlled chaos in its walls through unscripted collaborations onstage and wandering buskers in the audience; and why SXSW producers search for ways to limit their disorder by trying to dissuade unofficial events. In this way, the physical pattern sets the stage for certain interactions and attempts to foreclose others.

The discussion provides a map of how festivals relate to their locales, and how many local organizations and individuals relate through these temporary events. It also displays how these three patterns seem well suited for their respective cities, and therefore reinforce their cities' brands: as a wealthy resort separate from Providence, Newport is a kind of citadel, whereas Nashville's "leather and lace" persona is emplaced as a mix of organized music business and funky honkytonks, and Austin does host a raucous blend of cultural weirdness.

Conclusions
Festivalization as Good Policy

Concrete and Liquid Urban Culture

When learning a song, you listen to the lyrics and catch a few memorable lines. You identify the various parts: the intro, the verses, the chorus, and the bridge. You absorb the rhythm. And, soon enough, you develop an understanding of its overall meaning. Based upon our understanding of the patterns and rhythms of these festivals—and therefore of festivalization as a *process*—these final pages offer a few arguments for thinking about temporary events as a part of an urban cultural *policy* beyond mere economic merit. I will, then, conclude with a final sense of the meaning of festivalization put to use.

What is certain is that this book is not a piece of sheet music for culture workers and placemakers to follow note-for-note for similar outcomes. Without comparable long-standing musical histories, few cities could reproduce what Newport, Nashville, and Austin have done. And yet, all cities have local communities with culture to share, governments with some funds for arts and cultural initiatives, parks and streets to utilize, commercial entities hoping to promote their brands, and municipal entities like CVBs, chambers of commerce, and city halls with their agendas too. There is, then, much to take away from the idea of festivalization as an urban cultural policy.

Cultural policy is a messy term, meaning a great many things, but it often highlights government engagement with the production (the financing, solicitation, distribution, etc.) and consumption of cultural goods and services, as well as the variety of organizations (trade unions, universities, social movements, community groups, foundations, and businesses) that play a role in funding, promoting, and evaluating cultural products and creative individuals.[1] The substantive focus of these policies may include promoting arts education or cultural trade; developing media, communication, or cultural infrastructure and networks; improving quality of life; stimulating tourism; crystallizing a national or city identity; preserving cultural heritage; shaping a foreign policy; or addressing environmental and land-use issues.[2]

The disinvestment in US cities, leading to poorer municipal coffers (discussed in chapter 1), alongside a decades-long push for privatizing public assets, established a de facto neo-liberal cultural policy for urban revitalization, often through building culture- and tourism-based institutions. Between 1976 and 1986, 250 "convention centers, sports arenas, community centers and performing arts facilities were constructed or started, at a cost of more than $10 billion," many of which were for-profit projects heavily subsidized by municipal financing and incentivizing.[3] As stated at the outset, some of these were geographically bundled as amenity-rich districts and tourist attractions, called *cultural clusters* or *tourist bubbles*.[4] Urbanist Lyn Lofland uses Anselm Strauss's term *counter-locales* to describe such spaces: places that are carefully monitored and controlled so as to minimize unwanted and untoward interactions.[5] These strategies, which I'll call simply *concrete urban culture*—meaning large entertainment districts and coordinated infrastructure developments—are exercises in counterlocale composition.

A good example of one such place is the public-private, quasi-theme park of Baltimore's Inner Harbor, which also happened to be perhaps the most significant project that Struever Brothers, Eccles, and Rouse participated in to date. The development is a mixture of natural resources (the waterfront), commercial spaces (the Hard Rock Café and ESPN-Zone in the redeveloped Pratt Street Power Plant; the nearby Camden Yards), public institutions (the Baltimore Museum of Industry), and private nonprofit organizations (the Maryland Science Center; the National Aquarium), wrapped under a thin layer of cultural heritage (i.e., the city's shipping past). This massive, coordinated maneuvering of concrete urban culture is a particularly spectacular illustration of a common approach to the postindustrial "experience-based economy."[6]

The Inner Harbor counterlocale is one of many famously derided examples of similarly designed entertainment and leisure districts that have been carefully constructed to attract a certain subset of the population—those who will travel and perhaps even relocate based on the quality of an area's lifestyle and consumption opportunities. In an era of intense intercity competition, municipal image- and placemaking like this are key weapons in a city's arsenal. And while concrete urban culture draws lots of headlines for its attempts to redesign and refresh seemingly broken urban places, I suggest that a festival-focused strategy as we've seen it here, founded on flexible, temporary arts-based events, might better suit cities and their communities, so long as it attends to a few simple but elusive requirements and separates itself from a few common "mega event" strategies.

In comparison with public-private partnered, fixed-asset capital investments, earlier chapters clarify how the ephemeral nature of fairs and festivals makes them reconfigurable machines for resource development that mix existing public resources like parks and streets, and private, corporate interests. As mentioned in chapter 1, Seattle's city hall launched Bumbershoot to address civic concerns about the decline in their aerospace industry, and Chicago recognized that its Blues Fest is a good focal point for its transition from a manufacturing- to a consumer-based economy. Chapters 5 and 6 presented examples that served similar purposes: from broader claims of economic impact in all three locations to specific initiatives like the 2010 CMA Fest donating *all* of its profits to help Nashville recover from an epic downtown flood. Such strategies indicate that festivals are more than frivolous confections. Though they rarely last more than a weekend, the crafting of temporary cultural and entertainment-based spaces is a serious cultural strategy, and unlike concrete culture, festival programming can more fluidly respond to the changing needs of the city, its residents, and the audience that attends. As a contrast, let us call this *liquid culture*.

Liquid culture is not without its troubling effects. The World Cup, the Olympics, the Super Bowl, and the like have, time and time again, shown themselves to offer few tangible benefits to the communities they are placed within and serve as a significant boon to the operating organizations (e.g., FIFA; the International Olympic Committee), corporate sponsors, and local growth-machine elites.[7] Although temporary, mega events are primarily known for the more liquid activities of the festivities themselves; they have their concrete culture too, as they often require massive new spatial resource projects (e.g., housing blocks, stadiums, infrastructure improvements). They also make for bad policy: mega events impose laws and regulations that may not suit, and often run counter to, local needs. The 2014 World Cup, for example, made headlines for forcing Brazil to overturn established laws that prohibit alcohol sales at their events, since a major sponsor was Budweiser. When recalling the recommendation for Austin and SXSW to establish a "Clean Zone" downtown, one can realize that music festivals might be swayed by the allure of these policies too. Such developments threaten the greater potential of festivalization.

And so, as certain public urban spaces are redesigned into experiential marketplaces for shopping and consumption and massive events impose unwelcome new logics on local communities, careful policy models are needed to make sure the public good is considered in how these cultural goods are deployed. Unlike these mega events, smaller festivals could and should serve as a critical pivot for a variety of interests, and not focus on exploiting spatial resources and extracting economic ones for elite local groups and major corporations. At the same time, entertainment districts like downtown Austin and Nashville, which serve as the settings for festivalization, have *some* permanent legal distinctions (e.g., noise ordinances, hours of operation, commercial and residential zoning changes, parking regulation, relaxed open-container laws) as well as temporary ones (e.g., street closings, allowances of temporary structures/stages, etc.).

Cultural economist Lily Kong offers four key benefits of flagship arts developments and high-profile events as cultural policy: they (a) generate investment in infrastructure and cultural districts, (b) attract "cultural tourism," (c) reboot urban public spaces, and (d) nurture public-private partnerships in the city.[8] Festivalization can provide each of these as long-term benefits while also being low risk and offering few short-term costs. With these concerns in mind, a festival-based policy can be refracted through the lens of our now-familiar four resources:

An economic resource argument: Festivals attract money through sponsors and visitor spending, and can potentially draw new business and taxpaying residents.

A spatial resource argument: Festivals maximize the use of publicly held spatial resources (e.g., parks, streets, parking lots, convention centers) within a limited time period, potentially increasing the value of those public goods, while also nurturing proximate, related amenities (e.g., music venues, cafés, retail stores, etc.).

A social + cultural resource argument: Festivals can promote and reinforce local creative communities, while also attracting new participants from both near and far.

A symbolic resource argument: Festivals help brand place and attract media attention while the symbolic "buy-in" of corporations—although it might be troubling to scholars, critics, and musicians—can be minimally noticed by festivalgoers.

When seen in this fashion, festivals fit well with contemporary cultural policies as cities blend "quality of life" campaigns with more neo-liberal instincts: festivals provide a resonant image for place; make cities appear to be fun and exciting places to live and visit; bolster local nonprofits; and extract economic resources from corporations eager to hitch their name to a hip or family-oriented event without much complaint from participants.[9] Liquid and concrete urban culture can even be mutually supportive, as I showed in examples like the CMA Fest utilizing Nashville's convention center and other cultural institutions.

The preceding chapters offer some tangible costs, benefits, and warnings to the more humble, changeable, and responsive urban cultural policy approach that this liquidity brings. Over time and with some key variations, Newport, Nashville, and Austin have established entertainment zones that balanced more relaxed noise ordinances and curfews with affordable and mixed-use housing; highlighted their distinctive character and community; eased the pathway for culture-based entrepreneurialism; and invested in health and housing services for working musicians. Austin and Nashville developed cultural offices within their city halls with amounts of bureaucratic power while also connecting with and supporting their local arts communities. Local government agencies are making moves to better coordinate temporary cultural activities in conjunction with such events (e.g., streamlining permitting, managing multiple events over the calendar year, targeting particular municipal resources for use, offering legal and health-based services for musicians). And chapter 2 outlined a series of Nashville institutions—including the Schermerhorn Symphony Center, Country Music Hall of Fame and Museum, two stadiums, and a new convention center, the Music City Center—that "solidified" the city's position as a music locale, literally and symbolically. Meanwhile, in Newport, the burgeoning Rhode Island music scenes seek to find their place in and around their festivals, gaining some notoriety and getting a say in the festivals' planning, resource distribution, and cultural impact—for example, as they redefine what "folk" as a genre means, and helping with local community groups.

These benefits, however, could not possibly play out perfectly in every instance, and any festivalization strategy should be wary of these pitfalls. The Newport Folk Festival, the CMA Fest, and SXSW were not selected as exemplary cases, but rather because there is room in all three for greater adaptability, public assessment, community discussion, and representation.[10] Some festivals likely contribute more to their local creative communities, becoming entwined with their local place character, and proving to be solid economic endeavors in hard economic times. And there are other festivals that are much less connected. Researchers, indeed, often identify festivals that diminish, overwhelm, homogenize, obscure, or exclude local culture.[11] Some of what has been presented here, particularly in the case of Nashville's Gulch, would certainly support the notion that festivals can link up with and support urban counterlocale-style redevelopment. And at the ground level, festivals like the CMA Fest may champion the city's musical heritage but at the same time alienate local musicians who feel their own community's signature event has no place for them. Furthermore, corporations can use festivals to wedge their way into the landscape with unofficial events or with sponsors attempting to dictate festival booking (in the case of Milwaukee's

Summerfest); municipal stakeholders should be wary of overly corporate festivals, which add to already glutted urban landscapes.[12]

As I spoke with musicians and local stakeholders about these costs and benefits, they often responded with examples from other, international, locales. A few other cases, culled from those interviews and my own experiences, can show what other relationships these events can have with their communities.

Making Music in Other Countries

Visiting Paris for the first time, in June 2002, I remember being overcome with joy at seeing so many street musicians in the Montmartre district: a jazz quartet on a stoop, an accordionist on a corner. There was a mind-boggling amount of street life at nearly every turn. "Sure," I thought, "it's a Friday night, and it *is* Paris . . . but there's just *so much music*." I spent hours watching the performers, but also watching crowds gather to laugh and sing along to songs I had never heard before. Knowing no one in town, I left the city dumbfounded, and yet with a keen respect for the city's cultural life.

It was not until a decade later, in an interview where Newport Folk performer David Wax was recounting his experiences with festivals he had attended or performed at, that I learned that I had stumbled into Fête de la Musique. The Parisian festival, which began in 1982, places hundreds of amateur and professional musicians around the city on sidewalks, in parks, and on stoops every June 21, the longest day of the year. And in its hundreds of permutations around the world, the object of the event is to infuse music into public spaces and promote the local culture. The word *fête* means festival, but its homophone in French is *faites*, which means "to make"—which is, Wax explained, why the New York City version is called Make Music New York.

My interviews with musicians and festival producers were filled with mentions of other festivals. Some I had heard of, like Pop Montreal or Oslo's Øyafestival, and others, like São Paulo's Virada Cultural and the Winnipeg Folk Festival, I had not. Chats about these events served as touchstones for comparison, for it was most often the case that interviewees would describe the differences between international and US festivals.

European governments, and France's in particular, play a far more central and active role in the promotion of culture than in the United States.[13] Far from being the product of some grassroots movement, Fête de la Musique was the brainchild of Jack Lang, France's Minister of Culture—a cabinet-level position in charge of monuments, arts, and maintaining a national identity. Expanding the influence of his position, Lang promoted cultural institutions (helping develop a five-year plan for restoring cathedrals and historical monuments) and cultural centers (*maisons de culture*), but he also founded Fête de la Musique as well as cofounded the expansive European Capitals of Culture (ECoC) program, which might well be the most dramatic urban cultural policy initiative in history. Since 1985, the ECoC awards billions of euros of funding for concrete cultural infrastructure redevelopment and yearlong liquid events programming as it moves from city to city each year.[14]

According to Jimi Nilsson, a geographer researching Swedish music festivals, Scandinavian cities invest a good deal of money into major summer events as opportunities for employment and local business growth.[15] Nilsson points out that the Hultsfred municipality stepped up to save Sweden's biggest festival from bankruptcy and that several cities bid for another festival. And when I traveled across the border to Norway, I interviewed an administrative staffer in charge of promoting one of the country's biggest festivals, Øyafestival. On the issue of commercial and public funding, festival employee Birgitte Mandelid told me, "I think you would be hard pressed to find a festival in Western Europe without significant public funding," but noted exceptions like Barcelona's Primavera Sound, which is "paid in full" by a brand. She continued:

We have some commercial sponsors at Øya, but we also receive about 2.5 million Norwegian kroner [roughly US$450,000] in state support every year. There are restrictions regarding the money, for example, that they can't be used on booking bands or to reduce the admission price or get cheaper beer or anything like that. Rather, it's for making the festival more environmentally friendly, to help promote Norwegian bands abroad, to educate our own people when it comes to security issues, etc. We have to submit an extensive report every year, where every krone is accounted for.

Øya's funding constraints are self-imposed, and how money gets used is part of how the festival markets itself.

One could compare the public financing of a single year, 2007: the Hultsfred festival and Øyafestival attracted 30,000 and 65,000 festivalgoers, respectively, and were bolstered by US$1.5 million and US$450,000 of public support. One could compare this with Austin's municipal support for the much larger SXSW, which received closer to US$90,000.[16]

The higher level of investment does not make European festivals impervious to economic challenges. Jimi Nilsson noted that these festivals might be reaching their limits. Despite different levels of public funding, Hultsfred and Peace and Love declared bankruptcy in 2010 and 2013, respectively, due to meager ticket sales.[17] Nilsson told me that there has been a healthy debate over the value of public investment in these events. Even with a long-standing tradition of Scandinavian summer music festivals, he described their difficulties as "a kind of mass death" after 2008. In addition to the global economic downturn, the European festival market might be oversaturated.[18]

((( )))

Many of the musicians I interviewed compared their experiences in the United States with those in Canada and Latin American countries, and the connection between public funding and what they saw as a richer use of place often came up.

David Lamb, for example, spoke of performing at São Paulo's state- and municipally funded Virada Cultural (*cultural turn*).[19] He said his experience there was like no other. Founded by Mayor José Serra and run by city hall with over a thousand events all scheduled within a twenty-four-hour period and attended by over four million people (in a city of twenty million), he told me that São Paulo seemed to be "full of too many experiences to ever fully appreciate."[20] "They use corners and sidewalks and everything they can," he said, "and the streets are packed for twenty-four hours." Lamb's description of Virada Cultural's use of center-city spaces paralleled Fête de la Musique and also Pop Montreal.

Pop Montreal—a festival with a music conference similar to South by Southwest, in Canada's second-largest city—was cofounded by Dan Seligman, the brother of a member of a popular rock band called Stars. A few months before the 2012 event, he told me that "the Canadian government recognizes that culture actually has a pretty significant economic impact on the city, the province, and the country." He told me that the wealth of funding for the arts comes from "a Canadian ethos of the welfare state connecting communities and culture in a way that just doesn't exist in the US." He felt his festival had to prove itself and become a nonprofit (in 2004, its third year) to solidify steady support from the city of Montreal, the province of Quebec, and the federal government. This funding keeps his nonprofit festival tied to its communities, and allows him to rely less on other kinds of financial backing, particularly corporate sponsorships. Unlike Virada Cultural, which is completely supported by the government, Seligman said that Pop Montreal still has corporate sponsorships. Still, the funding means he "doesn't need to work with Pepsi-Cola or Chevrolet." He acknowledges that Pop Montreal couldn't be what it is without government funding, which provides for everything from paying staff and administrative costs to booking bigger headliners.

This backing makes it easier for Seligman and his team to petition for the use of public places and to get permits for unconventional private spaces. Permitting and negotiation of non-music-venue locations creates a different festival imprint. He explained how the city's Cultural Bureau and Festival and Cultural Events office allows Pop Montreal to use spaces differently. The support means Pop Montreal is "not like a generic festival, but one that is really part of the city's landscape" because the city government "clearly sees the economic impact of what we're doing, so it's so much easier than in other places." This is the how and why, as Seligman explained in the introduction to this book, Pop Montreal has a rare opportunity to use unorthodox urban spaces, like churches or spaces under bridges. It's also necessary for the festival's expansion: while both Montreal and Austin have rich music cultures, and both festivals use a confetti pattern, Montreal does not approach Austin's number of live-music venues. For a comparison of the resultant events, the 2012 Pop Montreal had 600 performers in over forty venues (at a ratio of 15 to 1), whereas the 2012 SXSW had 2,200 acts performing in over a hundred venues (22 to 1). (SXSW's unofficial activities use a wide variety of spaces, however, similar to Pop Montreal.)

Seligman explained that this financial backing shapes the festival's use of space and mandates collaboration with local community groups and bands.[21] Newport Folk musicians David Wax and Dom Flemons talked about similar experiences at other Canadian festivals. Wax spoke of the outreach and education at the Winnipeg Folk Festival, which is more heavily invested in music education than Pop Montreal:

> We had to do a mentorship program. Not everybody had to do it, but part of our contract was: "You have to come and spend the day with these young singer-songwriters, then help them, then they do a performance." You mentor them. It was amazing. It was like "Whoa, this is using us in a different way: as a resource." That's possible in Canada in a way that is hard to imagine in the US.

Comparing festivals, Wax noted that there's "an educational and collaborative aspect" to Canadian festivals, where there is a greater expectation for artists to stay longer and participate in workshops in order to build collaborations among musicians, create social networks across bands, and learn more about folk traditions. He sees Newport Folk slowly moving in that direction (and Joe Fletcher's experience with the Boys and Girls Club shows that there is more work to be done), though Wax notes that Newport only really requires one performance, whereas Canadian festivals require as many as five or six commitments. Recalling how he drew in other musicians to play songs with him at the Calgary Folk Festival, he says these different expectations give artists "the time and space to interact, talk to people, talk about collaborating, and have the time to actually practice something." He notes that Jay Sweet wants younger and more local musicians at the Newport Festival because, in part, they are more eager to stay through the festival, collaborate with other artists, and come onstage for the annual Sunday night finale.

Dom Flemons, from the Carolina Chocolate Drops, talked about forging interpersonal connections at these festivals too and, again, brought up funding:

> I always wonder: "Where's the money coming from?" It's always the big question. See, when it comes to the Canadian ones, they have all these government subsidies. When we went into Winnipeg for the first time, we were like "Oh my god." You could tell that the government was backing it. It was like: great hospitality, great stages, great sound, lots of people who were either volunteering or they were getting paid. You could tell it was done in a way that everyone was really happy with. You could see the difference.

Flemons went further than David Wax, criticizing corporate sponsorships from Newport's Dunkin' Donuts to retail home-appliance and hardware-behemoth Lowe's sponsoring Wilkesboro, North Carolina's, Merlefest. While being careful not to say large corporations are inherently evil, he pointed out that there are fewer community-directed expectations attached to their sponsorships. "We don't do that government subsidy sort of stuff in the US," Flemons added. "We'd rather spend it on the military." Instead, Lowe's and Miller Lite pursue their interests by imprinting the visual field with their corporate iconography, while the Canadian government expects musicians to work with community groups and nurture social + cultural resources for their investment.

Still, Flemons hoped more workshops were on the way at Newport, believing that "you really gotta have people who are interested in going to those. In Canada, people do. At the Winnipeg, Vancouver, Edmonton, and Calgary festivals, they go to the same format [as Newport did in its earlier incarnation] with workshops." David Wax echoed Flemons's point, although he wondered how much his imagination has exaggerated how Newport once was: he admits this image is partially fueled by a scene in Martin Scorsese's Bob Dylan documentary, *No Direction Home*, wherein Dylan is leading a topical song workshop, and the constant behind-the-scenes references artists are exposed to at Fort Adams undoubtedly nurture similar expectations loosely grounded in history. But Wax also compares Newport with his experience of collaborating with a

Haitian folk band at two Canadian folk festivals. "Because the money's from the government," he told me, "festival coordinators are more ambitious in booking different kinds of bands." Wax felt that Newport would have difficulty bringing in a band with little name recognition because corporations would be more willing to sponsor an event with known acts that will draw more festivalgoers and lend "cool" status via an affiliation with their brand.

Lamb, Mandelid, Nilsson, Seligman, Wax, and Flemons all point to how publicly provided economic resources of international events allow for a bolstering of local physical, social, and symbolic goods. These conversations provide a broader understanding of how American festivals could do more to nurture connections between musicians as well as between festivals and local communities, to deepen education about music, and to craft curious and unique urban experiences. It seems there is a lot that attendees and US festival organizers could learn from these comparisons.

((( )))

Looking at smaller, neighborhood festivals shows the same issues over placemaking, and festivalization writ small. David Wax also encouraged me to look into the Jamaica Plain Music Festival in his hometown of Boston, which suggests that there may be stronger ties between place, community, and event at smaller-scale local festivals. I met with the festival organizers in a grimy and dark Boston bar called the Brendan Behan Pub, where local musician Rick Berlin, talent buyer Shamus Moynihan, and marketing agent Charles McEnerney first held their weekly planning meetings for the festival. I spoke with them in May 2012 when they were prepping for their second event.

With Newport Folk Festival bands like My Morning Jacket playing over the sound system, I asked why these organizers were interested in starting a festival in the first place. McEnerney explained that there were limited opportunities for local musicians, and as a marketing agent he knew it was a tough time for them to get noticed. Jamaica Plain really has only one music venue, the Midway Café, where Moynihan books bands. Indicating the initial interest from potential performers, McEnerney continued: "We had over a hundred applicants for twenty-four slots." A contact at city hall greased the wheels, and the city eventually offered the use of what Berlin described as an "underutilized nearby park." Their small organizing committee ran a series of fund-raising events throughout the year, from BBQs to Neil Young tribute nights, in order to pay for the event. Keeping it free and nonprofit was of paramount importance. Berlin added that they also emphasized "keeping it a local thing, because we like that all the people in the audience didn't know all the bands, but they all knew everyone was each other's neighbor." Place identity mattered: bands had to have at least one member who lived in Jamaica Plain.

Moynihan talked about how inspired he has been by music festivals he has attended, but how he also knew he had to learn from their limitations. Once festivals reach a certain size, he said, they become "money-making machines" where artists expect greater compensation and attendees expect more services. Though he liked the Newport Folk Festival in the years before it went nonprofit, he felt like he was "on an assembly line being pushed through a process"; SXSW was "ten times worse." Instead, he wanted to make sure their event was modest and matched "the scale of the neighborhood."

When asked if they would turn the money down if they were ever approached by a major sponsor, Moynihan replied, "We already have!" The three men almost rolled their eyes in unison as Moynihan explained the offer: "They said, 'We'll give you X amount if you call it the *Our Company* Jamaica Plain Music Festival.'" The three were uninterested in either expanding dramatically or succumbing to corporate financial temptations. They refused to let their festival be used to help soften corporate images, even that of a supposedly benign alternative corporation like Whole Foods.

Instead, the three of them put together a worksheet entitled "15 Steps to Starting a Local Music Festival (during a bad economy)" and put it up on their website:

1. Form a small, strong, determined committee who want to see local music get attention it deserves.
2. Become a non-profit.
3. Organize small fundraisers leading up to the big day.

4. Create some buzz.
5. Organize regular events at local music venues.
6. Organize a Kickstarter campaign.
7. Ask a local music retailer to donate backline drums and amps.
8. Keep production costs low.
9. Ask musicians and performers to play for free to help get the festival off the ground.
10. Find an outdoor space you can utilize for free.
11. Do strategic, inexpensive marketing.
12. Seek sponsor dollars from local restaurants, cafes, retailers, education outlets, etc.
13. Keep it free.
14. Have food available on-site for sale.
15. Document the event.[22]

Though most of these tips are economically driven in nature (i.e., finding clever fund-raising techniques, making the event accessible to all), they also address spatial (e.g., using outdoor spaces), social + cultural (e.g., building coalitions, finding volunteers), and symbolic resources (e.g., strategic marketing, creating buzz) too.

((( )))

These stories about the Peace and Love Festival, Fête de la Musique, Øyafestival, Virada Cultural, Pop Montreal, the Calgary and Winnipeg Folk Festivals, and even the modest-sized Jamaica Plain Music Festival all trace an alternative path through our four resources, showing how festivals can work for people and places in ways that are less common for major US festivals. These differences are as important to recognize as the similarities. Newport, Nashville, and Austin's festivals all depend on a greater amount of private sponsorship, whereas the foreign examples are more likely to be funded by municipal, provincial, or federal funds (although there are exceptions—Peace and Love received much less than its other Scandinavian peers, and Seattle's Bumbershoot and Chicago's Blues Festival receive significant public funding).[23] Whereas the US festivals covered here are limited in access and spatial dimensions, the international festivals mentioned are more likely to be open to the public (save for the more confined citadel of Borlänge's Peace and Love). These US festivals have limited connections between musicians and in support of their local communities (although Nashville's CMA gives a great deal to local music education programs), but the international festivals are more likely to bolster local, even amateur, cultural endeavors. At the same time, international festivals have been rocked by the economic downturn and perhaps an oversaturation in the summer tourism market despite heavy governmental support, whereas American festivals have strategically used commercialization and corporate branding to keep their productions afloat.

The Right to the Locale

There is some connection between the call for a more liquid urban culture and Richard Sennett's 1970 book, *The Uses of Disorder*, which longs to return to the ideas of community and identity through the chaos of urban life, in opposition to the more cocooned suburban life. It is, however, a limited relation. Although Sennett indeed searches for a "better arrangement of social materials," in the end I must loop back to Henri Lefebvre to ground an ethos of culture and everyday life in the assets of urban place.[24] Lefebvre's 1968 book, *Le droit à la ville*, claims in its title and throughout its text that people have a "right to the city." He suggests that citizens should not only have access to the city's resources, but also collectively have a voice in how those resources are used to shape the lives of residents and visitors, and in what comprises the city fabric itself. When millions of dollars are launched at sports stadiums and millions in tax incentives are given to lure corporations back to cities— all high-stakes gambles that can potentially be added to the growing list of strategic urban policy mistakes—what is needed is a call for a more publicly accountable and representative urban culture, one based upon tracking the range of community resources, not a charge for conflict and anarchy.[25]

Festivals are not the only way to ensure this kind of city access, but if they were open, changeable, democratic spaces, they could serve as places for both tradition and experimentation, and could become a model for a more responsive use of community resources. Festivals are certainly popular enough to make such an attempt worth the effort, for it is precisely their wide popularity that might make possible what Lyn Lofland calls *locales*. The inverse of counterlocales, locales are places for a less scripted intermingling of a variety of individuals. Examples here could include small, neighborhood events like Jamaica Plain's Music Festival or Newport's BridgeFest, but also larger-scale events too. It is ironic that SXSW is the most market-driven, commercial event and yet is the most discordant and locale driven of the three, particularly in comparison with the citadel event at Newport. The allure of a potential "Clean Zone"—a counterlocale measure if ever there was one—must be strong. Still, the examples touched on in this book hold mixed results, and more research is needed on this very point.

What is more certain is how few studies on urban development encourage these sorts of ephemeral and temporary cultural events. Perhaps building buildings is hardwired in our cultural DNA. Experience-based urban development, however, is possible and, perhaps, better. A festivalized urban cultural policy can be founded upon interpersonal collaborations—between musicians and fans, honkytonk bartenders and festival organizers, venue owners and volunteers, visitors and locals. As festivals increasingly become strategies for urban stakeholders to compete in the market of places, the costs and benefits of festivalization must be assessed beyond economic terms.

From the buskers and riots and unofficial venues to the programmed spaces and corporate branding at Newport Folk, the CMA Fest, and SXSW, the festival serves as a microcosm of the city in ways that the stakeholders who call these moments their city's "signature event" cannot fully comprehend. On the one hand, the older logics of city development ought not be quickly applied in the age of urban culture and experiences—through big cultural infrastructure—but at the same time, festivalization must not produce tightly controlled counterlocales either. The tension between firm control and production of these festivalized spaces and the more entropic activities at the ground level is the critical struggle for understanding not just these events but urban culture writ large.

Encore
Toward a Sociology of Occasions

Divergent Perspectives, Many Motivations, One Event

As I talk with a former advertising representative during the 2013 Newport Folk Festival—the ad rep is telling me that he used to work with the
festival for the organic snack food company Clif Bar—a performer who
calls himself Father John Misty[1] begins his set onstage. Between songs,
Misty offers a running commentary on his own songs, the music of other
acts at the festival, and the very institution of Newport itself. Though he
starts off with self-deprecating irony—admitting that his first song does
not really qualify as "folk" music, he humorously proclaims: "Let the sa-
tanic Norwegian Death Metal commence!"—it is not long before he
launches into an extended lamentation. He stops in the middle of his
second song, "Funtimes in Babylon," to criticize another festival act:

> I want to say something. And it's not cute, and it's not fucking funny. It's
> not really meant for your entertainment. But, if you are making fuckin'
> millions off the artifice of some old-timey bullshit and you're wear-
> ing vests and fedoras and you have a huge platform and you've made a
> comfortable living for yourself and you have a couple of Priuses in the
> driveway.... You have a fucking responsibility to the music that you claim
> to play to say something that fucking matters. And give up this "me me
> me/I work at a coffee place" bullshit.

He concludes the speech by claiming that he was only invited to Newport because he is "a white guy with a beard who has some acoustic guitar on his album."

And this turns out to be just the beginning. He goes on to fulfill what he teasingly refers to as his childhood dream of "shitting all over a very important cultural institution" by questioning folk music's reception in contemporary culture and attacking the site sacralization of the fort itself: "It's crazy, man. People used to get blacklisted by their government for playing what was considered folk music. Now they are ushered into the upper tier of luxury and acceptance from the mainstream. And we have our folk festivals in stinking memorials to nationalistic imperialism." He continues by critiquing the corporate sponsorship of music—expressing an over-the-top faux relief that the festival is subsidized by Honest Tea rather than some other, more corporate brand—and even insults the audience directly: "Is this a camping thing or do you all go back to the yachts and get a good night's sleep?" He finally closes his set with a half-apologetic admission that he has been "preachy" and "antagonistic," yet each and every salvo has been met with gleeful cheers from an audience only eager for more.

Father John Misty's willingness to bite the proverbial hand seems like an attitude more familiar to rock 'n' roll, but his negative assessment of the earlier, Dunkin' Donuts incarnation of the festival echoes the viewpoints of many other folk musicians, and points to the now-familiar tension between music and the commercialization that seems to be necessary for its existence, at least at public festivals. It is also another reminder of the divergent perspectives and motivations among participants. This moment at Newport resonated with others in my research: seeing a SXSW volunteer curled up asleep on a folding chair while a conference panel continued to her left; or a few hours later in a beautiful room at St. David's Episcopal Church, seeing an Arkansas crooner named Adam Faucett singing passionately enough to keep the audience on the edges of their seats while the sound engineer struggled to hold his head up, working another long night at the soundboard.

This mixture of experiences may not be surprising, but it points to the difficulties of fully comprehending and analyzing a complex and adaptable sociological phenomenon that involves thousands of people. On the one hand, there are moments of cohesiveness—for example, for organizers who might rally around a certain vision of city marketing, or for audiences as they cycle through a particular spatial arrangement of activities. And yet, on the other hand, festivals can never wield complete control of the experiences and interactions of all participants. There are always incongruities and departures from the official narrative: from antagonistic or contrarian moments (e.g., attendees reacting to branding, locals bristling at the crowds, protesters picketing the event), to alternative activities that exist alongside official proceedings (e.g., the Fader Fort at SXSW or Lois Vaughan's BridgeFest), to simple juxtapositions wherein two different people have two very different experiences alongside each other (e.g., Misty and the Clif Bar representative), to people occupying different roles at the same event (e.g., the aspiring musician volunteering at SXSW). This is obviously not just a challenge for understanding festivals, of course. Any collective social event is a convergence of harmonious and conflicting motivations and perspectives, a knot of people's lives and experiences in contemporaneous activity. This book concluded with this very point.

For social scientists, however, coordinated activities like these—so central to placemaking in this study, but also to lived social activity in general—could be explained within a larger story of occasions. Occasions, in my opinion, can and should be a locus of sustained sociological study. As an encore, these additional pages address this puzzle, building on the preceding chapters to lay some groundwork for understanding events as foci for research. As such, I posit a few parting thoughts on moments by developing the frame of *patterns* and *resources* laid out in the introduction to (a) suggest looking at the dynamics of occasions I call *porosity*, *density*, and *turbulence* (illustrated by two familiar aspects of music festivals: alternative events and buskers) and (b) propose that occasions are a useful addition to sociological inquiry, as another social phenomenon that connects large-scale social forces and micro-level lived experiences, providing another link for understanding the multifaceted nature of social life through a tangible social phenomenon.

In so doing, this section aims to use the data in this book to refresh a conversation about a "sociology of occasions."

The Dynamics of Occasions

Occasions have been central to sociology, albeit implicitly so. Although there are several strands of sociology influencing my understanding of occasions, there is likely no more influential beginning to this focus of attention than Émile Durkheim's 1912 book, *The Elementary Forms of Religious Life*. Durkheim points to rites and rituals as flashes of charged sociality in which representations of the community are exchanged and the individual is sentimentally bound to the group. He mentions festivals as specific examples of "collective enthusiasm"—for instance, during the Crusades, the Renaissance, the Reformation, and the French Revolution.[2] Durkheimian anthropologist Radcliffe-Brown and his protégé, W. Lloyd Warner, whose *Yankee City* research informed this project, both maintained an interest in how ritual and ceremony shaped the collective sentiments of a community and inculcated solidarity. It is, however, Warner's master's and Ph.D. student (and research assistant when *Yankee City* was being prepared for publication) Erving Goffman who revised these themes further to broaden our view of social events and introduced a greater degree of sensitivity to variations within them.

Goffman's *Behavior in Public Places* drew from *Elementary Forms* and redirected sociology's attention from more elaborate religious events toward everyday interactions without sapping them of their relevance to both participants and social scientists. He writes of fleeting social moments replacing those onetime supernaturally infused rituals, and differentiates the *social occasion* from other, more common gatherings or situations. For Goffman, the social occasion is a

> wider social affair, undertaking, or event, bounded in regard to place and time and typically facilitated by fixed equipment; a social occasion provides the structuring social context in which many situations and their gatherings are likely to form, dissolve, and re-form, while a pattern of conduct tends to be recognized as the appropriate and (often) official or intended one.[3]

This definition pays acute attention to the forces giving these moments their structure, to how social occasions circumscribe many more minor interactions, as well as to their changing quality. This complex portrayal led to Goffman's 1967 book, *Interaction Ritual*, which makes an outright call for a *sociology of occasions*, explaining that events could be a "subject matter in their own right, analytically distinguished from neighboring areas, for example, social relationships, little groups, communication systems, and strategic interaction."[4] The radical nature of Goffman's claim should not be diminished by his mid-century gendered writing: he insisted that our studies are not of men and their moments, but rather of "moments and their men."[5]

Other sociologists from different perspectives have paid some attention to occasions, including George Herbert Mead, William I. Thomas, Harold Garfinkel, Guy Debord, Randall Collins, and Henri Lefebvre. But for now, an account of occasions—based on this book and through this limited lens—can be stated plainly. There are key stakeholders (e.g., municipal governments, nonprofits, trade organizations) within a particular social and geographic area (e.g., a block, neighborhood, or city) that can mobilize *resources* (e.g., funding, locations, local talent, and symbolic images) to create an occasion (e.g., a block party, a parade, or an Olympics) for a finite time period. Participating actors require more accomplices than they may ever meet in person, and everyone is bound together in a temporary but repeatable ballet of *patterned*, semi-organized activity that holds a shape and activates the intentions of its planners (e.g., to bring industry professionals to town, attract tourists, or raise visibility of a community), without ever being able to dictate each participant's motivations and interpretations of said events.

Pushing beyond the outline of patterns and resources articulated in this book, however, I would like to posit a set of three dynamics that could help guide our understanding of the processes of social activity in and around occasions: *porosity, density,* and *turbulence*. These dynamics pay special attention to the kinds of discordant moments like the one of Father John Misty at Newport: activities wherein participants asymmetrically "buy into" the event, traffic in competing intended and unintended meanings and "official" and "unofficial" statuses, and poach resources for their own purposes. Although these are perhaps unusual terms for the social sciences, they extend the theme of "liquid culture" from the conclusion, and in truth, their essence runs through much of the discourse on occasions, only some of which can be mentioned here.

An attention to these dynamics should not just help in understanding the mixture of activity in any given occasion, but also assist in comparing occasions more generally. They may also add to our comprehension of how symbolic, spatial, social + cultural, and economic resources flow through the three organizational patterns—citadel, core, and confetti—described in the introduction.

((( )))

As I have shown, festivals, in their design and enactment, behold a kind of fluidity of access. When thinking about occasions more generally, I call the degree of entrée and engagement common to Goffman's work on social situations *porosity*: regardless of the degree to which an occasion's activities are formal and planned, there will always be an amount of openness to whatever occurs within and around them.[6] Additionally, festivals specifically and occasions more generally have a kind of *density*—an idea from Randall Collins, who used an elaboration of the Durkheimian value of *social density*—which indicates the greater or lesser extent to which actors spend time in each other's physical co-presence: a quality of prolonged engagement in which participants maintain a degree of attention to and membership in an activity.[7] *Turbulence* is a third and altogether different quality, having to do with the range of harmonious or discordant activities and motivations occurring within and around a particular occasion. Like porosity and density, turbulence is inherently neither good nor bad, but it differs from them in addressing not just the access to moments and their shared co-presence but also their propensity for countervailing activity: what in Goffman's terms would be *in*appropriate, or *un*official activity.[8]

Although these dynamics are well suited for understanding occasions in general, let us build on this study of festivals to explain them. In brief: the *porosity* of the festival addresses the levels of regulation over resources arranged in patterns and the resultant accessibility of and to such temporary events; *density* concerns the space and time of festival activities, plotted spatially on a map and temporally in a schedule—i.e., whether spaces are small or large, or enclosed or open; whether events take place at day or night, during the week or on the weekend, concurrent

One of several signs at the perimeter of the CMA Fest indicating acceptable activities and the distribution of resources.

or consecutively, etc.; and *turbulence* has to do with the harmony or discord of activity in and around the festivals.

Some comparisons could be made across the cases mentioned in this book. Newport's Folk Festival and Borlänge's Peace and Love Festival serve as good examples of lower levels of porosity, with physical walls and spatial distances, whereas festivals like Fête de la Musique position free music on disparate street corners in a highly porous fashion. The low permeability of citadel-like events generally means less accessibility, and seems to result in lower levels of turbulence. Such low porosity often corresponds to a high density of experiences, packed within a confined space. Meanwhile, a confetti-patterned festival like SXSW allows for a greater variety of both unofficial and official participation, with a low density of activity and lots of turbulence. This turbulence could be indicated by the music activity seeping through chain-link fences of confetti festivals, allowing for a variety of uncontained activity—ones that even operate counter to the primary event itself. Somewhere in between lies the core-patterned festival, which in Nashville expresses itself through open honkytonk windows and doors and a somewhat monitored public sphere where police begrudgingly tolerate buskers and protesters.

With this quick sketch of patterns, resources, and dynamics in mind, a set of relationships could be mapped out. Tighter control of festival resources means lower porosity of the event, whereas less control over resources means greater access to those assets. The more impermeable these festivals are, the greater the control over the content itself. As porosity increases, from low levels in the citadel to high levels in the confetti pattern, organizers hold less jurisdiction over the landscape, leading

Boaters outside the 2012 Newport Folk Festival, listening to music for free while a park ranger observes.

	CITADEL	CORE	CONFETTI
POROSITY	Low	Medium	High
DENSITY	High	Medium	Low
TURBULENCE	Low	Medium	High

A simplification of occasion patterns and dynamics.

to greater turbulence. As festivals attempt to more tightly contain their activities by limiting or at least regulating participation, porosity and turbulence become major challenges. Sketching these relationships between festival patterns and these dynamics produces a deceptively tidy framework.

And yet, the reality is never so orderly. The Father John Misty story, for example, highlights a critique of the low-porosity, low-turbulence Newport Festival from its second-largest stage, challenging the symbolic resources of authenticity and questioning the meaning of the fort in a way that contrasts with other participants (for example, Jim James, who called Fort Adams "sacred ground"). Such discordance is common, and two familiar moments from my festival data may serve to illustrate these dynamics for greater comparability and generalizability: guerilla events and buskers.

First, there are the unofficial, shadow events. Founders and organizational figures like Jay Sweet (Newport Folk), Ed Benson (CMA), and Roland Swenson (SXSW) sought to limit activities around their occasions, yet individuals and groups appropriated assets for unofficial purposes. SXSW, arranged in the highly porous confetti pattern, presented the greatest challenges to organizers, who were interested in maintaining and controlling their brand. Because of its rather low density, SXSW could not book each venue and provide programming for every empty lot in the downtown Austin area, nor place a gate around the entirety of the central business district and, as such, had to develop strategies to curb unofficial activities from moving into those programming vacuums: notifying city inspectors of alternative events, discouraging artists from participating in them, and sending legal notices to groups that used the SXSW brand in their promotional materials. Despite these efforts, outside organizations still hold dozens of unofficial events, taking advantage precisely of the porous nature of the confetti pattern. Although the festival organizers saw guerilla events as detracting from the festival, many music fan attendees found the "Mardi Gras for hipsters" atmosphere to be a positive attribute and barely noticed the difference between official and unofficial events. A third viewpoint was held by music industry professionals, who saw an unintended benefit insofar as unofficial events deflected nonindustry people from the official showcases they needed to attend, as well as providing additional opportunities to see bands outside official events.

The core pattern of the CMA Fest became less porous with its recent move downtown, though clearly the nestling of official activities within Lower Broad's old honkytonks augments the overall experience. Although the musicians and locals understood the difference between the honkytonk singers and the acts on the Riverfront stage, most fans told me they didn't care—or even notice—that they were crossing an official/unofficial boundary. This was best evidenced by the fact that out-of-town festivalgoers rarely adapted to the local norms of tipping honkytonk performers. Festival organizers seemed more concerned with people selling illegal merchandise on the streets around the festival than in the alternative events themselves: unlike in Austin, these alternative events were more clearly value added for most participants.

And then there is the low porosity of the Newport Festival. Despite its fort-like pattern, organizers were still figuring out how to address BridgeFest, the alternative event planned outside its boundaries. Organizers of the grassroots local affair, though, hoped its activities would complement and augment rather than detract from or compete with the official jazz and folk festivals. Over its first few years, BridgeFest organizers developed a relationship with the Newport Festival organization, including hosting a "conversation" with festival founder George Wein and longtime producer Bob Jones in 2012. Moreover, current festival producer Jay Sweet expressed interest in being more involved with BridgeFest in the near future, which indicates some desire to syncopate the turbulence around the event with the events inside, and to decrease the density of activities, though he expressed wanting a stronger role in that relationship to maintain control of the brand.

A second example of porosity at festivals is buskers. Less porous occa-

A couple of buskers during the 2011 CMA Fest on Second Avenue, minutes before politely being asked to pack it up by the Metro Nashville Police.

sions provide an opportunity for this kind of social activity, and buskers often stand within and on the margins of the grounds at SXSW and the CMA Fest to play for tips from festivalgoers on their way to and from the events. Despite the sheer number of SXSW participants and the many additional opportunities to participate in alternative events, these folks are still there, who seem to range from eccentric locals (a man in a Lone Star flag cape and matching thong) to itinerant backpackers. In contrast, the core arrangement in Nashville allows the CMA to program Lower Broad spaces with a density of corporate-curated events and activities in specific zones of activity. Buskers, in this case, were uncontained but did not seem to last long before police came to disperse them so they would not detract from the official activities. Finally, there was Newport's citadel arrangement: a carefully coordinated, more condensed set of activities around the grounds of Fort Adams. Though this organization could be sterile, organizers incorporated buskers into the event to add the appearance of some measure of unfocused whimsy. Newport buskers weren't independent entrepreneurs, but *contained* entertainers. Sanctioned by the festival itself and even sponsored by a guitar manufacturer, these buskers—along with the Berklee College gospel choir and the What Cheer? Brigade—filled in between the formal acts onstage. The sponsored open-mic tent could be another example of *contained* turbulence. Comparable to SXSW's rather rowdy activity, there was a need to increase the turbulence in what some could argue was a more staid set of events at Fort Adams.

These two examples illustrate how one could gauge the activities of events relationally. Less containment and less density seem to create more opportunities for occasional turbulence. Turbulence is not chaos, however, nor is it a purely negative quality. Its costs and benefits depend upon one's position within the occasion. For festival organizers, a turbulent activity can be a drain on resources. On the other hand, turbulence provides a kind of richness to a less orderly, confettied event like SXSW, in which festivalgoers might not even notice the untidy nature of such activity, or might even see it as value added. Therefore, although there will always be struggles over unofficial activity, and over the definition of what should be legitimate and what should be prohibited in these areas, such activities can generate any number of interpretations. These dynamics demonstrate how organizers and participants use occasions. They even indicate some desire for a measure of dissonance or disorder.

A sociology of occasions, then, is based upon the idea that different patterns of social activity provide distinctive ways to access and distribute resources, and how they do so can be understood in terms of porosity, density, and turbulence. These dynamics provide a language for the struggles over the boundaries of occasions and the efforts to gain control of, or access to, economic, spatial, social + cultural, and symbolic resources.

The Betweenness of Occasions

Finally, one ought to consider how occasions sit within the larger sociological universe: as a part of what sociologists call the "meso-level" of society, the strata of our lives that links individual actions with the greater forces in our social worlds. Examining occasions in this way means understanding them as conduits that connect the experiences of individuals and our heterogeneous social activities with larger social institutions, processes, and histories.

Certainly, the research in this book was framed within a broader social and historical context—the transformation of the US economy and its effects on cities, the increasing importance of live performances to the music industry, and the rise of festivals as consumer experiences—and other macrosociological factors were touched on throughout, most notably recent urban redevelopment strategies, the rise of urban "quality of life" campaigns, and the 2008 economic downturn. Individual and group activities were then set within this landscape: how a loose community of Providence musicians was able to take advantage of the Newport Festival's post-2008 economic challenges and to gain greater notoriety through the event's newfound interest in regional music; how local Nashville organizations built a signature event that merged with a city trademark to unseat the city's old Athens of the South brand; and how musicians weave through a confetti of SXSW events to build a career. The festival, as a moment of collaborative meaning making, is a junction point of both those larger forces and more local actions, tying the creative activities of individuals and the constraining and empowering forces of social structures: as a platform for urban economic development, cultural careers, and performances, and organic and corporate-stylized symbolic landscapes, for example.

Such linking of the micro and macro levels of social life makes the occasion what sociologists call a *mesostructure*. Like other social foci in the same layer of social thought—roles, groups, social movements, networks, and organizations—occasions incorporate multiple dimensions, which makes them useful tools for understanding social life. I see occasions harmonizing with other mesostructures, and four main facets to their utility.[9]

1. The aforementioned micro-macro link serves a *gap-bridging function*.[10] In this spirit, looking at occasions is a good way to avoid over-romanticizing "micro vs. macro" and "agency vs. structure" arguments to instead examine how structural and historical issues are funneled to individuals through social interactions and activities and, conversely, how actions within occasions potentially shape bigger organizational and historical change.

2. Occasions are like roles, groups, and organizations in their *universality*. Randall Collins, when asking rhetorically, "What *isn't* a ritual?" admits that he is more apt to see rituals everywhere rather than seeing them as a limited phenomenon.[11] By the same token, occasions could be described similarly: there is some true applicable power in the generalizability of occasions.

3. Akin to social movements, groups, and organizations, occasions are *scalable* and *mutable*. There can be big occasions and small ones, complex and simple ones. Most importantly, the resources, patterns, and dynamics outlined in this research could be used to analyze them regardless of their sizes and shapes.

4. Like groups and networks, but unlike roles and social movements, occasions nest. Occasions sit within other occasions, with smaller ones reproducing some of the qualities of the bigger, and vice versa.

In sum: theoretically, occasions bridge the constructed dichotomies of social analysis; substantively, they allow scholars to leap across diverse phenomena; analytically, occasions are highly dynamic and versatile; and conceptually, they allow researchers not just to compare across cases but also to telescope in and out of particular experiences in and around these moments.

And yet, Goffman wrote that occasions should be "analytically distinguished" from other sociological foci like "social relationships, little groups, communication systems, and strategic interaction."[12] I suspect that what gives occasions a more distinctive quality is what was discussed at the outset: their ability to encompass and activate multiple motivations and positions. The dynamics of porosity, density, and turbulence indicate that meaning and experience might vary at different levels of and proximity to diverse social activity, and comparisons of smaller experiences within larger occasions. Turbulence, perhaps in particular, shows the vitality of occasions. One could even argue that multiple perspectives are required for such large-scale social phenomena to occur at all. A sociology of occasions in this sense—as dynamic, unfocused, richly social products of many actors who may never meet, and this as unlikely to produce solidarity among the wide array of participants— offers a unique window into our social worlds.[13]

((( )))

Why should one be concerned about occasions as meso-level social life? I see at least two reasons. First, these structures have a purpose for the practice of sociology. Neil Smelser's *Problematics of Sociology* notes that this is the "most vague" level of sociological analysis, and I hope that the above framework is a step in the direction of envisioning occasions as useful tools for sociological analysis. They might be unique, but occasions are also ubiquitous and consequently allow for connections across a range of sociological studies. Examples abound, offering an eruption of comparisons: religious and cultural holidays like St. Patrick's Day, Mardi Gras, or *Día de los Muertos*;[14] rites of passage like Mexican *quinceañeras*, Filipino debutante balls, cotillions, bar and bat mitzvahs, collegiate graduations, or New Orleans jazz funerals;[15] community gatherings like neighborhood block parties and multifamily garage sales, or large county fairs;[16] culture- or identity-based group outings like the Puerto Rican Day Parade or Pride;[17] political events like marches, protests, picket lines, and strikes;[18] community-building spaghetti dinners at the VFW, 5K fundraiser runs, and barn raisings;[19] individual and small-group activities like street performances and funeral processions;[20] illegal activities akin to back-alley drug deals and mass riots;[21] cultural events like art walks and "smart mobs";[22] large organization undertakings like annual conferences and conventions;[23] and more commercial occasions such as restaurant weeks, sporting events, and farmers' and flea markets, grand openings, and everything-must-go closing sales.[24] The connections and comparisons across these studies are well beyond the scope of this encore, but I hope to take them on in the near future.

There is a secondary value to mesostructures such as occasions, too. Smelser notes that society needs mesostructures. He finds an "undeniable decline" in the significance of extended families, churches, and similar associations, leading to a "crisis at the meso-level of social organization" that serves as our "most problematic feature of society."[25] In his view, these social forms hold a civic importance in addition to their value to the social sciences. Within an article entitled "The Sociology of the Local," Gary Alan Fine explains that mesosociological structures are useful in everyday life because they serve as "both a stage and a lens": a stage occupied by meaningful exchanges and also a lens for people to understand "typifications of groups, gatherings, or publics" and "establish boundaries and divisions."[26] Mumford notes that urban culture itself is "the stage and the drama" for the rituals of our communities.[27] Indeed, the activities in and around these festival patterns work as places for various stakeholders and outsiders to struggle over resources, and more generally as a prism through which participants understand the place and culture of Music City.

David Maines summarizes both contributions: mesostructure works "as the arena in which people carry out activity and as a sociological focus for research and inquiry."[28] I believe that occasions serve both purposes. And, furthermore, I believe that a perspective based upon patterns, resources, and the dynamics of porosity, density, and turbulence may help in the effort to better understand and compare moments of similarly heightened social interaction. For sociologists, more examples are needed to illustrate how occasions can be sites wherein actors from local organizations, communities, and corporations come together; where these groups varyingly consume, distribute, and take advantage of resources through heightened moments of sociality; and where collective activities and individual identities are shaped. And society needs to understand how these occasions can be better used for collective purposes.

Appendix A
The Lineup (Methodological Note and List of Interviewees)

Before offering a detailed list of the people who were interviewed for this book, a few words are needed to explain the relevance of using their real names.

Overall, *Music/City* draws on data collected from 110 formal interviews with key stakeholders around the idea of urban culture, dozens of unstructured interviews with festival participants, and hundreds of hours of observations over seven years. Midway through my research I was confronted with very real methodological problems of how to tell this story within the confines of the sociological convention of omitting or obscuring key markers that might identify participants. Could I hide Nashville as "a southern city well known for a certain genre of music" or Newport as "an elite northeastern historical harbor town with two music festivals"? And, with regard to my interviewees: Should I obscure the names of sitting mayors, festival producers and impresarios, or headlining performers? Both strategies would limit deeper understandings of particular strategies and activities in and around these events.

Lending anonymity is traditionally used in social research to assure respondents that they can participate without fear of repercussion. Confidentiality—collecting identifying information but making an effort to ensure that no one outside a research team knows the identity of respondents—is such a concern that many scholars have refashioned cities themselves with new names like "Yankee City" and "Middletown." And yet, when detailing the specific places and events in this book, assuring confidentiality to respondents—which would require not just new names but perhaps inserting them into different positions in and around festivals or "placing" them within different or unrecognizable social contexts—would have undermined the value of much of this book's information. The data used here are clearly relevant, as they relate specifically to understanding Newport, Nashville, and Austin as Music Cities, and interviewees' perspectives on cultural production are relevant with regard to the particular maneuverings of the particular people who actively create these festivals.

In several instances, including those in which respondents' comments were less consequential to the analysis, I used only a pseudonym without a surname. This was the case for several festivalgoers, volunteers, locals, and some passersby (e.g., Katy, Thomas, and Josh in chapter 2; Jay, Bill, Pete, Sarah, and Traci in chapter 3; Isabella, Ben, and Tina in chapter 4). But for the majority of the respondents, I wanted to use people's real names and felt that doing so would improve the quality of the research.

Although pseudonyms are the norm in qualitative research, a few scholars have recently questioned their value. Mitchell Duneier's *Sidewalk* serves as the most commonly cited example, wherein he used respondents' real names to vouchsafe the veracity of the data (1999: 348; see also Marwell 2007). Guenther details the complexities of using real names and suggests that it might be worthwhile so long as analytic rigor is maintained without posing significant harm to research subjects (2009). I felt that using real names in this case did not pose substantial risk, especially since most informants in *Music/City* were used to being interviewed and were not as disadvantaged as, for example, Duneier's homeless sidewalk vendors. In fact, most respondents were very powerful women and men in their political and cultural spheres. Additionally, I believed, like Duneier, that using real names would increase accountability on the part of respondents, since they then held a vested interest in providing me with accurate data. This required a greater effort to assure respondents as to the value and validity of the research at the beginning of our interviews and a heightened level of accountability from both researcher and participants throughout the process, up to and including a final draft.

Despite believing that people's actual identities could help both lay and scholarly readers understand my analysis, I still offered participants the chance to use a pseudonym to protect their identities. In only one case did an interviewee take the opportunity at the outset: the manager of a major artist who did not want to attract attention to his client ("Fred," quoted in chapter 1). In fact, most of the people I interviewed—as people who have built their names and identities in media, politics, or the music industry—expressed disappointment when I merely introduced the idea of anonymity at the time of our initial interview. Almost everyone had some experience with journalists, was comfortable in the interview setting, and hoped to be quoted "on the record."

Although most participants had a great deal of familiarity with the media, there are important methodological differences between media journalists and the ethnographic method of interviewing. The process here required multiple conversations, and due to the annual rhythm of festivals, they were often years apart. Just as with my previous book, *The Tour Guide*, after interviews and observations I followed up with each interviewee to review the data and requested that they sign an additional waiver indicating that they had reviewed the materials as presented and permitted my use of their real name in future publications. This was the most important part of the process regarding the use of real names.

Accustomed to journalists, who seldom return to a field site, take only days or weeks to craft their final products, and rarely if ever review drafts pre-publication, respondents were often surprised when I contacted them again. Most were puzzled at the opportunity to revisit what they had said in interviews, but were happy to review the sections in which they were presented. In a few cases, interviewees' perspectives changed slightly, usually because years had passed since our initial contact, and they were able to offer new information. Such a process not only assured accountability for me as a researcher, it also allowed me to affirm and clarify details. Only one respondent was interested in reverting to a pseudonym at this final stage: a woman who was concerned that her opinions might incur negative attention from South by Southwest organizers ("Sofia," quoted in chapter 4). She wanted her perspective included, but was concerned that the festival might target her new business partners, who still work in the cultural and music industries. In this case, as well as

Fred's, I felt comfortable including their interview data even with pseudonyms, so long as I indicated in the text why they did not want their real names to be included.

There is an important caveat to this issue of confidentiality, however. When I first began collecting these data in 2006, most of the interviewees in and around the CMA Fest granted me access contingent on complete confidentiality under normal research protocols. But with my growing interest in using real names, I contacted them after those initial interviews during follow-up visits to Nashville in 2012 and 2013 with new IRB approval from the University of Massachusetts–Amherst. In those visits, and in a few cases via email when in-person meetings could not be arranged, I asked that they opt to participate in this research in the same fashion as everyone else: signing a new wavier stating that they had reviewed the materials as presented and granting me permission to use their real names, just as I had asked of respondents in Newport and Austin. This change allowed for a continuity of presenting these data across all settings.

Finally, I should mention that I interviewed many more people than are mentioned in the book. Many lent critical background information, and perhaps most importantly reinforced data from other interviews that allowed me to make confident claims. Stories from bloggers, venue owners, reporters, gallery owners, fiddle makers, radio DJs, and independent radio promoters provided deeper understandings of the social world of music festivals, but could not be included in the interest of space. Some of these data could provide additional ways of understanding festival culture: music bloggers could have lent a better understanding of new media's role in archiving temporary moments, and a focus on local craftsmen could illustrate how non-musicians use festivals for their own gains. It is my hope that these gaps will be filled by other researchers.

Of the over 110 people interviewed, the following are the 64 named sources in the book.

Newport and Providence, Rhode Island

Debbie Bailey, Boys and Girls Clubs of Newport County
Cady Drell, WERS Radio promotions director

Kathryn Farrington, vice president of marketing for the Newport County Convention and Visitors Bureau

Dom Flemons, singer-songwriter for the Grammy Award–winning Carolina Chocolate Drops until 2013, when he embarked on his solo career

Joe Fletcher, singer-songwriter

Jim Gillis, arts and culture reporter for the *Newport Daily News* from 1980 to 2013

John Hirschboeck, board member of the Newport Arts and Cultural Alliance of Newport County

David Lamb, singer-songwriter for Brown Bird

Edward Lavallee, Newport city manager (2005–2012) and Venice, FL, city manager (2012–present)

Didi Lorillard, Newport socialite and daughter of Newport Jazz Festival founders Elaine and Louis Lorillard

Cris Offenberg, board member of the Newport Arts and Cultural Alliance of Newport County

Scott Pingeton, organizer of the "Newport Nightcap" and producer of a benefit album, *Long Distance Salvation*

Jim Quinn, Newport Blues Café owner

Frank Shea, executive director, Olneyville Housing Corporation

Betsy Siggins, founder and director of the New England Folk Music Archives

Jody Sullivan, executive director of the Newport County Chamber of Commerce

MorganEve Swain, singer-songwriter for Brown Bird

Jay Sweet, managing director of the Newport Folk Festival

Lois Vaughan, pianist and BridgeFest founder

David Wax, singer-songwriter for the David Wax Museum

George Wein, founder of Newport Jazz and Folk Festival

Nashville, Tennessee

Ed Benson, CMA executive director (1992–2005) and chief strategic officer (2005–2008)

Terry Clements, vice president of the Nashville Convention and Visitors Bureau

Karl Dean, mayor of Nashville (2007–present)

Jim Foglesong, president of Dot, MCA, Capitol, and ABC Records, and
    Country Music Hall of Fame inductee
Kim Fowler, independent label executive
Joe Galante, chairman of Sony BMG Nashville
Honey Hopkins, director of the Music City Music Council
Buddy Killen, Grand Ole Opry bassist, songwriter, and producer, and Country
    Music Hall of Fame inductee
Travis Mann, singer-songwriter of the Travis Mann Band
Todd Mayo, cofounder of *Music City Roots*
Alan Mayor, photographer
Molly Nagel, independent label executive
Mike Neal, Nashville Chamber of Commerce president and CEO
    (2002–2006), Tulsa Regional Chamber president and CEO
    (2006–present)
Wendy Pearl, CMA vice president of communications
Ronnie Pugh, author and former Country Music Hall of Fame historian
Jonah Rabinowitz, executive director of the W. O. Smith Music School
Kerrigan Skelly, pastor at Pinpoint Evangelism
Hazel Smith, country music historian, television, and radio host. For seven
    years, Smith hosted a Country Music Television show called *Southern
    Fried Flicks*, in which she hosted folks like Wynonna Judd, Brad Paisley,
    Garth Brooks, Alison Krauss, and George Jones in her kitchen for
    conversation and a movie.
Jeff Walker, CEO/president of AristoMedia Group and CMA board member
John Walker, cofounder of *Music City Roots*

Austin, Texas

Allen Chen, editor-in-chief of Austinist
Ronda Chollock, AAA format radio promotions for independent label artists
Erik Courson, indie label A&R rep
Justin Gressley, college radio promotions at Advanced Alternative Media, now
    project manager at Domino Records
Lila Johnson, director of outreach and marketing communications at SIMS
    Foundation
Brendan Leith, talent booker, Iron Horse Entertainment Group

Dani Linnetz, singer-songwriter

Sofia, pseudonym for an events promoter

Roland Swenson, cofounder and managing director of SXSW

Mike Watt, bass player for the Minutemen and the Stooges

Will Wynn, mayor of Austin (2003–2009)

From Places Here and There

Rick Berlin, musician and cofounder of the Jamaica Plain Music Festival

Fred, pseudonym of a manager for a top-tier musician

Birgit Hedkvist, Borlänge councilwoman

Birgitte Mandelid, head of marketing at Øyafestival

Charles McEnerney, principal and founder of Layers Marketing and cofounder of the Jamaica Plain Music Festival

Erin McKeown, singer-songwriter and frequent NPR contributor

Shamus Moynihan, talent buyer at the Midway Café and cofounder of the Jamaica Plain Music Festival

Jimi Nilsson, geographer at Uppsala University

Dan Seligman, cofounder and managing director for Pop Montreal

Charles Thompson (aka Frank Black, Black Francis), singer-songwriter, the Pixies and Frank Black and the Catholics

Kristin Thomson, cofounder of Future of Music Coalition

Tom Weyman, label owner and manager of Supply and Demand Music, cofounder of the Columbus Cooperative, talent buyer for the Columbus Theatre, and Brown Bird manager

Appendix B
Music City Set List

"The Whole of the Moon," the Waterboys

"Mabel Grey," Brown Bird

"Too Many Doors," Joe Fletcher and the Wrong Reasons

"Rye Whiskey," Frank Fairfield

"Trouble in Your Mind," Carolina Chocolate Drops

"Heartbreak Hotel," Elvis Presley

"Boondocks," Little Big Town

"This Is Country Music," Brad Paisley

"Save a Horse (Ride a Cowboy)," Big and Rich

"Baggage Claim," Miranda Lambert

"Down on the Street," the Stooges

"Blunderbuss," Jack White

"Mic Tester," Northern State

"Going Down the Road Feeling Bad," Woody Guthrie

NOTES

Introduction

1. While early European festivals would highlight role reversals, corporate festivals are more one dimensional, and unlikely places of catharsis (Bakhtin 1984).

2. Other research on music examines the recording and radio industries (Ahlkvist and Faulkner 2002), musician-audience interactions (Becker 1951), digital piracy (Marshall 2004), consumption and status (Hennion 2001), and authenticity (Peterson 1997; Grazian 2003).

3. Eighty-one percent of all outdoor arts festivals have music as a component—as compared with crafts (67%), dance (42%), and film (8%)—and festivals with music as its primary focus are the most common (22%) (Rosenstein 2010: 9).

4. Rural areas exploit their place-based musical heritages too: Virginia promotes a 300-mile stretch of Blue Ridge Mountain road called the Crooked Road as a "Heritage Music Trail" (Wildman 2011). Comparisons could be made with film festivals, but Tribeca, Park City, Soho, and Venice aren't tied to a particular film genre.

5. There are certainly a few touring festivals, like the Vans Warped Tour or Lollapalooza. There are also subcultural genres and scenes that are certainly emplaced but transcend locale as well: Deadheads, raves, and goth scenes are translocal (see Gardner 2004; Bennett and Peterson 2004).

6. Although it is difficult to adequately measure the geography of musicians (mostly due to only being able to glean employment numbers from Census data), Nashville was not in the top five locations of musicians in 1970 (Florida and Jackson 2009: 15).

7. Chicago and New Orleans have rich musical heritages, studied by Grazian (2003), and Gotham (2007), both of whom spend some time on festivals.

8. Second Tier Cities (STCs) "are spatially distinct areas of economic activity where a specialized set of trade-oriented industries takes root and flourishes," providing "relatively good" jobs that are more stable over time and across income levels and are more responsive to political change (Markusen, Lee, and DiGiovanna 1999: 12; see also Sassen 1991; Currid-Halkett and Stolarick 2011). There are other factors to consider, like population, major universities, and transportation hubs. The aforementioned NEA study also found that 77% of outdoor festivals were in towns with less than 250,000, and only 17% in cities with a population over half a million (Rosenstein 2010: 11).

9. Habermas describes church gatherings, rock concerts, interactions in bars and cafés, and sidewalk interactions as similar moments of the public sphere that could
allow for democratic public discourse (1996: 374).

10. Becker (my emphasis, 2008 [1982]: x, 1, 4). He makes a call for complexity and
richness over generalizability (xix).

11. Two other significant inspirations: Halle and Tiso's study of New York's Chelsea art
district is a multidimensional examination of the perspectives of gallery owners,
artists, audiences, and even the art objects themselves (2014); DeNora's studies of
music point to their "contexts of use," claiming that "we have very little sense of
how music features within social process and next to no data on how real people
actually press music into action in particular social spaces and temporal settings"
(2000: x).

12. Specifically, I attended the 2007, 2011, 2012, and 2013 Newport Folk Festival; the
2006, 2009, and 2012 Country Music Association Music Festival; and the 2007,
2008, 2009, 2011, and 2012 South by Southwest Music Festival. In addition, I performed at SXSW in 2008, was given a SXSW Media Pass in 2011, and received a
Staff Pass for the Newport Folk Festival in 2012.

13. See Stoller 2001, Wacquant 2003, and Wynn 2011.

14. The Austin and Newport surveys were administered in 2007, and the Nashville
data were collected in 2008. These surveys were done with the assistance of one
or two local graduate and undergraduate students, who, alongside the author, interviewed festivalgoers and locals in public spaces in and around festivals. These
data improved my confidence in making claims throughout the book, although a
forthcoming article will provide greater depth.

15. Häussermann and Siebel 1993.

16. Twenty-six percent of music festivals pay their artists (as compared with 2% of arts
and crafts festivals and 4% of visual arts festivals), and 39% of music festivals have
expenses over $100,000 (as compared with 12% of arts and crafts festivals and 18%
of visual arts festivals) (Rosenstein 2010: 37, 42–43). Nonprofits organize 80% of
festivals (ibid.: 41).

17. Lefebvre sees social space as encompassing relationships and interactions, offering
opportunities for order and disorder and "permitting fresh actions to occur, while
suggesting others and prohibiting yet others" (1991: 73).

18. Pearson 1987: 107.

19. Rosenstein 2010: 25.

20. See Ravenscroft and Matteucci 2003. Gotham uses Lefebvre and David Harvey's
work to identify how the physical environment can be a resource or an impediment to capital investment and accumulation (2009).

21. This is an oversimplification of very complex and interconnected concepts, but it is a conflation that Bourdieu himself periodically made (1984, 1985) and is more akin to Lefebvre's idea of multidimensional social space (1991; see also Soja 1996).

22. Again, there is a connection that could be made with Bourdieu's symbolic capital (1984).

23. Comaroff and Comaroff 2009, Grams 2010, Markusen 2004, and Verlegh 2010.

24. Suttles 1984.

25. Evans 2003 and Hitters 2007.

26. The 2010 New England population is fourteen million and, if you add the New York City Metropolitan Statistical Area's twenty million, this is a fair estimation.

27. Weber writes that "it is necessary for the sociologist to formulate pure ideal types of the corresponding forms of action which in each case involve the highest possible degree of logical integration by virtue of their complete adequacy on the level of meaning. But precisely because this is true, it is probably seldom if ever that a real phenomenon can be found which corresponds exactly to one of these ideally constructed pure types" (1978: 20). See also Ruth Benedict's classic *Patterns of Culture* (1934).

28. Technically and historically, a citadel is part of a walled fortress surrounding a city. Urban sociologists also used the idea of the citadel to explain spatial concentrations of wealth and power (Marcuse and van Kempen 2002).

29. *Amenities* are resources for "all firms as well as citizens in the area. They often enhance the local distinctiveness (of architecture or a waterfront) by improving the locality, rather than just making it cheaper for one business," including natural resources (e.g., water, climate, etc.), built resources (e.g., restaurants, museums, libraries, opera houses, etc.), social resources (e.g., diverse populations, talented residents, etc.), and ideological resources (e.g., tolerance, "cultured" populations, diversity of lifestyles, etc.) (Clark 2003: 107–11).

Chapter One

1. Shackelford 1978.

2. Sisario 2009.

3. Weber 1978.

4. Logan and Molotch 1987 and Molotch 1996, 1999.

5. Jonas and Wilson 1999.

6. The story of deindustrialization and the rise of postindustrial cities has been chronicled in many different ways (see Garreau 1991; Sassen 1994).

7. Zukin 1989: 40–41.

8. Lloyd and Clark 2001.

9. Eisenschitz 2010 and O'Connor and Wynne 1995.

10. Grazian 2004; see also Crawford 1995; Hannigan 1998; Judd 1999; Lash and Urry 1994.

11. Less optimistic assessments of cities abound, including Sharkey 2013 and Sampson 2012, which detail how inequalities persist and are even exacerbated by these recent changes.

12. Florida 2002: 166.

13. Lloyd 2005 and Montgomery 2005; see also Florida 2013. Glaeser questions Florida's "gay index" and suggests that it is likely more a product of education than of homosexuality or any particular bohemian lifestyle (2005).

14. Storper 2013: 14–31, 181–82.

15. Corporations create cities "in their own image" (Mumford 1966: 144, 191, 194–95), and "internalize market culture" (Zukin 1991: 7).

16. A *brand* is a product or a service that is "made distinctive by its positioning relative to the competition and by its personality, which comprises a unique combination of functional attributes and symbolic values" (Hankinson and Cowking 1993: 10). In the industrial era, chambers of commerce in cities from Atlanta to Birmingham, UK, attempted to attract industry by promoting their pleasant workforces and cleaner air (Ward 1998: 198–200).

17. See Molotch, Freudenburg, and Paulsen 2000: 793, and Lee's description of a "habitus of location" (1997: 132; see Kearns and Philo 1993). Hannigan finds three interrelated dimensions to city branding: instant recognition, comfort and certainty, and an identifiable place as the designated focus for consumption (2002: 187).

18. Whereas "Big Apple" was an older cultural image with unclear origins and was revived by the city's CVB, the strategic branding of "I♥NY" played a huge role in tourism and promotion (Greenberg 2009).

19. Connolly and Krueger 2006: 4; see also *Bloomberg BusinessWeek* 2010.

20. Future of Music Coalition 2012. The study notes that 42% of respondents report receiving no income from live performances either.

21. See Peterson and Berger 1996 and Lopes 1992.

22. An Exxon geophysicist adapted sound-wave technology for oil prospecting to invent Auto-Tune. The software, initially designed to seamlessly adjust performances to a particular key, was transformed into a desired aesthetic for musicians. Unaltered digital and live performances are increasingly rare: sound engineers can add slight errors to make a song sound more authentic on CD, and there is now a "live" version so a singer can still deliver a live performance and have his or her voice auto-corrected in real time.

23. By 2007, thirty-six million Americans (27% of Internet users) downloaded music or video illegally, and big record companies lost significant power outside their ability to find and promote superstar-level musicians (see Madden and Rainie 2005).

24. Licensing opportunities range from television shows, commercials, and films to new venues, like videogames and cellphone ringtones. A song placed on primetime television can net a band $5,000 to $50,000. On performance rights and copyright laws, see Krasilovsky, Gross, and Shemel 2003.

25. By 2005, over 80% of recorded music was produced by four labels—EMI, Warner Music Group, Sony BMG, and Universal Music Group—in a process that mirrored the overall consolidation of the cultural industries at the same period (Dowd 2004). The 1980s saw fifty albums sell over six million copies, whereas only three albums sold more than two million copies in 2011. As digital sales rose, physical sales declined: album sales dropped from 2000's 785 million to 2011's 330 million (Moscaritolo 2012; Hracs 2012).

26. For a more detailed model of this system, see Scott 1999.

27. Including the American Federation of Musicians union and the Screen Actors Guild–American Federation of Television and Radio Artists union, the Recording Academy, the American Association of Independent Music, and SoundExchange.

28. Bertoni 2012. Also, *Billboard* claims that Spotify drove a 75% bump in streaming revenue in 2013 (Adegoke 2014).

29. Krukowski 2012.

30. Calculating compensation from these services can be mind-boggling (Macias 2012; Samson 2011; Abebe 2012). Pandora's founder responded to critics by claiming their service can be a "meaningful" revenue stream for artists, reporting that Pandora was expected to pay 2,000 artists over $10,000 in 2012 and that top-tier musicians can make up to $3 million (Westergren 2012). SoundExchange (a nonprofit) attempts to improve this new uneven digital landscape by collecting and distributing royalties from new media.

31. Christman 2013.

32. Mortimer, Nosko, and Sorensen also find that smaller acts have seen a smaller decline in record sales and greater concert revenues (2012: 4).

33. Dekel 2010.

34. Even at a high-water mark of recorded-music consolidation, the 1980s saw a small "indie" community of punk bands like the Pixies, Sonic Youth, and the Minutemen use zines, college radio, a loose network of friends' couches, and a little bit of money from smaller labels like SST to leave an indelible mark on American culture with little commercial label and radio support (Azarrad 2001).

35. Kafka 2003.

36. Byrne 2012: 207.

37. Chmielewski, Fritz, and Lewis 2010.

38. See Andrews 2009, Seabrook 2009, and Ratliff 2011. *Billboard*, however, reported that so-called 360° deals did not live up to their promise, and dragged down Live Nation profits (Peoples 2010).

39. Not all CVBs are "quasi-governmental entities," but are independent nonprofit organizations funded from hotel taxes.

40. Frith 2001: 45–46.

41. Morton 2008: 85.

42. The director of the Seattle Mayor's Office of Film + Music said the growth of the city's music scene "happened in spite of the city. The city wasn't doing anything to get behind it, and I don't think the industry even understood how the city as a government could help" (Johnson 2005).

43. Richards and Wilson quoted in Hitters 2007: 283; see also Waterman 1998: 59.

44. Rosenstein 2010: 37, 42–43.

45. Early radio lured advertisers away from magazines and newspapers, hosting shows like the *Maxwell House Hour* and the *General Motors Family Party*, often explicitly controlling content, and independent stations followed suit even to the point of a musician taking on a particular sponsored persona (Peterson 1997: 120–22, 128). Companies would sponsor touring bands by booking gigs and paying for expenses.

46. Rosenstein 2010: 37.

47. Research indicates that corporate sponsorship of arts festivals can constrain festival policies (Quinn 1996), or create "performance[s] for money" (Greenwood 1989: 178).

48. Rosenstein 2010: 34.

49. Knopper 2012.

50. Stinchcombe 1965.

51. Durkheim 1966: 488–96.

52. Warner 1959: 107. There is a close connection between cultural events, place, and symbolism, as well as "civil rights marches in southern cities, women's marches to 'Take Back the Night' or win abortion rights, and Gay and Lesbian Pride parades in major cities," which stake claims on public space (Hayden 1997: 38).

53. Woronkowicz et al. 2012.

54. See Delaney 2003 to understand the criticisms over sporting arenas, and Marwell 2007 for a community response to redevelopment in Brooklyn, New York.

55. *Cultural policy* is a focus on the levels of the cultural worker, commercial firms, nonprofits, public cultural institutions, educational institutions, government agencies, international organizations, and consumers (Throsby 2010: 23–24).

Chapter Two

1. Morton 2008: 81.
2. Myers 2010.
3. Wein notes in his autobiography that he didn't hear any complaints from the folk community about the organization turning for-profit (2003: 232, 447–49).
4. Pareles 1998.
5. The Jazz Festival lineup also diversified, including funk and rock acts through the '60s.
6. Szwed claims the axe story is apocryphal (2010: 354).
7. See Cohen 2008: 161, 209. Contra to the belief in an "authenticity" in folk, Lomax crafted folk music paragon Huddie "Lead Belly" Ledbetter (who first recorded, among dozens of folk standards, "Goodnight Irene") as an authentic, southern, "raw Negro" by forcing him to perform in overalls and to sing imperfectly (Byrne 2012: 91).
8. Pennell 2002.
9. In 1960, Elaine Lorillard and Charles Mingus organized the "Rebel Jazz Festival," a rogue, counter-festival critiquing the commercialization of the Jazz Festival and, in Nat Hentoff's estimation, its racism. Lorillard was also suing the board for having been voted off it (Cohen 2008: 93).
10. On the relationship between folk music and the civil rights movement, see Roy 2010.
11. Wein 2003: 192.
12. The Lorillard fortune, interestingly, came from a line of several tobacco brands, including Newport and not including KOOL.
13. Evans 1997.
14. Ratliff 2007. Shields aimed to exploit small city brands: "When you think about Monte Carlo, Jackson Hole, Nantucket, Newport, there's brand in the names already" (ibid.).
15. Ratliff 2009. Wein also remained unpaid (Massimo 2009).
16. Sisario 2009; see also G. Smith 2011.
17. Klepper 2012.
18. There are heavy metal and noise rock scenes in Providence as well.
19. See Zafirau 2008. This is slightly different from Goffman's *impression management* (1959) due to its fusion of status and social capital in the cultural industries.
20. Szwed 2010: 349–50. Sweet did scout bands at unofficial and official SXSW events.
21. WMVY 92.7FM radio interview, Friday, August 4, 2006. Wax told me Sweet books bands that are "peaking at particular moments that correspond to when the festival occurs."

22. Hobsbawm 1983: 1, 13.

23. MacCannell 1976: 43–45, 111–12.

24. Bourdieu 1984: 26.

25. In comparison with the other festivals, Sweet went on to say: "I guess you could say that 'We're a SXSW artist,' although I don't know what that means."

26. Quinn's Blues Café works on the model of holding residencies—bands playing a block of dates, rather than just one show. He says that this format, more common in the jazz community, makes it difficult for him to work with BridgeFest as compared with Deer Tick's late-night after-parties.

Chapter Three

1. These are reminiscent of old-fashioned church fans, often used at the CMA as advertisements, and collected by some festivalgoers.

2. Even a more traditional country singer like Alan Jackson actively brands (and rebrands) songs. He repurposed the old blues song "Mercury Boogie" into "Mercury Blues" and changed his own lyrics from "crazy 'bout a Mercury" to "crazy 'bout a Ford truck" for a Ford commercial.

3. In 2002, when Gaylord Entertainment changed WSM's format from country music to sports and talk to coincide with Nashville's new NFL team, there was a successful protest by locals, country fans, and musicians alike (Havighurst 2007: xiii).

4. Kreyling 2005: 12.

5. Many WSM employees had side projects and used their expertise to establish their own music firms. Buddy Killen, for example, left playing bass at the Opry for Tree Publishing, matching a song called "Heartbreak Hotel" with Elvis and becoming a hugely influential Music Row figure.

6. This group grew from the short-lived Country Music Disc Jockey Association.

7. Pecknold 2007: 135.

8. There are other institutions worthy of mention. The Bluebird Café (and to a lesser extent, the Broken Spoke, the Hall of Fame Lounge, and Bean Central) is where newcomers hope to be discovered, as Garth Brooks once was, and where established stars mix with aspiring newcomers for singer-songwriter nights. The Station Inn is a bluegrass mecca, too.

9. Hattie Louise "Tootsie" Bess and her husband, "Big Jeff" Bess, were tied to the music industry, and because of Tootsie's proximity to the Ryman, musicians like Patsy Cline and Webb Pierce would visit often. The back room used to be "industry only."

10. Hight 2010.

11. Huxtable 1973; see also Hill 2011. Ryman renovations did not begin until the 1990s rebirth of Second Avenue and Lower Broad.
12. Hight 2010.
13. Robert's Western World was a steel guitar warehouse and showroom, then a liquor store, a Western apparel shop, and finally, in 1999, a honkytonk.
14. Carey 2001a.
15. Technically, the "Nashville Convention and Visitor's Corporation."
16. Arango 2007.
17. These feelings, however, have mellowed. Recent media offers positive press, and locals note that the CMA has worked to neutralize the relationship.
18. The CMA Fest pays backing musicians and technicians, not headlining artists. If musicians appear on the television special, they do earn performance fees.
19. Pugh 1996.
20. A reporter described these meals as "the crappiest food in the world," characterizing it as "big old sausages floating in coagulated grease." He noted that organizers knew what was best for them and started getting a different caterer for the press area.
21. Technically, the "Metropolitan Government of Nashville and Davidson County." The two merged in 1963.
22. Stinchcombe notes that these organizational forms established at the founding are basic features that can be identified later (1965: 153; see also Johnson 2007).
23. See Wynn 2012 on the commercialization in country music lyrics.
24. Cooper 2006.
25. Foglesong pointed to the close relationship between artists and DJs: musicians often worked closely with DJs, and without label assistance, which led to more airtime when DJs had greater freedom in what they played.
26. Greenberg 2012.
27. Scholars studying jazz and blues performers detail similar complaints about audiences (Becker 1951; Grazian 2003).
28. One interviewee, Hazel Smith, asked the first question of our interview: "Is that your car with the New York plates in the parking lot?"
29. Country musicians successfully sold everything from "laxatives and patent medicines to work clothes, farm equipment, and live chicks" (Havighurst 2007: 85; see also Peterson 1997: 120).
30. Pushing the pun further: Sharpie was the official sponsor of country star Mark Willis's 1999 "Permanently" tour.
31. See Peterson and Beal 2001 and Broome and Tucker 1990.

32. See Lloyd 2011 on East Nashville's music scene.

33. Chris Thile was performing with his new band, and Sara Watkins was a solo act. Their reunion was a surprise for fans. Both were returning Newport Folk artists: Thile's band performed in 2010, and Watkins performed with the Decemberists in 2011.

34. The Opry was deeply invested in cross-promotional marketing from the beginning as well (Havighurst 2007: 67).

35. Peterson 1997; see also Hemphill 1970.

Chapter Four

1. Selling merchandise is a priority: T-shirts, CDs, and buttons help pay for gas, food, and lodging to complement the small compensation from the festival itself.

2. SXSW 2013.

3. Fonarow 2006: 79–153.

4. Humphrey 1983.

5. See Stimeling 2011, Orum 2002, and Grodach 2012.

6. Created in 1981, the AMAC—and the Texas Music Alliance before it—addressed what it saw as the decline of country music in the state. The Texas Music Alliance worked to convince the chamber that musicians were pro-growth as well, rather than antiestablishment radicals (Shank 1994: 193, 200).

7. Shank 1994: 198–208. One of the early attempts to support the local music scene was a Love Your Band marketing campaign. Then there was "Austin: You Make It Live," which led to the current "Live Music Capital of the World" motto.

8. Other business-oriented festivals include the Folk Alliance Festival, Non-COMMvention, and FMQB (Friday Morning Quarterback) Conference.

9. Louis Meyers went on to become the executive director of the Folk Alliance.

10. According to Shank, SXSW "demonstrates the complete modernization of music-making in Austin, Texas. The music festival allows recording company executives to act out their remembered fantasies of fandom, while the panels and the activities in the hotel lobby work to discipline musicians into the expectations and assumptions of the national industry" (1994: 235).

11. Martin 1988. Swearingen details the long fight between development and conservation shaping the quality of life in Austin and beyond (2010).

12. Florida and Gates 2004: 214.

13. Jarnow 2012.

14. Attal was the guitarist in a punk band, then found partners to open Stubb's. SXSW approached them to use the space for an event, and he realized that he wanted to

get into the booking business. In 2007 he founded C3 Presents, which has promoted and booked the Austin City Limits Music Festival, Chicago's Lollapalooza festival, and even President Barack Obama's 2009 election night celebration.

15. Corcoran 2006. The city's offer to relocate the Liberty Lunch fell through, but the venue support program was revived again in 2005 as the "Music Venue Relocation Program for Downtown Development" to help rebuild a popular African American–owned venue called Midtown Live after a fire. The offer again crumbled, this time under public pressure for "giving away taxpayers' money" to private businesses, especially bars. The offer of a $750,000 forgivable loan caused controversy and sparked racial tensions in the city (King 2005).

16. Long 2010: 15.

17. Austin's Live Music Task Force notes that the government had a "largely laissez-faire relationship" with the music scene, with the community generally concerned over sound ordinances and development (Freeman 2008).

18. SXSW co-owner Louis Black said that many of their perennial problems and roadblocks were alleviated when Toby Futrell became city manager in 2002 (Black 2007); she paved the way for a strong central business district and support of the festival.

19. Zaragosa 2007.

20. One task force member claimed that audiences had declined 60–70% since 1990 while the city's population doubled, and yet there was a modest uptick in the number of venues (Gregor 2008).

21. Live Music Task Force 2008.

22. Dunbar 2012.

23. Sherman 2011; see also Hernandez 2013.

24. Gregor 2008.

25. SXSW Music is spread over a hundred venues, whereas the film festival is held at nine.

26. Beach 2008.

27. Artist and Repertoire, A&R, are label scouts assigned to find talent and nurture artists' careers.

28. SXSW, like Newport, would not disclose to me the contract terms for their headlining acts.

29. Foreign governments and quasi-governmental groups (like the New Zealand Music Commission) are increasingly offering travel grants and subsidies for acts and music executives, prompting an increase in SXSW international visitors—up to 20% of all registrants (Leeds 2007a).

30. There is a dizzying array of topics, including "Are Metalheads Smart Enough to

Be Online?," "I Love College: Booking College Shows and Festivals," "Oh Canada: Your Guide to Touring in Canada," "Super Fans as a Marketing Force Amplifier," and "Women in the Recording Studio."

31. For studies of musicians' careers, see Faulkner and Becker 2009 and Faulkner 1983.

32. Lack of "walkability" was, according to organizers, one of factors leading to the collapse of New York's New Music Seminar.

33. Beach 2008 and SXSW 2012. SXSW claims other local businesses benefit similarly.

34. Kelso 2007.

35. Popov and Popov 2007; see also Swenson 2011 and Sutter and Toohey 2011. This wasn't the first time PACE agents shut down venues before SXSW (see Lieck 2002).

36. Corcoran 2008.

37. In 2014, for example, a drunk driver attempted to avoid a police checkpoint and ended up driving through a crowd of SXSW attendees, killing two people and injuring twenty-three.

38. Leeds 2007b.

39. Shank 1994: 89.

40. If there's an indie ethos, it might be the Minutemen's evocation of "jamming econo": touring and performing on the cheap. As one Minutemen song famously declares: "Let the products sell themselves, fuck advertising, commercial psychology."

41. Sisario 2011.

42. Hoffberger 2014. In 2013, the New Orleans ACLU successfully contested the Clean Zone strategy, even though it has been used at big baseball games and the Super Bowl.

43. Populous 2014. A 2014 postmortem by Austin's city manager came to similar conclusions.

44. SXSW 2014.

45. Austin's other big music event, the Austin City Limits Festival, is held within nearby Zilker Park, usually in October, and hews to the citadel pattern.

Chapter Five

1. Lefebvre 1991: 89–93. As I am uninterested in orthodoxy, there is, again, a bit of a conflation here. Lefebvre wrote of the mental (*espace conçu*), social (*espace vécu*), and physical spheres (*espace perçu*), which I refigure here as symbolic, human, and spatial.

2. Tyrrell and Johnston 2001: 99.

3. The report, requested by the Rhode Island Department of Environmental Manage-

ment (which operates Fort Adams Park), found that 89% of attendees would not be in the state if not for the festivals. Newport Jazz had fewer attendees, but they spent more than those at the folk festival; whites were 95% of the folk festival audience; and 10% of Newport festivalgoers attended more than ten times (Advantage Marketing Information 2013).

4. Oermann 2011 and CMA 2013.

5. Loftsgaarden 2012. Austin City Limits brought $37 million to the city in 2008 (Freeman 2008) and $73 million in 2011 (Dinges 2012).

6. Loftsgaarden 2012 and SXSW 2014.

7. Howkins 2001.

8. Americans for the Arts 2012.

9. Raines and Brown also note that festival attendees (who account for 35% of the city's annual visitors) stayed over five days and spent an average of $1,500 (2006).

10. Harper and Cotton 2013: 17.

11. TXP 2012: 6.

12. Greenberg 2012.

13. Plohetski 2011.

14. City of Newport, Planning and Development Profile 2010.

15. Americans for the Arts 2012.

16. Gedan 2007.

17. Sernovitz 2009. The developers claim one of the contributing factors was a change in the state's reimbursement to homeowners and developers with historic projects. The tax credit was reduced from 27.75 to 22% in 2008 (Vernon-Sparks 2009).

18. Bai 2013.

19. Quoted in Lloyd and Christens 2012: 126. The Nashville Housing Authority designated the majority of the area's housing as substandard and paved the way for the Capitol Hill Redevelopment Plan, which razed the predominantly African American community. In 1949, the transformation of the Capitol area (four blocks north of Broadway) was the first urban renewal plan to receive congressional approval.

20. See Carey 2001b and Spinney 1995.

21. *Kiplinger* named Nashville the smartest city in America to live in 2006 (Rheault 2006). Nissan's headquarters relocation from Los Angeles to Nashville (bringing 1,300 jobs at an average salary of $80,000) alongside Gateway and Dell's planned expansion in manufacturing and sales staff further bolstered Nashville's economy.

22. The Music City Music Council organizes public-private partnerships, philanthropists, music industry folks, and other business owners.

23. Phillips 2010: 272.

24. Ladendorf 2010 and City of Austin 2010.

25. Swearingen 2010: 42.

26. The Austin Technology Incubator is a nonprofit based out of the University of Texas at Austin and has raised over $725 million of investor capital (Measley and Mangum 2010).

27. Freeman 2008.

28. Wynn continued: "States spent real public dollars giving kids a quality education and they can do anything and go anywhere and they come to Austin. Most cities wring their hands about brain drain. Well, Austin is its number-one beneficiary."

29. Most employees were moved to Facebook's Palo Alto offices.

30. Munir 2012.

31. Ladendorf 2012.

32. Hudgins 2012.

33. Berube et al. 2010. Success here is gross value added, employment, and population.

34. Debord 1956. Though less doctrinaire a comparison than some would like, there are commonalities: Debord's *dérives* and Lefebvre's concept of *rhythmanalysis* both focused upon physical and social spaces and their effects on everyday practices, through repetition, comparison, contradictions, and conflicts (Lefebvre 2004 [1974]: 205–7).

35. During a performance by the Canadian rock band Great White, pyrotechnics set fire to flammable soundproofing, and an inadequate sprinkler system and poorly marked exits led to 100 deaths. The tragedy was an unimaginable disaster for the survivors, resulted in prison sentences for the venue owners and the band's tour manager, made national media headlines, and also radiated new safety measures across the city's venues (Walker 2012).

36. Inspectors found eight of a possible ten violations at another nearby arts collective (Donnis 2004).

37. M. R. Smith 2011.

38. The funds include $25 million to assist with land acquisitions, and a 62.5% property tax discount, all equaling $245.5 million over a twenty-year period (Cass 2012).

39. See Metropolitan Planning Department 2007: 3.

40. TIFs use future tax gains to fund current public (e.g., infrastructure) or private (e.g., a sports stadium) urban development projects in targeted districts, with the controversial aim of enhancing areas perceived to be blighted or in need.

41. Lloyd and Christens 2012: 122.

42. Burns 2008. Across the train tracks, the Mercy Lounge (opened in 2003, in a historical building called the Cannery) filled a void in the local music scene when City Hall closed, and served as the location for the first Southland conference.

43. *USA Today* 2006.

44. Allyn 2012.

45. Although growth was seen as impinging on the music scene, it should be noted that these music venues also provided a strong tax base for growth; in this case, a TIF program to add to a voter-approved bond for a $127.5 million public works project. James Moody, who owns the Mohawk—just outside the TIF district—expressed his excitement for the redevelopment project with regard to parking and public safety, but notes, "there's a big difference between cleaning an area and sanitizing it, and I don't think [the city has] done a great job of taking into account the cultural impact and the creative class that's already been developed there." He worries that any project could jeopardize Red River's status as "the only true music street where you have interconnected venues" (Powell 2010).

46. Gregor 2009a. For the past forty years, a property owner could buy the development rights and zoning opportunities (e.g., for additional height, bought through a Transfer of Development Rights) from another owner, which "allows communities to achieve preservation goals and protect property rights, without spending public funds" (Gregor 2009b).

47. According to the 2010 Census, all three cities have become less segregated from 2000 to 2010: Providence's White-Black Index of Dissimilarity (which measures the likelihood of a neighbor being of a different racial group, with a higher number indicating a higher likelihood of the two groups living in different Census Tracts) dropped from 68.2 to 50.8, Nashville's from 65.2 to 55, and Austin's from 64.8 to 48.4.

48. Allyn 2013.

49. Long 2010: 111.

50. For comparison, a refrigerator emits 40 dBs, traffic noise, 80 dBs, and a plane overhead, 103 dBs.

Chapter Six

1. Face-to-face interactions, and therefore strong urban densities, nurture greater chances for innovation and human and intellectual capital (Storper and Venables 2004).

2. Lloyd 2011.

3. Providence, however, has not kept pace with Austin and Nashville: Census data show that between 2000 and 2010, Austin and Nashville saw population growth of 37.33 and 21.20%, respectively, while Providence's MSA had only 1.13% growth.

4. See Brown-Saracino 2009, Ocejo 2011, and Vigdor 2010.

5. One exception is the Throwing Muses, a band formed in 1981 by stepsisters Tanya Donelly and Kristin Hersh (who graduated from Newport's Salve Regina

University) that gained a national reputation at the height of the early 1990s indie rock crescendo. Neither the band nor the sisters individually played the festival.

6. McCauley's own rise to prominence in his home state is impressive: his parents brought him to the festival as his first concert, in 1988, and he's now on its advisory board.

7. Havighurst 2007: 73, 168–69.

8. "Chevrolet the official ride of Country Music is proud to support tomorrow's Country Music stars through the Keep the Music Playing program," said Caruso, manager of Chevrolet promotions. "Chevrolet's 100 years of history have long been celebrated in song. Combining our support for Country Music and education was an easy decision" (CMA 2012).

9. Benefactors of this program include Mike Curb (founder of Curb Records), the Gibson Foundation (a nonprofit run by Gibson Guitars), and Martha Ingram (local philanthropist, chairman of Vanderbilt's Board of Trust, worth over $2 billion).

10. Nashville ranks fourth on a list of the top fifty most populous US cities in philanthropic giving, whereas Austin ranks thirty-second and Providence ranks last (*Chronicle of Philanthropy* 2012).

11. Freeman 2008.

12. This is below average, but slightly better than musicians nationwide: 44% of musicians don't have health insurance, twice the national average (Future of Music Coalition 2013: 4).

13. Gregor 2008.

14. AMP is a 501(c)(6) nonprofit—a designation for business organizations (e.g., chambers of commerce) to convene under the 501(c) umbrella for some federal tax exemption.

15. Mommaas 2004.

16. *Austin Daze* 2006.

17. Schudson 1986: xii.

18. Of note: these surveys were conducted in 2007 and 2008, before Newport became a not-for-profit. Analysis was greatly assisted by Ayse Yetis-Bayraktar. Each survey was coded and recorded, and the analysis is conducted in Stata 9. The sample sizes for Austin, Newport, and Nashville locals were 42, 42, and 73. Because of the small sample sizes, this serves as *descriptive* data for comparison with the interview and participant-observation data, across the three festival locations. The survey questions and a more detailed discussion about these data are available on my personal website: jonathanrwynn.com.

19. *Austin Daze* 2006: 17–18.

20. Specifically, only 7% of Newport festivalgoers attending for their first time and 4% of Nashville attendees who had attended fewer than four times agreed that they would like the festival better if it were in New York or Los Angeles. Additionally, *none* of the first-year attendees or people who went more than four times liked the idea of these events leaving their cities.

21. Herbert Gans used the phrase *fallacy of physical determinism* to critique Jane Jacobs (Fowler 1987).

Conclusion

1. Miller and Yúdice 2002: 1.

2. Throsby 2010: 131–32.

3. Judd 1999: 36; see also Metzger 2001. The largest American culture organization, the National Endowment for the Arts, was under siege in the 1990s. Only 13% of nonprofit arts organizations' funding comes from the public sector (Cherbo, Vogel, and Wyszomirski 2008: 18).

4. There are certainly attempts to spark amenity growth through distinctive architectural monuments alone (e.g., Calatrava's Milwaukee Art Museum; I. M. Pei's Rock and Roll Hall of Fame and Museum in Cleveland).

5. Lofland uses the locale/counterlocale framing to warn that carnivals and the like can be a form of *camouflaged control* (1998: 216; see also Judd 1999).

6. Desfor et al. 2011. Crafting urban spaces requires walking a knife-edge between "preserving fixed social structures that underpinned and supported past capital investments and destroying these structures in order to create new opportunities for investment" (Gotham 2009: 356).

7. Much of this pessimism over temporary events is rightly based upon the questionable value of these expensive "mega events" (see Andranovich, Burbank, and Heying 2001; Hiller 2000).

8. Kong 2000: 387; see also Richards and Wilson 2004: 1932.

9. Some note that festivals provide positive exposure of a region (Schuster 2001) and lend a sense of city pride and self-esteem.

10. Some argue that creative cities need *less* government, but a good example might be Chicago, where festival planning and management was moved from the Department of Cultural Affairs to a new Mayor's Office of Special Events (Andersson 2011; see also Clark and Silver 2013: 36).

11. See Hannigan 2002: 354–55. Other research posits that festivals are a poor use of municipal resources (Ward 1998: 203).

12. Zukin 1991: 19. "NikeTowns" and "Disney Worlds" have arisen within the contemporary city, and the rebirth of a place like Times Square has been "re-presented as offices and showplaces of corporate culture industries" (Zukin 1995: 276).

13. The Arts Council of Great Britain (now the Arts Council of England) distributed £310 million (over US$507 million) in grants to different cultural spheres in correspondence with local communities.

14. Lang worked with his counterpart in Greece to found the ECoC. According to the EU Council's resolution, the program is designed to "open up to the European public particular aspects of the culture of the city, region, or country concerned" and "highlight the richness and diversity of European culture and the features they share as well as to promote greater mutual acquaintance between European citizens" (quoted in Palmer/Rae Associates 2004: 47; see also Richards 2000, 2007). Launched in Athens in 1985, the ECoC has landed in over fifty cities; 77.5% of ECoC total funds are from the public sector (i.e., national, city, regional, and EU sources), and only 13.2% are from private sponsorships (Palmer/Rae Associates 2004: 19).

15. I contacted Birgit Hedkvist, Borlänge's municipal councilwoman who handles most of the contact with the festival. Through Nilsson's translation, she told me the municipal government has only provided a small investment (US$43,000) to improve the local campsite for festivalgoers and logistical coordination with police, fire, and emergency services. Borlänge turistbyrå (Borlänge and Co.) is 25% owned by the municipal government, and the rest is privately held. She noted that locals were initially suspicious of the festival's benefits, but with continued success the city has embraced it. It turns out that Borlänge was more of an outlier in this regard. In addition, the Association of Swedish Festivals promotes hundreds of events across the country annually (see Aldskogius 1993 for a better understanding of the Scandinavian festival scene).

16. The city of Austin waived $14,000 worth of security deposits and application and permitting fees, and authorized $76,000 of payments to the police department. Comparatively, Austin contributes $5,000 for the Fiesta de Independencia, $7,000 for Martin Luther King Jr. Day, $9,000 for Veterans Day, $15,000 for Celebrate Texas (Texas Independence Day), and $36,000 for Juneteenth (Alexander 2007).

17. Both Hultsfred and Peace and Love emerged from bankruptcy.

18. Kuchler 2012.

19. Cultural theorist Fredric Jameson described contemporary life as "saturated with the image of culture," calling it the *cultural turn*, writing that what was once known as culture—as a place for tradition and experimentation—is now a part of everyday life (1998: 111).

20. The event was inspired by Nuit Blanche, a French all-night arts festival (Caldeira 2012).
21. The festival received $20,000 in 2011 and $25,000 in 2012 from the Canada Arts Presentation Fund, for example, and similar amounts from the city's Festival and Cultural Events office in 2010 and 2012. There are many other funding sources in Canada. "Building Communities through Arts and Heritage" provides support for local festivals through three programs. The Local Festivals program, for example, supports recurring events involving the entire community, offering opportunities to local artists and artisans, or celebrating local history and heritage.
22. JP Music Festival 2011.
23. Swenson told me that SXSW benefits from other countries' public expenditures on exporting their music: he sees the British as the most successful at it, saying, "There's no one [in the government] helping us, but we receive the benefits of— I don't want to call it socialism, but the public support for bands to be sent to the US."
24. Sennett 1996 [1971]: 189.
25. Mitchell offers a more expansive view of this notion (2003).

Encore

1. This is the stage name of Joshua Tillman, former drummer for Newport alums Fleet Foxes.
2. Durkheim 1966: 285. He sees that any rite "can only serve to sustain the vitality of these beliefs, to keep them from being effaced from memory, and in sum, to revivify the most essential elements of collective conscience. Through it, the group periodically renews the sentiment which it has of itself and of its unity; at the same time, individuals are strengthened in their social natures. The glorious memories which are made to live before their eyes, and with which they feel that they have a kinship, give them a feeling of strength and confidence: one is surer of one's faith when one sees to how distant a past it goes back and what great things have transpired" (1965: 420).
3. Goffman 1963: 18. Goffman's "The Neglected Situation" defines the *social situation* as a more refined version of the *occasion*, as "an environment of mutual monitoring possibilities, anywhere within which an individual will find himself accessible to the naked senses of all others who are 'present,' and similarly find them accessible to him," and continues by defining a *gathering* as a somewhat more divided and looser aggregate of participants (1964: 135).
4. Goffman 1967: 2.

5. Goffman 1967: 3. As Becker (another sociologist indebted to Warner) reminds us, "collective action and the events they produce are the basic unit of sociological investigation" (2008 [1982]: 370).

6. Goffman 1967: 146. He described "tight" social occasions wherein attitudes and interactions are more restricted, and more relaxed "loose" occasions (1963: 198–215).

7. Collins 2005: 116. *Interaction Ritual Chains* unifies the Durkheim/Goffman and the Interactionist threads by placing what he calls the "ritual mechanism" at the center of his microsociology (2005: xi, 3).

8. This emphasis cuts across these traditions: Goffman develops another dyad, *contained* and *disruptive activity*, to describe kinds of adjustments in mental health facilities (1961), as Debord (1994), with far more explicit political purpose, encourages disruption of the consumerist agenda.

9. Smelser notes that "even though the micro, meso, macro, and global levels can be identified, it must be remembered that in any kind of social organization we can observe an interpenetration of these analytic levels" (1997: 29; see also Collins 1988; Giddens 1986).

10. Krause's article reviews "gap bridging" theories like Giddens's linking of structure and agency and Bourdieu's habitus, which connects structuralism and phenomenology (2013: 144), and indicates that there is still the necessity for alternative theories of social space. See also Collins's critique of binary-based thinking (1992).

11. Collins 2005: 15. Situations, for Collins, move from small, micro-level phenomena to meso-level sociology when they are partially replicated (with or without the same actors) or when they link up with other situations via Interaction Ritual Chains.

12. Goffman 1967: 2.

13. This certainly differs from Collins's preconditions for rituals that, in his lights, do not require various motivations or even a limited awareness of the bounds of activity (2005: 115–18, 131).

14. Etzioni 2000, Gotham 2002, and Small 2004.

15. Rodriguez 2013, Knudsen 1968, Horowitz and Schwartz 1974, Lidz 1991, and Regis 1999.

16. Deener 2012 and Herrmann 2006.

17. Flores 2000 and Kates and Belk 2001.

18. Lukes 1975 and Fantasia 1988.

19. Johnson-Weiner 2010 and Filo, Spence, and Sparvero 2013.

20. Tanenbaum 1995.

21. McPhail and Wohlstein 1983.

22. Wasik 2006.

23. Hiller 1995.
24. Maisel 1974.
25. Smelser 1997: 47–48.
26. Fine 2010: 372; 2012; see also Turner 2005.
27. Mumford 1966: 60.
28. Maines 1982: 276.

REFERENCES

Abebe, N. 2012. "Grizzly Bear Are Indie Rock Royalty, But What Does That Buy Them in 2012?" *New York Magazine*. http://www.vulture.com/2012/09/grizzly -bear-shields.html.

Adegoke, Y. 2014. "Spotify Drove Universal Music's 75% Jump in Streaming Revenue Last Year." *Billboard*, February 25. http://www.billboard.com/biz/articles/news /5915732/spotify-drove-universal-musics-75-jump-in-streaming-revenue-last-year.

Advantage Marketing Information. 2013. "Newport Festivals Foundation: An Economic Impact Study." http://www.newportfestivalsfoundation.org/img /EconomicImpactStudyFinal2012.pdf.

Ahlkvist, J. A., and R. Faulkner. 2002. "'Will This Record Work for Us?' Managing Music Formats in Commercial Radio." *Qualitative Sociology* 25:189–215.

Aldskogius, H. 1993. "Festivals and Meets: The Place of Music in 'Summer Sweden.'" *Geografiska Annaler: Series B, Human Geography* 75(2):55–72.

Alexander, K. 2007. "Austin Waives $90,000 in Fees for SXSW." *Austin American-Statesman*, March 10.

Allyn, B. 2012. "Reversing Years of Neglect on a Hill above Nashville." *New York Times*, May 8, B4.

———. 2013. "As High Dollar Houses Crowd onto Tiny Lots, Teardown Fever Is Sickening Neighborhoods across Nashville." *Nashville Scene*, December 19.

Americans for the Arts. 2012. "Arts and Economic Prosperity IV: The Economic Impact of Nonprofit Arts and Culture Organizations and Their Audiences in the City of Providence." http://www.buyartprovidence.com/images/RI_CityOf Providence_AEP4_FinalReport.pdf.

Andersson, D. E. 2011. "Creative Cities Need Less Government." In *Handbook of Creative Cities*, edited by D. E. Andersson, A. E. Andersson, and C. Mellander, 327–42. Cheltenham, UK, and Northampton, MA: Edward Elgar.

Andranovich, G., M. Burbank, and C. H. Heying. 2001. "Olympic Cities: Lessons Learned from Mega-Event Politics." *Journal of Urban Affairs* 23(2):113–31.

Andrews, A. 2009. "Changes Rock the Music World as '360' Deals Rise." *The Telegraph*, February 6.

Arango, T. 2007. "Cashville USA." *Fortune Magazine*, January 29. http://money.cnn .com/magazines/fortune/fortune_archive/2007/01/22/8397980/.

Austin Daze. 2006. "Louis Black on SXSW '06." http://www.austindaze.com/2006/08 /29/louis-black-on-sxsw-2006/.

Azarrad, M. 2001. *Our Band Could Be Your Life: Scenes from the American Indie Underground, 1981–1991*. New York: Back Bay Books.

Bai, M. 2013. "Thrown for a Curve in Rhode Island." *New York Times*, April 20, BU1.

Bakhtin, M. 1984. *Rabelais and His World*. Translated by H. Iswolsky. Bloomington: Indiana University Press.

Beach, P. 2008. "The Beginnings of SXSW. " *Austin American-Statesman*, March 8.

Becker, H. 1951. "The Professional Dance Musician and His Audience." *American Journal of Sociology* 57(2):136–44.

———. 2008 [1982]. *Art Worlds*. Berkeley: University of California Press.

Benedict, R. 1934. *Patterns of Culture*. New York: Houghton-Mifflin.

Bennett, A., and R. A. Peterson, eds. 2004. *Music Scenes: Local, Trans-Local, and Virtual*. Nashville: Vanderbilt University Press.

Bertoni, D. 2012. "Spotify's Daniel Ek: The Most Important Man in Music." *Forbes Magazine*, January 16. http://www.forbes.com/sites/stevenbertoni/2012/01/04 /spotifys-daniel-ek-the-most-important-man-in-music/5/.

Berube, A., A. Friefhoff, C. Nadeau, P. Rode, A. Paccoud, J. Kandt, T. Just, and R. Schemm-Gregory. 2010. "Global Metro Monitor: The Path to Economic Recovery. Metropolitan Policy Program, Brookings Institution, and LSE Cities, London School of Economics and Political Science." http://www.brookings.edu/~/media /research/files/reports/2010/11/30%20global%20metro%20monitor/1130_global _metro_monitor.

Black, L. 2007. "Page Two: Scratching the Surface." *Austin Chronicle*, March 2.

Bloomberg BusinessWeek. 2010. "Who Says the Music Industry Is Kaput?" *Bloomberg BusinessWeek Magazine*, May 27. http://www.businessweek.com/magazine /content/10_23/b4181077568125.htm.

Bourdieu, P. 1984. *Distinction: A Social Critique of the Judgment of Taste*. Translated by R. Nice. Cambridge, UK: Polity.

———. 1985. "The Forms of Capital." In *Handbook of Theory and Research for the Sociology of Education*, edited by J. G. Richardson, 241–58. New York: Greenwood.

Broome, P. J., and C. Tucker. 1990. *The Other Music City: The Dance Bands and Jazz Musicians of Nashville 1920 to 1970*. Nashville: American Press Print.

Brown-Saracino, J. 2009. *A Neighborhood That Never Changes*. Chicago: University of Chicago Press.

Burns, J. 2008. "City Hall to Leave Gulch, Urban Outfitters Will Take over Space." *Nashville Business Journal*, April 30. http://www.bizjournals.com/nashville /stories/2008/04/28/daily22.html?page=all.

Byrne, D. 2012. *How Music Works*. San Francisco: McSweeney's.

Caldeira, T. P. R. 2012. "Imprinting and Moving Around: New Visibilities and Configurations of Public Space in São Paulo." *Public Culture* 24(2):385–419.

Carey, B. 2001a. "A City Swept Clean: How Urban Renewal, for Better and for Worse, Created the City We Know Today." *Nashville Scene*, September 6.

———. 2001b. "A Quiet Downtown." *Nashville Scene*. http://www.nashvillescene.com /nashville/a-quiet-downtown/Content?oid=1186060.

Cass, M. 2012. "Nashville's Omni Hotel Shows Off Model Rooms." *The Tennessean*, August 21. http://www.tennessean.com/article/20120821/BUSINESS01/308200041 /Nashville-s-Omni-Hotel-shows-off-model-rooms.

Cherbo, J. M., H. Vogel, and M. J. Wyszomirski. 2008. "Toward an Arts and Creative Sector." In *Understanding the Arts and Creative Sector in the United States*, edited by J. M. Cherbo, R. A. Stewart, and M. J. Wyszomirski, 9–27. New Brunswick, NJ: Rutgers University Press.

Chmielewski, D. C., B. Fritz, and R. Lewis. 2010. "Ticketmaster–Live Nation Merger Gets Justice Department's Approval." *Los Angeles Times*, January 10.

Christman, E. 2013. "US Album Sales Hit Historic Lows." *Billboard*, August 2. http:// www.billboard.com/articles/news/5638056/us-album-sales-hit-historic-lows.

Chronicle of Philanthropy. 2012. "Generosity of America's 50 Biggest Cities: A Ranking." http://philanthropy.com/article/Generosity-in-Americas-50/133675/.

City of Austin. 2010. "Austin: Top Creative Center in the US." July 22. http://www .ci.austin.tx.us/news/2010/top_creative_center.htm.

City of Newport. 2010. "Planning and Development Profile." http://www.cityof newport.com/departments/planning-development/profile/economy.htm.

Clark, T. N. 2003. "Urban Amenities: Lakes, Opera, and Juice Bars: Do They Drive Development?" In *The City as an Entertainment Machine*, vol. 9 of *Research in Urban Policy*, edited by T. N. Clark, 103–40. New York: JAI Press/Elsevier.

Clark, T. N., and D. Silver. 2013. "Chicago from a Political Machine to an Entertainment Machine." In *The Politics of Urban Cultural Policy: Global Perspectives*, edited by C. Grodach and D. Silver, 28–41. London: Routledge.

CMA. 2012. "CMA Foundation Donates $1.4 Million to Music Education through CMA's Keep the Music Playing Music Education Campaign." http://www .cmaworld.com/news/newsitemdetail/2012/02/01/cma-foundation-donates-$1.4 -million-to-music-education-through-cma's-keep-the-music-playing-music -education-campaign.

———. 2013. "CMA Music Festival Direct Visitor Spending Reaches New High— $31.5 Million." http://www.cmaworld.com/news/2013/09/cma-music-festival -direct-visitor-spending-reaches-new-high-31-5-million/.

Cohen, R. D. 2008. *A History of Folk Music Festivals in the United States*. Lanham, MD: Scarecrow Press.

Collins, R. 1988. "The Micro Contributions to Macro Sociology." *Sociological Theory* 6:242–53.

———. 1992. "The Romanticism of Agency/Structure versus the Analysis of Micro/Macro." *Current Sociology* 40(1):77–79.

———. 2005. *Interaction Ritual Chains*. Princeton, NJ: Princeton University Press.

Comaroff, J., and J. L. Comaroff. 2009. *Ethnicity, Inc*. Chicago: University of Chicago Press.

Connolly, M., and A. B. Krueger. 2006. "Rockonomics: The Economics of Popular Music." In *Handbook of Arts and Culture*, vol. 1, edited V. A. Ginsburgh and D. Throsby, 667–719. Amsterdam: Elsevier.

Cooper, P. 2006. "A Little Rock, a Lot Country." *USA Today*, May 12. http://usatoday30.usatoday.com/life/music/news/2006-06-11-roadtrip-cma-festival_x.htm.

Corcoran, M. 2006. "Restaurant to Expand Music Operations with New Indoor Venue, Bigger Outdoor Stage." *Austin American-Statesman*, December 13.

———. 2008. "Fight for Control at SXSW." *Austin American-Statesman*, February 5.

Crawford, M. 1995. "Contesting the Public Realm: Struggles over Public Space in Los Angeles." *Journal of Architectural Education* 49(1):4–9.

Currid-Halkett, E., and K. Stolarick. 2011. "Cultural Capital and Metropolitan Distinction: A View from Los Angeles and New York." *City, Culture, and Society* 1(4):217–23.

Debord, G. 1956. "Theory of the *Dérive*." *Les Lèvres Nues* 9 (November). Translated by Ken Knabb. Reprinted in *Internationale Situationniste* 2 (December 1958).

———. 1994. *Society of the Spectacle*. New York: Zone Books.

Deener, A. 2012. *Venice: A Contested Bohemia in Los Angeles*. Chicago: University of Chicago Press.

Dekel, J. 2010. "Jack White Doesn't Suffer Internet 'Cowards'" Gladly. *Spinner*, July 13. http://www.spinner.ca/2010/07/13/jack-white-interview-dead-weather/.

Delaney, K. 2003. *Public Dollars, Private Stadiums*. Piscataway, NJ: Rutgers University Press.

DeNora, T. 2000. *Music in Everyday Life*. Cambridge, UK: Cambridge University Press.

Desfor, G., J. Laidley, Q. Stevens, and D. Schubert. 2011. *Transforming Urban Waterfronts*. New York: Routledge.

Dinges, G. 2012. "Report: SXSW's 2012 Economic Impact Was $190 Million." *Austin American-Statesman*, October 4.

Donnis, I. 2004. "Citywatch: Olneyville Artists Face Abrupt Eviction." *Providence*

Phoenix, January 23. http://www.providencephoenix.com/features/tji/documents /03543331.asp.

Dowd, T. J. 2004. "Concentration and Diversity Revisited: Production Logics and the U.S. Mainstream Recording Market, 1940 to 1990." *Social Forces* 82(4):1411–1455.

Dunbar, W. 2012. "What Will Austin's Soundproofing Program Do for Downtown Clubs?" *KUT News*, January 31. http://www.kutnews.org/post/what-will-austin %E2%80%99s-soundproofing-program-do-downtown-clubs.

Duneier, M. 1999. *Sidewalk*. New York: Farrar, Strauss & Giroux.

Durkheim, E. 1966. *The Elementary Forms of Religious Life*. New York: Free Press.

Eisenschitz, A. 2010. "Place Marketing as Politics." In *International Place Branding Yearbook 2010*, edited by F. Go and R. Govers, 21–30. New York: Palgrave Macmillan.

Etzioni, A. 2000. "Toward a Theory of Public Ritual." *Sociological Theory* 18(1): 44–59.

Evans, G. 2003. "Hard-Branding the Cultural City—From Pardo to Prada." *International Journal of Urban and Regional Research* 27(2):417–40.

Evans, M. R. 1997. "Newport, Rhode Island—America's First Resort: Lessons in Sustainable Tourism." *Journal of Travel Research* 36(2):63–68.

Fantasia, R. 1988. *Cultures of Solidarity: Consciousness, Action, and Contemporary American Workers*. Berkeley: University of California Press.

Faulkner, R. R. 1983. *Music on Demand*. New Brunswick, NJ: Transaction.

Faulkner, R. R., and H. Becker. 2009. *"Do You Know…" The Jazz Repertoire in Action*. Chicago: University of Chicago Press.

Filo, K., K. Spence, and E. Sparvero. 2013. "Exploring Properties of Community among Charity Sport Event Participants." *Managing Leisure* 18(3):194–212.

Fine, G. A. 2010. "The Sociology of the Local: Action and Its Publics." *Sociological Theory* 28(4):355–76.

———. 2012. "Group Culture and the Interaction Order: Local Sociology on the Meso-Level." *Annual Review of Sociology* 38:159–79.

Flores, J. 2000. *From Bomba to Hip Hop: Puerto Rican Culture and Latino Identity*. New York: Columbia University Press.

Florida, R. 2002. *The Rise of the Creative Class*. New York: Perseus Book Group.

———. 2012. "The Geography of America's Music Scenes." *The Atlantic Cities*. http://www.theatlanticcities.com/arts-and-lifestyle/2012/08/geography-americas -music-scenes/2709/#slide1.

———. 2013. "More Losers Than Winners in America's Economic Geography." *The Atlantic Cities*, January 30. http://www.theatlanticcities.com/jobs-and-economy /2013/01/more-losers-winners-americas-new-economic-geography/4465/.

Florida, R., and G. Gates. 2004. "Technology and Tolerance: The Dependence of Diversity to High-Technology Growth." Brookings Institution Survey Series, June.

Florida, R., and C. Jackson. 2009. "Sonic City: The Evolving Economic Geography of the Music Industry." *Journal of Planning Education and Research* 29(3):310–21.

Fonarow, W. 2006. *Empire of Dirt: The Aesthetics and Rituals of British Indie Music.* Middletown, CT: Wesleyan University Press.

Fowler, E. P. 1987. "Street Management and City Design." *Social Forces* 666(2): 365–89.

Freeman, D. 2008. "Music Deportment: Assessing the Live Music Task Force Recommendations." *Austin Chronicle*, Nov 21. http://www.austinchronicle.com/music /2008-11-21/704796/.

Frith, S. 2001. "The Popular Music Industry." In *The Cambridge Companion to Pop and Rock*, edited by S. Frith, W. Straw, and J. Street, 26–52. Cambridge, UK: Cambridge University Press.

Future of Music Coalition. 2012. FMC Artist Revenue Streams Project. http://money .futureofmusic.org/.

———. 2013. Artists and Health Insurance Survey. http://futureofmusic.org/sites /default/files/Artistsandhealthinsurancereport1013.pdf.

Gardner, R. O. 2004. "The Portable Community: Mobility and Modernization in Bluegrass Festival Life." *Symbolic Interactionism* 27:155–78.

Garreau, J. 1991. *Edge City: Life on the New Frontier.* New York: Doubleday.

Gedan, B. 2007. "Royal Mills Loses Steam." *Providence Journal*, June 21.

Giddens, A. 1986. *The Constitution of Society.* Cambridge, UK: Polity Press.

Glaeser, E. L. 2005. Review of Richard Florida's *The Rise of the Creative Class. Regional Science and Urban Economics* 35(5):593–96.

———. 2011. *Triumph of the City: How Our Greatest Invention Makes Us Richer, Smarter, Greener, Healthier, and Happier.* New York: Macmillan Publishers.

Goffman, E. 1959. *The Presentation of Self in Everyday Life.* Garden City, NY: Doubleday.

———. 1961. *Asylums.* New York: Anchor.

———. 1963. *Behavior in Public Places: Notes on the Social Organization of Gatherings.* New York: Free Press.

———. 1964. "The Neglected Situation." *American Anthropologist* 66(6):133–36.

———. 1967. *Interaction Ritual: Essays on Face-to-Face Interaction.* Garden City, NY: Doubleday.

Gotham, K. F. 2002. "Marketing Mardi Gras: Commodification, Spectacle, and the Political Economy of Tourism in New Orleans." *Urban Studies* 39(10):1735–1756.

———. 2007. *Authentic New Orleans.* New York: NYU Press.

———. 2009. "Creating Liquidity out of Spatial Fixity: The Secondary Circuit of Capital and the Subprime Mortgage Crisis." *International Journal of Urban and Regional Research* 33(2):355–71.

Grams, D. 2010. *Producing Local Color: Art Networks in Ethnic Chicago.* Chicago: University of Chicago Press.

Grazian, D. 2003. *Blue Chicago.* Chicago: University of Chicago Press.

———. 2004. "The Production of Popular Music as a Confidence Game: The Case of the Chicago Blues." *Qualitative Sociology* 27:137–58.

Greenberg, M. 2009. *Branding New York: How a City in Crisis Was Sold to the World.* New York and London: Routledge.

Greenberg, P. 2012. "Police, Organizers Prep CMA Fest Security Measures, Take Aim at Bootleggers." *The City Paper,* June 3. http://nashvillecitypaper.com/content/city -news/police-organizers-prep-cma-fest-security-measures-take-aim-bootleggers.

Greenwood, D. J. 1989. "Culture by the Pound: An Anthropological Perspective on Tourism as Cultural Commodification." In *Hosts and Guests: The Anthropology of Tourism,* 2nd ed., edited by V. Smith, 171–86. Philadelphia: University of Philadelphia Press.

Gregor, K. 2008. "Rockin' Solutions: A Four-Piece Combo: Highlights of Solutions Emerging from the Four Live Music Task Force Subcommittees." *Austin Chronicle,* July 18.

———. 2009a. "Can This District Be Saved?" *Austin Chronicle,* September 11.

———. 2009b. "How Does TDR Work?" *Austin Chronicle,* September 11.

Grodach, C. 2012. "City Image and the Politics of Music Policy in the 'Live Music Capital of the World.'" In *The Politics of Urban Cultural Policy: Global Perspectives,* edited by C. Grodach and D. Silver, 156–75. New York and London: Routledge.

Guenther, K. M. 2009. "The Politics of Names: Rethinking the Methodological and Ethical Significance of Naming People, Organizations, and Places." *Qualitative Research* 9(4):411–21.

Habermas, J. 1996. *Between Facts and Norms: Contributions to a Discourse Theory of Law and Democracy.* Cambridge, UK: Polity Press.

Halle, D., and E. Tiso. 2014. *New York's New Edge.* Chicago: University of Chicago Press.

Hankinson, G., and P. Cowking. 1993. *Branding in Action: Cases and Strategies for Profitable Brand Management.* Maidenhead, UK: McGraw-Hill.

Hannigan, J. 1998. *Fantasy City: Pleasure and Profit in the Postmodern Metropolis.* London: Routledge.

———. 2002. "Cities as the Physical Site of the Global Entertainment Economy." In *Global Media Policy in the New Millennium*, edited by M. Raboy, 181–95. Luton, Bedfordshire: Luton University Press.

Harper, G., and C. Cotton. 2013. "Nashville Music Industry: Impact, Contribution, and Cluster Analysis." Nashville Chamber of Commerce. http://www.nashville chamber.com/docs/default-source/research-center-studies/nashville-music -industry-study.pdf?sfvrsn=4.

Häussermann, H., and W. Siebel. eds. 1993. "Festivalization of Urban Policy: Town Development by Large Projects." *Leviathan* 13. Opladen: Westdeutscher Verlag.

Havighurst, C. 2007. *Air Castle of the South: WSM and the Making of Music City*. Chicago: University of Illinois Press.

Hayden, D. 1997. *The Power of Place: Urban Landscapes as Public History*. Cambridge, MA: MIT Press.

Hemphill, P. 1970. *The Nashville Sound: Bright Lights and Country Music*. New York: Simon and Schuster.

Hennion, A. 2001. "Music Lovers: Taste as Performance." *Theory, Culture & Society* 18(5):1–22.

Hernandez, R. 2013. "Emo's Sold: C3 Presents Adds Another Jewel to Its Concert Promotions Crown." *Austin Chronicle*, February 11. http://www.austinchronicle .com/blogs/music/2013-02-11/emos-sold/.

Herrmann, G. M. 2006. "Garage Sales Make Good Neighbors: Building Community through Neighborhood Sales." *Human Organization* 65(2):181–91.

Hight, J. 2010. "How Tootsie's Orchid Lounge Helped Change Country Music and Nashville, in Just 50 Years." *Nashville Scene*, November 4. http://www.nashville scene.com/nashville/how-tootsies-orchid-lounge-helped-change-country-music -and-nashville-in-just-50-years/Content?oid=1919387.

Hill, J. 2011. "Country Music Is Wherever the Soul of a Country Music Fan Is: Opryland U.S.A. and the Importance of Home in Country Music." *Southern Cultures* 17(4):91–111.

Hiller, H. H. 1995. "Conventions as Mega-Events: A New Model for Convention–Host City Relationships." *Tourism Management* 16(5):375–79.

———. 2000. "Toward an Urban Sociology of Mega-Events." *Research in Urban Sociology* 5:181–205.

Hitters, E. 2007. "Porto and Rotterdam as European Capitals of Culture: Towards the Festivalization of Urban Cultural Policy." In *Cultural Tourism*, edited by G. Richards, 281–302. Binghamton, NY: Hawthorne Press.

Hobsbawm, E. 1983. "Invented Traditions." In *The Invention of Tradition*, edited by E. Hobsbawm and T. Ranger, 1–14. Cambridge, UK: Cambridge University Press.

Hoffberger, C. 2014. "Wrestling with SXSW." *Austin Chronicle*, October 10. http://www.austinchronicle.com/news/2014-10-10/wrestling-with-sxsw/.

Horowitz, R., and G. Schwartz. 1974. "Honor, Normative Ambiguity, and Gang Violence." *American Sociological Review* 39(2):238–51.

Howkins, J. 2001. *The Creative Economy: How People Make Money From Ideas*. New York: Penguin.

Hracs, B. 2012. "Creative Industry in Transition: The Rise of Digitally Driven Independent Music Production." *Growth and Change* 43(3):443–62.

Hudgins, M. 2012. "In Texas's Capital, Construction on Many Corners." *New York Times*, August 15, B6.

Humphrey, D. C. 1983. "Prostitution and Public Policy in Austin, Texas, 1870–1915." *Southwestern Historical Quarterly* 86:473–516.

Huxtable, A. L. 1973. "Only the Phony Is Real." *New York Times*, May 13, AL138.

Jameson, F. 1998. *The Cultural Turn: Selected Writings on the Postmodern, 1983–1998*. Brooklyn, NY: Verso.

Jarnow, J. 2012. *Bid Day Coming: Yo La Tengo and the Rise of Indie Rock*. New York: Penguin.

Johnson, G. 2005. "In 35th Year, a City's Changing Attitude Toward Music." *USA Today*, June 9.

Johnson, V. 2007. "What Is Organizational Imprinting? Cultural Entrepreneurship in the Founding of the Paris Opera." *American Journal of Sociology* 113(1): 97–127.

Johnson-Weiner, K. M. 2010. *New York Amish*. Ithaca, NY: Cornell University Press.

Jonas, A. E. G., and D. Wilson, eds. 1999. *The Urban Growth Machine: Critical Perspectives Two Decades Later*. Albany: State University of New York Press.

JP Music Festival. 2011. http://www.jpmusicfestival.com/resources/15-steps-to-a-local-music-festival.pdf.

Judd, D. R. 1999. "Constructing the Tourist Bubble." In *The Tourist City*, edited by D. R. Judd and S. S. Fainstein, 35–53. New Haven, CT: Yale University Press.

Kafka, P. 2003. "Celebrity 100, the Road to Riches." *Forbes.com*, July 7. http://www.forbes.com/forbes/2003/0707/078.html.

Kates, S. M., and R. W. Belk. 2001. "The Meanings of Lesbian and Gay Pride Day: Resistance through Consumption and Resistance to Consumption." *Journal of Contemporary Ethnography* 30(4):392–429.

Kearns, G., and C. Philo. 1993. *Selling Places: The City as Cultural Capital, Past, and Present*. Oxford: Pergamon Press.

Kelso, J. 2007. "Buy a Wristband or South by Southwest Will Turn You In to the Authorities." *Austin American-Statesman*. Sunday, March 25.

King, M. 2005. "Point Austin: The Fire This Time." *Austin Chronicle*, March 25. http://www.austinchronicle.com/news/2005-03-25/264138/.

Klepper, D. 2012. "Newport Folk Fest Rides a Wave of Success." *Kansas City Star*, July 27. http://www.kansascity.com/2012/07/27/3725501/newport-folk-fest-rides-a -wave.html.

Knopper, S. 2012. "Music Festivals Enjoy a Record Expansion in 2012." *Rolling Stone*, September 28.

Knudsen, D. D. 1968. "Socialization to Elitism: A Study of Debutantes." *Sociological Quarterly* 9(3):300–308.

Kong, L. 2000. "Culture, Economy, Policy: Trends and Developments." *Geoforum* 31(4):385–90.

Krasilovsky, M. W., J. M. Gross, and S. Shemel. 2003. *This Business of Music: The Definitive Guide to the Music Industry*. 9th ed. New York: Billboard Books.

Krause, M. 2013. "Recombining Micro/Macro: The Grammar of Theoretical Innovation." *European Journal of Social Theory* 16(2):139–52.

Kreyling, C. 2005. *The Plan of Nashville: Avenues to a Great City*. Nashville: Vanderbilt University Press.

Krukowski, D. 2012. "Making Cents." November 14. http://pitchfork.com/features /articles/8993-the-cloud/.

Kuchler, H. 2012. "Revelers Desert Music Festivals." *Financial Times*, July 13.

Ladendorf, K. 2010. "Quietly, Apple Keeps Growing in Austin." *Austin American-Statesman*, January 24.

———. 2012. "Tech Companies Say They Got a Boost from SXSW Interactive." *Austin American-Statesman*, March 14.

Lash, S., and J. Urry. 1994. *Economies of Signs and Space*. London: Sage.

Lee, M. 1997. "Relocating Location: Cultural Geography, the Specificity of Place and the City Habitus." In *Cultural Methodologies*, edited by J. McGuigan, 126–41. London: Sage.

Leeds, J. 2007a. "Auditioning for the World Stage at an Austin Festival." *New York Times*, March 17.

———. 2007b. "The Fort." *New York Times*, March 18.

Lefebvre, H. 1991. *The Production of Space*. London: Blackwell.

———. 2004. *Rhythmanalysis: Space, Time, and Everyday Life*. London: Continuum.

Lidz, V. 1991. "The Sense of Identity in Jewish-Christian Families." *Qualitative Sociology* 14(1):77–102.

Lieck, K. 2002. "Dancing about Architecture." *Austin Chronicle*, February 1. http:// www.austinchronicle.com/music/2002-02-01/84518/.

Live Music Task Force. 2008. City of Austin. http://www.ci.austin.tx.us/council /downloads/lmtfreport.pdf.

Lloyd, R. 2005. *Neo-Bohemia: Art and Neighborhood Redevelopment in Chicago.* New York: Routledge.

———. 2011. "East Nashville Skyline." *Ethnography* 12(1):114–45.

Lloyd, R., and B. D. Christens. 2012. "Reaching for Dubai: Nashville Dreams of a 21st-Century Skyline." In *Global Downtowns*, edited by M. Peterson and G. Mc-Donogh, 113–35. Philadelphia: University of Pennsylvania Press.

Lloyd, R., and Clark, T. N. 2001. "The City as an Entertainment Machine." In *Critical Perspectives on Urban Redevelopment*, edited by Kevin Fox, vol. 6 of *Research in Urban Sociology*, 357–78. Oxford: JAI Press/Elsevier.

Lofland, L. H. 1998. *The Public Realm: Exploring the City's Quintessential Social Territory.* New York: Aldine de Gruyter.

Loftsgaarden, B. 2012. 2012 "South by Southwest City of Austin Economic Impact Analysis." http://sxsw.com/sites/default/files/attachments/2012%20SXSW%20 Economic%20Impact%20Analysis%20-%20FINAL.pdf.

Logan, J., and H. Molotch. 1987. *Urban Fortunes.* Berkeley: University of California Press.

Long, J. 2010. *Weird City: Sense of Place and Creative Resistance in Austin, Texas.* Austin: University of Texas Press.

Lopes, P. D. 1992. "Innovation and Diversity in the Popular Music Industry, 1969 to 1990." *American Sociological Review* 57:56–71.

Lukes, S. 1975. "Political Ritual and Social Integration." *Sociology* 9(2):289–308.

MacCannell, D. 1976. *The Tourist: A New Theory of the Leisure Class.* Berkeley: University of California Press.

Macias, D. 2012. "Making Dollars: Clearing Up Spotify Payment Confusion." http:// www.hypebot.com/hypebot/2012/11/clearing-up-spotify-payment-confusion.html.

Madden, M., and L. Rainie. 2005. "Music and Video Downloading." *Pew Internet & American Life Project*, March 23. http://www.pewinternet.org/Reports/2005 /Music-and-Video-Downloading.aspx.

Maines, D. R. 1982. "In Search of Mesostructure: The Negotiated Order." *Urban Life* 11(3):267–79.

Maisel, R. 1974. "The Flea Market as Action Scene." *Journal of Contemporary Ethnography* 2(4):488–505.

Marcuse, P., and R. van Kempen. 2002. *Of States and Cities: The Partitioning of Urban Space.* Oxford: Oxford University Press.

Markusen, A. 2004. *The Distinctive City: Evidence from Artist and Occupational Profiles.* Minneapolis: Humphrey Institute of Public Affairs, University of Minnesota.

Markusen, A. R., Y.-S. Lee, and S. DiGiovanna. 1999. *Second Tier Cities: Rapid Growth beyond the Metropolis*. Minneapolis: University of Minnesota Press.

Marshall, L. 2004. "The Effects of Piracy upon the Music Industry: A Case Study of Bootlegging." *Media, Culture & Society* 26:163–81.

Martin, S. 1988. "Mayoral Candidates See Money in Music." *Austin Chronicle*, May 6.

Marwell, N. 2007. *Bargaining for Brooklyn: Community Organizations in the Entrepreneurial City*. Chicago: University of Chicago Press.

Massimo, R. 2009. "Lineup for Folk Festival, 50 Features Mix of Young and Old." *Providence Journal*, May 5.

McPhail, C., and R. T. Wohlstein. 1983. "Individual and Collective Behaviors within Gatherings, Demonstrations and Riots." *Annual Review of Sociology* 9:579–600.

Measley, T., and C. Mangum. 2010. "Which City Will Be Silicon Valley 2.0?" *ABC News*, August 26. http://abcnews.go.com/Technology/austin-nyc-silicon-valley/story?id=11480847#.UD962tBYs4N.

Metropolitan Planning Department. 2007. "Downtown Community Plan 2007."

Metzger, J. T. 2001. "The Failed Promise of the Festival Marketplace: South Street Seaport in Lower Manhattan." *Planning Perspective* 16:25–46.

Miller, T., and G. Yúdice. 2002. *Cultural Policy*. Thousand Oaks, CA: Sage.

Mitchell, D. 2003. *The Right to the City: Social Justice and the Fight for Public Space*. New York: Guilford Press.

Molotch, H. 1996. "L.A. as a Design Product: How Art Works in a Regional Economy." In *The City: Los Angeles and Urban Theory at the End of the Twentieth Century*, edited by A. Scott and E. Soja, 225–75. Berkeley: University of California Press.

———. 1999. "Growth Machine Links: Up, Down, and Across." In *The Urban Growth Machine: Critical Perspectives Two Decades Later*, edited by A. E. G. Jonas and D. Wilson, 247–66. Albany: State University of New York Press.

Molotch, H., W. Freudenburg, and K. Paulsen. 2000. "History Repeats Itself, But How? City Character, Urban Tradition, and the Accomplishment of Place." *American Sociological Review* 65:791–823.

Mommaas, H. 2004. "Cultural Clusters and the Post-Industrial City: Towards the Remapping of Urban Cultural Policy." *Urban Studies* 41(3):507–32.

Montgomery, J. 2005. "Beware the 'Creative Class': Creativity and Wealth Creation Revisited." *Local Economy* 20(4):337–43.

Mortimer, J. H., C. Nosko, and A. Sorensen. 2012. "Supply Responses to Digital Distribution: Recorded Music and Live Performances." *Information Economics and Policy* 24:3–14.

Morton, J. F. 2008. *Backstory in Blue: Ellington at Newport '56*. Piscataway, NJ: Rutgers University Press.

Moscaritolo, A. 2012. "Internet Radio Closing In on Traditional Music Listening." *PCMag.com*, November 8. http://www.pcmag.com/article2/0,2817,2411889,00.asp.

Mumford, L. 1966. *The Culture of Cities*. New York: Harcourt Brace Jovanovich.

Munir, H. 2012. "Travis County Approves Apple Incentives Deal." *KUT Radio*. http://kut.org/2012/05/travis-county-approves-apple-incentives-deal/.

Myers, M. 2010. "Riot in Newport, 1960." *Wall Street Journal*, July 1.

Novak, S. 2008. "Urban Urges: The Burbs No Longer Beckon Residents Who Want to End Commutes and Be Close to It All." *Austin American-Statesman*, February 10.

Ocejo, R. E. 2011. "The Early Gentrifier: Weaving a Nostalgia Narrative on the Lower East Side." *City & Community* 10(3):285–310.

O'Connor, J., and D. Wynne. 1995. *From the Margins to the Centre*. London: Arena.

Oermann, R. K. 2011. "CMA Fest by the Numbers." June 14. http://www.musicrow.com/2011/06/cma-fest-by-the-numbers/.

Orum, A. 2002. *Power, Money, and the People: The Making of Modern Austin*. Eugene, OR: Wipf and Stock Publishers.

Palmer/Rae Associates. 2004. *European Cities and Capitals of Culture: Study Prepared for the European Commission*. Brussels: Palmer/Rae Associates.

Pareles, J. 1998. "Critic's Notebook; Newport Folk, How It's Changed." *New York Times*, August 4.

Pearson, N.W. Jr. 1987. *Goin' to Kansas City*. Urbana: University of Illinois Press.

Pecknold, D. 2007. *The Selling Sound: The Rise of Country Music*. Durham, NC: Duke University Press.

Pennell, G. 2002. "Newport Folk Festival 1965." http://farinafiles1.tripod.com/Newport.htm.

Peoples, G. 2010. "TicketsNow, 360 Deals a Drag for Live Nation." *Billboard*, May 10. http://www.billboard.com/biz/articles/news/touring/1207078/ticketsnow-360-deals-a-drag-for-live-nation.

Peterson, R. A. 1997. *Creating Country Music: Fabricating Authenticity*. Chicago: University of Chicago Press.

Peterson, R. A., and B. A. Beal. 2001. "Alternative Country: Origins, Music, World-View, Fans and Taste in Genre Formation." *Popular Music and Society* 25:233–49.

Peterson, R. A., and D. G. Berger. 1996. "Measuring Industry Concentration, Diversity, and Innovation in Popular Music." *American Sociological Review* 61:175–78.

Phillips, R. J. 2010. "Arts Entrepreneurship and Economic Development: Can Every City Be 'Austintatious'?" *Foundations and Trends in Entrepreneurship* 6(4):239–313.

Plohetski, T. 2011. "SXSW Crowds, Traffic Cause Frustration and Safety Fears." *Austin American-Statesman*, March 18. http://www.statesman.com/news/entertainment/music/sxsw-crowds-traffic-cause-frustration-and-safety-2/nRYR9/.

Popov, L., and T. Popov. 2007. "An Open Letter from Factory People: We Love You Austin and SXSW, but You're Freaking Us Out." *Austinist.com*, March 21. http://austinist.com/2007/03/21/an_open_letter_from_factorypeople_we_love_you _austin_and_sxsw_but_youre_freaking_us_out.php.

Populous. 2014. "SXSW and the City of Austin: Report on Assessment and Visioning Workshop." http://sxsw.com/sites/default/files/attachments/Executive%20 Summary%20-%20Populous%20Report.pdf.

Powell, A. 2010. "Off the Record: Music News." *Austin Chronicle*, May 7. http://www .austinchronicle.com/music/2010-05-07/1025376/.

Pugh, R. 1996. *Ernest Tubb: The Texas Troubadour*. Durham, NC, and London: Oxford University Press.

Quinn, B. 1996. "Re-Thinking Arts Festival Policy in Ireland." *Cultural Policy* 3:91–107.

Raines, P., and L. Brown. 2006. *The Economic Impact of the Music Industry in the Nashville-Davidson-Murfreesboro MSA*. Nashville: Belmont University and Nashville Area Chamber of Commerce.

Ratliff, B. 2007. "George Wein Sells Company That Produces Music Festivals." *New York Times*, January 25.

———. 2009. "Wein Seeks to Regain Control of Newport Festivals." *New York Times*, March 3.

———. 2011. "Metal, Electronica, Country and Jazz Are All on Tour." *New York Times*, February 17.

Ravenscroft, N., and X. Matteucci. 2003. "The Festival as Carnivalesque: Social Governance and Control at Pamplona's San Fermin Fiesta." *Tourism, Culture & Communication* 4:1–15.

Regis, H. A. 1999. "Second Lines, Minstrelsy, and the Contested Landscapes of New Orleans Afro-Creole Festivals." *Cultural Anthropology* 14(4):472–504.

Rheault, M. 2006. "#1 Nashville." *Kiplinger*. http://www.kiplinger.com/features /archives/2006/05/nashville.html.

Richards, G. 2000. "The European Cultural Capital Event: Strategic Weapon in the Cultural Arms Race?" *Journal of Cultural Policy* 6(2):159–81.

———. 2007. "The Festivalization of Society or the Socialization of Festivals? The Case of Catalunya." In *Cultural Tourism: Global and Local Perspectives*, edited by G. Richards, 257–80. New York: Haworth Press.

Richards, G., and J. Wilson. 2004. "The Impact of Cultural Events on City Image: Rotterdam, Cultural Capital of Europe, 2001." *Urban Studies* 41(10):1931–1951.

Rodriguez, E. I. 2013. *Celebrating Debutantes and Quinceañeras: Coming of Age in American Ethnic Communities*. Philadelphia: Temple University Press.

Rosenstein, C. 2010. "Live from Your Neighborhood: A National Study of Outdoor Arts Festivals." Research Report No. 51. Washington, DC: National Endowment for the Arts.

Roy, W. G. 2010. *Reds, Whites, and Blues: Social Movements, Folk Music, and Race in the United States*. Princeton, NJ: Princeton University Press.

Sampson, R. J. 2012. *Great American City: Chicago and the Enduring Neighborhood Effect*. Chicago: University of Chicago Press.

Samson, J. D. 2011. "I Love My Job but It Made Me Poorer." *Huffington Post*, October 5. http://www.huffingtonpost.com/jd-samson/i-love-my-job-but-it-made_b_987680 .html.

Sassen, S. 1991. *The Global City: New York, London, Tokyo*. Princeton, NJ: Princeton University Press.

———. 1994. *Cities in a World Economy*. London: Pine Forge Press.

Schudson, M. 1986. *Advertising, the Uneasy Persuasion*. New York: Basic Books.

Schuster, J. M. 2001. "Ephemera, Temporary Urbanism, and Imaging." In *Imaging the City: Continuing Struggles and New Directions*, edited by L. J. Vale and S. B. Warner Jr., 361–97. New Brunswick, NJ: Center for Urban Policy Research, State University of New Jersey Press.

Scott, A. J. 1999. "The US Recorded Music Industry: On the Relations between Organization, Location, and Creativity in the Cultural Economy." *Environment and Planning A* 13:1965–1984.

Seabrook, J. 2009. "The Price of a Ticket." *New Yorker*, August 10, 33–47.

Sennett, R. 1996 [1971]. *The Uses of Disorder*. London: Faber and Faber.

Sernovitz, D. J. 2009. "Struever Bros., Eccles & Rouse Stops Work on Baltimore Projects." *Baltimore Business Journal*, June 8.

Shackelford, R. 1978. "The Yaddo Festivals of American Music, 1932–1952." *Perspectives of New Music* 17(1):92–125.

Shank, B. 1994. *Dissonant Identities: Rock 'n' Roll Scene in Austin, Texas*. Hanover, NH: University Press of New England.

Sharkey, P. 2013. *Stuck in Place: Urban Neighborhoods and the End of Progress toward Racial Equality*. Chicago: University of Chicago Press.

Sherman, M. 2011. "Emo's Owner on Famed Austin Club's Closure: 'What Makes a Venue Is Not Four Walls.'" *Billboard*, September 29. http://www.billboard.biz /bbbiz/industry/touring/emo-s-owner-on-famed-austin-club-s-closure-1005377 682.story#4FcjxuO8f2pS5Q76.99.

Sisario, B. 2009. "New York Loses Its Jazz Festival." *New York Times*, May 19, C1.

———. 2011. "In Austin, Music Lovers Get Parallel Universes." *New York Times*, March 15, C1.

Small, M. 2004. *Villa Victoria*. Chicago: University of Chicago Press.

Smelser, N. 1997. *Problematics of Sociology: The Georg Simmel Lectures*. Berkeley and Los Angeles: University of California Press.

Smith, G. 2011. "New Genre-Bending Music Club Gets a Boost from Providence." *Providence Journal*, October 6.

Smith, M. R. 2011. "With Eye on Legacy, Newport Festivals Go Nonprofit." *Associated Press*, January 25.

Soja, E. 1996. *Thirdspace: Journeys to Los Angeles and Other Real-and-Imagined Places*. Oxford: Wiley-Blackwell.

Spinney, R. G. 1995. "Municipal Government in Nashville, Tennessee, 1938–1951: World War II and the Growth of the Public Sector." *Journal of Southern History* 61(1):77–112.

Stimeling, T. 2011. *Cosmic Cowboys and New Hicks: The Countercultural Sounds of Austin's Progressive Country Music Scene*. New York: Oxford University Press.

Stinchcombe, A. L. 1965. "Social Structure and Organizations." In *Handbook of Organizations*, edited by J. G. March, 142–93. Chicago: Rand McNally.

Stoller, P. 2001. *Money Has No Smell: The Africanization of New York City*. Chicago: University of Chicago Press.

Storper, M. 2013. *Keys to the City*. Princeton, NJ: Princeton University Press.

Storper, M., and A. Venables. 2004. "Buzz: Face-to-Face Contact and the Urban Economy." *Journal of Economic Geography* 4:351–70.

Sutter, M., and M. Toohey. 2011. "City Cracks Down on Venues as Promised." *Austin 360.com*, March 17. http://www.austin360.com/blogs/content/shared-gen/blogs /austin/music/entries/2011/03/17/city_cracks_down_on_venues_as.html.

Suttles, G. 1984. "The Cumulative Texture of Local Urban Culture." *American Journal of Sociology* 90:283–304.

Swearingen, W. S. Jr. 2010. *Environmental City: People, Place, Politics, and the Meaning of Modern Austin*. Austin: University of Texas Press.

Swenson, R. 2011. "OP ED: SXSW Manager Responds to Criticism." *The Horn*, April 15. http://www.readthehorn.com/local/4019/sxsw_manager_speaks_out_about_free _events.

SXSW. 2012. "Statistics for SXSW Music 2012." http://sxsw.com/sites/default/files /attachments/STATISTICS%20FOR%20SXSW%20MUSIC%202012.pdf#overlay -context=resources.

———. 2013. "SXSW 2013 Marketing." http://sxsw.com/sites/default/files/attachments /SXSW_Marketing_Deck.pdf.

———. 2014. "SXSW 2014 Economic Impact Report." http://www.sxsw.com/sites

/default/files/attachments/2014%20SXSW%20Economic%20Impact%20Analysis
.pdf.

Szwed, J. 2010. *Alan Lomax: The Man Who Recorded the World.* New York: Penguin.

Tanenbaum, S. 1995. *Underground Harmonies: Music and Politics in the Subways of New York.* Ithaca, NY: Cornell University Press.

Throsby, D. 2010. *The Economics of Cultural Policy.* Cambridge, UK: Cambridge University Press.

Turner, J. 2005. *Theoretical Principals of Sociology.* Vol. 3, *Mesodynamics.* New York: Springer.

TXP, Inc. 2012. "The Economic Impact of the Creative Sector in Austin—2012 Update."

Tyrrell, T. J., and R. J. Johnston. 2001. "A Framework for Assessing Direct Economic Impacts of Tourist Events: Distinguishing Origins, Destinations, and Causes of Expenditures." *Journal of Travel Research* 40:94–100.

USA Today. 2006. "Jack White Leaves 'Super-Negative' Detroit." May 25. http://www
.usatoday.com/life/people/2006-05-25-jack-white_x.htm.

Verlegh, P. W. J. 2010. "Country Images: Why They Influence Consumers." In *International Place Branding Yearbook 2010*, edited by F. Go and R. Govers, 45–51. New York: Palgrave Macmillan.

Vernon-Sparks, L. 2009. "Developer Struever Bros. Owes Millions to Rhode Island Companies." *Providence Journal*, April 26.

Vigdor, J. L. 2010. "Is Urban Decay Bad? Is Urban Revitalization Good?" *Journal of Urban Economics* 68(3):277–89.

Wacquant, L. 2003. *Body and Soul: Notebooks of an Apprentice Boxer.* Oxford: Oxford University Press.

Walker, A. 2012. "Meet Nick Bauta, the Designer-Entrepreneur Driving Providence's Industrial Renaissance." April 22. http://www.fastcompany.com/1834668/meet
-nick-bauta-designer-entrepreneur-driving-providences-industrial-renaissance.

Ward, S. V. 1998. *Selling Places: The Marketing and Promotion of Towns and Cities, 1850–2000.* London: Routledge.

Warner, W. L. 1959. *The Living and the Dead.* New Haven, CT: Yale University Press.

Wasik, B. 2006. "My Crowd, or, Phase 5: A Report from the Inventor of the Flash Mob." *Harper's Magazine* 312(March):56–66.

Waterman, S. 1998. "Carnivals for Elites? The Cultural Politics of Music Festivals." *Progress in Human Geography* 22:54–75.

Weber, M. 1978. *Economy and Society: An Outline of Interpretive Sociology.* Berkeley: University of California Press.

Wein, G. 2003. *Myself among Others: A Life in Music*. Cambridge, MA: Da Capo Press.

Westergren, T. 2012. "Pandora and Artist Payments." October 9. http://blog.pandora
.com/pandora/archives/2012/10/pandora-and-art.html.

Wildman, S. 2011. "On Virginia's Crooked Road, Music Lights the Way." *New York
Times*, May 20.

Woronkowicz, J., et al. 2012. "Set in Stone: Building America's New Generation of
Arts Facilities, 1994–2008." *Cultural Policy Center Report*. Chicago: University of
Chicago Press.

Wynn, J. 2011. *The Tour Guide: Walking and Talking New York*. Chicago: University
of Chicago Press.

———. 2012. "Sociology of Music." *Everyday Sociology*, October 22. http://www
.everydaysociologyblog.com/2012/10/sociology-of-music.html.

Zafirau, S. 2008. "Reputation Work in Selling Film and Television: Life in the Hollywood Talent Industry." *Qualitative Sociology* 31:99–127.

Zaragosa, S. 2007. "Red River Clubs Swelling Up." *Austin Business Journal*, July 8.

Zukin, S. 1989. *Loft Living: Culture and Capital in Urban Change*. New Brunswick, NJ:
Rutgers University Press.

———. 1991. *Landscapes of Power*. Berkeley: University of California Press.

———. 1995. *The Cultures of Cities*. London: Blackwell.

INDEX

ambush marketing, 154, 164. *See* official vs. unofficial

amenities: built, 4, 12–13, 25, 43, 133, 181–82, 230, 271n29; natural, 26, 172, 195. *See also* music venues, honkytonks

Artist & Repertoire (A&R), 140, 144, 146–47, 158, 279n27

audiences: admission of, 160; and class, 90–91, 105, 205; creating intimacy for, 72, 103–9; and festivals, generally, 8, 22–23, 32, 37, 39, 132, 137–38, 280–81n3; and gender, 100; industry members as, 130; interactions between musicians and, 66–69, 72, 90–91, 97–99, 103–4, 111–13, 126, 148; and race, 56, 275nn9–10, 279n15; as volunteers, 130–31, 138–40, 147–48, 171; zones of participation, 127–28, 157

authenticity, 54, 60, 142, 251, 269n2; of any event, 50–51, 70, 251; of music, 113, 122, 149, 200, 275n7; in relation to branding, 121, 212

badges, 125, 127–28, 139, 140, 147–49, 155, 160

Becker, Howard, 9–10, 148

Bonnaroo Music and Arts Festival, 8, 22, 23, 73, 78, 81, 176, 206

Bourdieu, Pierre, 13, 271n21

branding: brand activation, 116, 151; corporate sponsorship, 37–38, 45–50, 56, 59, 73, 113–17, 121, 126, 150, 152, 159–63, 210–12; definition of, 272n16; event branding, 73, 93, 155–57, 212–13, 251; manufacturing-age, 28; musician

as brand, 38, 105; territorial trademarking and place branding, 4, 8, 14–16, 28, 42–43, 84, 116–17, 133, 135, 163, 197, 211–19, 255, 269n4, 272n17

Brown Bird, 45, 60–64, 66–68, 183, 208–9

Bumbershoot, 17, 22, 37, 228, 240

Business Improvement Districts, 178, 187

careers: of aspiring and established musicians, 25, 34, 58, 112, 130, 139, 143–44; career foothold, 131; festival performance as way to start or build, 43, 60–64, 66, 106–7, 141, 216; income and compensation, 29–30, 33–35, 76; labels developing, 31–32, 202; medical and mental health care, 207–10; working odd jobs to maintain music career, 61

Carolina Chocolate Drops, 35, 46–47, 69, 71, 237

chain migration, 63

chamber of commerce: as active supporters, 10, 39, 116–17, 132, 135, 137, 175; as impediment to music scene growth, 58; using music scenes to attract businesses, 25, 39, 193, 206, 211

Chicago Blues Festival, 26, 228, 240

clean zones, 164, 166, 229, 242, 280n42

CMJ Music Marathon, 145

Coachella Valley Music and Arts Festival, 8, 22–23, 78, 81

collective representations, 42

community: festival's struggles with, 55, 75, 89, 118–19, 157–60; and local music culture, 40–41, 84, 205 concrete vs. liquid culture, 5–6, 24, 25–26, 42, 92, 226–32, 247, 285n4

convention and visitors bureau, 25, 65, 92–93, 116–17, 226

country vs. city, 23–24, 82–85, 94–95, 123

creative class, 26, 28–29, 60–63, 117, 131, 133, 137, 172–74, 183, 187, 199–200

cultural clusters, 85–87, 227

cultural policy: definitions of, 226, 229, 274n55; and festivals, 12, 19, 26–28, 42–43, 182, 206, 227, 279n15; international examples of, 232–38, 286n14; smaller-scale, 238–39

cumulative texture of the city, 14

Dylan "going electric," 33, 50, 54, 66

dynamics: density, 18, 56, 83, 220, 248, 283n1; as a guiding framework on occasions, 245–54; porosity, 17, 149–52, 165, 200, 222–24, 240, 248; turbulence, 76, 111, 123, 224, 242, 248

entertainment machines, 25, 86–89, 132

fallacy of physical determinism, 220

fan clubs, 99, 106–8

festivalization, 4, 11–16, 19, 43, 80, 124, 168, 193, 226–42

festivals: artist compensation, 36–38, 53, 107, 144, 277n18, 278n1, 279n25; as commercial enterprises, 94, 161–63; as conference, 127, 138–40, 143, 145, 149–50; constructing lineups, 61–64, 104–6, 126, 141; as coordinated activity, 7, 9–10, 35–41; and corporate sponsorship, 37–38, 45–50, 54–55, 59, 72–73, 155, 237, 239, 244; as counterculture, 2, 22, 40–41, 55–56, 61, 130, 162–63, 219, 244; as educational, 54, 69, 202, 236–38; history of, 21–23, 52–57, 89–92, 132–38; international

comparison, 37, 232–37; public funding of, 37, 39, 206, 227, 233–38, 240, 285n3, 287n21; as supporting local musicians, 202–3, 238–41

Fête de la Musique, 17, 18, 232–33, 235, 240, 249

genres: Americana, 60–61, 118, 121, 185; country, 8, 96, 112–13, 118–19, 123–24, 276n2; folk, 22, 49, 54, 63–64, 67; hip-hop, 83, 187; indie rock, 130–33, 149–50, 161; jazz, 8, 21–22, 53, 56, 74, 76; as social relationship, 73, 80, 231

gentrification, 25, 137, 183, 194–96, 199, 209

Goffman, Erving, 20, 246–47, 287n3

Grand Ole Opry, 84, 86–88, 90, 114, 116, 202

growth machines, 23, 229

historical districts, 129, 191

ideal type, 17–18, 271n27

invented traditions, 54–55, 65–70, 120

Jacobs, Jane, 27

law enforcement: interactions with non-sanctioned festival activities, 111, 136, 156, 250, 253–54; as paid festival security, 15, 37, 49, 53, 93, 170–71, 280n37

Lefebvre, Henri, 12, 168, 179, 241–42, 247, 270n17

Live Music Task Force, 136, 177, 207

Live Nation, 35

live performances vs. digitization, 30–35, 40, 76–77, 170, 272n22, 273n30

locale vs. counterlocale, 64, 227–28, 231, 242

Lollapalooza, 8, 17, 22, 40, 269n5

Lower Broad: as center of CMA Fest activities, 39, 97, 111, 115–16, 123, 160, 165; history and development of, 87–88, 174–76

media: alternative, 36, 132, 213, 273n34; conventional, 23, 25, 59, 61, 71–72, 86, 97, 120–21, 128; media areas at festivals, 65–68
mega-events, 163, 228–29
mesosociology, 255–58
methods, 10–11, 259–65, 270n12, 270n14
municipal government: establishing festivals, 228, 234; music/culture offices in city hall, 177, 179, 206–7, 231, 238–40; supporting festivals, 37, 56, 93, 132, 135–36, 199, 274n42, 279n18; supporting scenes, 39, 88, 176–77, 204, 206, 210, 279n17
Music City Music Council, 204
Music City Roots, 119–22, 210
music industry: connection with creative industries, 118, 170, 173–74; labels collaborating with festivals, 104–6; live music, 34–35, 87, 131–32, 136, 170; relationship with municipal agencies, 27, 37, 84, 85–86, 116; recorded, 30–32, 205–6, 273nn24–25; supporting musicians, 132–33, 202, 206–8; trade organizations, conferences, and conventions, 39, 90–91, 127–28, 140, 143, 145, 149–50; transformations of, 29–35; webcasting and streaming services, 32, 273n30
music venues, honkytonks, 1, 5, 10, 13, 18, 77–78, 87, 111, 129, 134, 137, 152, 183–84, 191–92, 235–36, 238–39

New Music Seminar, 132–33
"Newport Effect," 61, 63, 72

nonprofits: Boys and Girls Clubs of Newport County, 201–2; CMA Foundation, 204; festivals as, 59, 64, 71, 78, 113, 220, 235, 239, 270n16; festivals supporting, 15, 49, 69, 74–75, 201–4, 230; Health Alliance for Austin Musicians (HAAM), 207–8; Keep the Music Playing, 204; Nashville Alliance for Public Education, 203; New England Folk Music Archives, 69, 201; Olneyville Housing Authority, 182; as part of urban development, 182, 227; SIMS Foundation, 207–8; Steel Yard, 182; W. O. Smith Music School, 204–6

occasional public, 9
official vs. unofficial: alternative events, 74–81, 108–11, 118–22, 162, 197–98; BridgeFest, 74–78; buskers, 251–54; contrast of, 148–57; "meet and greet" or "howdy and shake," 99, 107–8; protesters, 164–65; street preachers, 109–11
organizational imprinting, 41, 94–95, 113–17

parades, 42, 82–83, 164–65, 257, 274n52
patterns: citadel, 1–2, 17, 46, 65, 73–74, 79–80, 92, 95; comparisons between, 16–19, 43, 219–25, 247–54; confetti, 18, 154, 164–66; core, 17, 83–84, 92–93, 95, 97, 123–24
Peace and Love Festival, 1–3, 17, 46, 234, 240–41, 249, 286n15
photography, 66–68, 100, 101–3, 104
place character, 26, 28, 56, 61, 80, 85, 89–90, 116, 123, 129, 177, 218–19, 239
place professionals, 28, 39
Pop Montreal Music Festival, 17, 18, 232, 235–36, 240
public spaces, 1, 8, 13, 17, 19, 24, 111, 150, 223, 235

"quality of life" campaigns, 137, 176–77, 227, 230, 255

religion, 2, 41–42, 61, 109–11, 123–24
reputational work, 60–64
resources: economic, 12, 53, 116, 134–35, 152, 168, 169–71; as framework for cultural policy, 229–30; social + cultural, 13–14, 36–37, 52, 75, 177, 199–210, 271n21; spatial, 13, 18, 52, 109, 128–29, 134, 180; symbolic, 14–15, 52, 72, 85, 114, 123, 133, 210–19; as theoretical framework, 12–16, 28, 219–25, 248
ritual, 41–42, 246, 256, 258

scenes: local, 13, 24, 51, 60–63, 111–12, 129, 131, 137, 200, 203; "underground" music, 181–82, 183, 194, 198, 278n7
second-tier cities, 8–9, 269n8
sight/site sacralization, 71–74, 87, 120, 220, 244, 251
social ties, 60–64, 72, 112
Swift, Taylor, 31, 83, 108, 109

Tax Increment Financing (TIF), 173, 186–87, 190, 191, 194–95, 282n40, 283n45

technology industries, 25–26, 135–36, 176–78, 192, 199, 282n26
themed spaces, 42, 86, 88, 97, 175, 227
Third Man Records, 189–90
touring, 34–35, 37
tourism, 5, 9, 15–16, 52, 58, 112, 136, 222
tourism set, 52, 70, 79–80
tourist bubbles, 227
transformation of US cities: affordable housing, 174, 181, 187, 194–95, 230; affordable housing for musicians, 189, 190, 193; Austin, 128–29, 133–38, 176–77, 178, 190–92; brownfield remediation and, 25, 182, 186–87, 189–90, 194; "jobs follow people," 26–28, 135, 177–78, 207; Nashville, 87–89, 93, 175–76, 178, 186–90, 281n19; Providence, 172–74, 178; residential real estate and music venues, 5–7, 186–88, 192, 196; urban redevelopment, 22–29, 193–96

walking, 11, 26, 179–96
W. O. Smith School of Music, 205–6

Yankee City, 246, 259, 260

zoning, 24, 181, 186–87, 196, 229, 283n46